Game Changers for Government Contractors

Insider Tips and Advice from the Industry's Top Experts

Michael LeJeune and Joshua P. Frank

Contributing Authors

Mark Amtower
Amtower & Company

Erin Andrew
Live Oak Bank

Michele Atkinson
Cavalry Consulting

Russ Barnes
Systro Solutions

Carroll Bernard
Govology

Judy Bradt
Summit Insight

Tim Burt
Tim Burt Media

Jenny Clark
Solvability

Chris Bobbitt
Technical Assent

Mario Burgos
Burgos Group

Bellandra Foster
BBFoster Consulting

Ashley Haass
The Daily Brief

Jay McConville
Privia

Mike McDermott
InquisIT

Michael McNulty
McNulty and Associates

Steve Meredith
SW PA Commission

Matt Miller
EMA, Inc.

David Neal
David Neal Consulting

Maria Panichelli
Obermayer Rebmann
Maxwell & Hippel LLP

Linda Rawson
DynaGrace Enterprises

Doug Reitmeyer
Government
Construction Experts

Rob Rosenberger
Blackdragon

Matthew Schoonover
Koprince Law

Kathleen Smith
CyberSecJobs.com

Courtney Spaeth
growth[period]

Carrie Ann Williams
Andana Consulting

Eric "Doc" Wright
Vets2PM

ISBN 978-1-7336009-4-1 (pbk)
ISBN 978-1-7336009-5-8 (ebk)

Printed in the United States of America
1 2 3 4 5 6 7 8 9 10

This book is dedicated to all of the co-authors that made this project possible. There is NO WAY that we could have pulled this off without you. Thank you for being Game Changers!

Contents

A Message from Joshua Frank

This book is more than simply a consolidation of lessons presented by industry thought-leaders. Whether you are new to government sales or been doing it for years, *you will likely recognize many of the authors*.

First, let me thank all of our colleagues responsible for writing this book. I am truly inspired by how we came together on this project.

Putting together a book of this magnitude is time-consuming. The level of coordination is extensive. There is strength in unity and value in collaboration. Nowhere else will you find this level of expertise from so many of our industry's top experts.

I can't thank Michael LeJeune enough for the hard work in putting this book together over the last twelve months. My business partner at RSM Federal and program lead for the Federal Access Knowledge-Base and Training Platform, Mike's relentless pursuit of excellence shines through in this book.

Some episodes will appeal to the business professional that is new to the government market. Other episodes are more complex and will provide value to the more experienced business professionals.

Like a newspaper, we hope you'll find several episodes that provide nuggets of wisdom and knowledge to shift one or more of your strategies into high gear.

Joshua Frank, Managing Partner, RSM Federal

Author's Introduction

My team and I at RSM Federal have helped our clients win over $2.6 Billion in government contracts. That number is staggering to me. That's a LOT of money no matter how you slice it. But it can also be intimidating.

If you are new to government contracting or struggling in your business, you may look at $2.6 Billion and think that you can't do it. You may think that you don't have the knowledge, skills, or background to make it happen. This is especially true if you don't have any contracts yet, only have a few contracts, or feel that you have reached a plateau.

I'm here to tell you that no matter where you are RIGHT NOW, YOU CAN DO IT! In fact, if I can do it, I think anyone can do it. I didn't have any special knowledge when I started my journey. To prove it, let me tell you where I came from.

My backstory isn't earth-shattering. I don't have a tragic life-changing incident to tell you about. I did not come from a wealthy privileged background. I grew up somewhat poor on a dying farm in Southwest Louisiana. My parents were older when they had me. I was totally a mistake. My mom was convinced it was just the flu. Nine months later, I came out swinging.

We never had a lot. When you grow up in a family like that, you learn the value of hard work. I spent long days on the farm running a tractor, driving a truck, and watching over the fields. I was somewhere around 8 or 9 the first time I stole my dad's truck to get us lunch. It just seemed easier than walking and a truck wasn't much different than driving a tractor.

I was the baby of four kids and there were 17 years between my brother and I. Don't forget, I was an accident. So, while I was treated a little like the baby, I was also bossed around by three older siblings. It didn't take long to figure out that *I had to fight for what I wanted.*

I bucked the system in a lot of ways. My sibling's hated school and all of them dropped out early. My dad didn't care. In fact, he quit school in the sixth grade. I sort of liked school. I liked using my brain more than my muscle. I was interested in math and science and business.

Interestingly, my mom started my love for business. She was a simple housewife born in the 1940's. That meant she "knew her place" in the home. But that didn't stop her from wanting more. She started a small greeting card and cookbook company when I was about four. That got us into craft shows.

And this is where it gets a little embarrassing. My mom convinced me to dress up like a clown and sell balloon bouquets at the craft shows. She bought the supplies, made the bouquets, and I walked around selling them. *We split the profits.*

Later on, I would develop my own line of silly duck greeting cards. They were ugly and kind of stupid (if I can be a bit harsh about my five-year-old self), but I wanted more money. Looking back, I wanted another revenue stream. And thus, an entrepreneur was born.

Let's fast forward a bit. I got out of the Army in 1999 with not much more than a security clearance and a desire to learn. Over the next few years, I learned computers, programming languages, and customer support skills.

Eventually, I was called over to the Dark Side – the sale team! I didn't know a lot about sales, but I wanted to earn more money and my mentor at the time, a retired Colonel and senior executive at General Dynamics, begged me to try sales. So, I reluctantly jumped in.

A few months later I was shattering sales records.

Shortly after 9/11, I woke up one day in charge of government sales for a small software company. The entire leadership team had been abruptly fired and I was foolish enough to volunteer and take over the team.

I should note that I had only been a part of the sales team for six months and had absolutely zero sales training. As the new manager, I didn't have much of a clue where to start. I foolishly decided to email everyone at the White House and Pentagon with an unsolicited proposal for a blanket license agreement for our software. I also followed up my email with a direct mail packet of our printed presentation. When I say everyone, I *mean everyone.* I got the President's email address from a friend and sent him a couple of emails and multiple packets. (Yes, the President of the United States.) I even faxed the President a packet directly to his War Room. Imagine sitting in the President's War Room when the fax machine kicks-on and out comes 75 pages of my marketing materials...

I'm fairly certain this email / fax stunt put me on the FBI's watch list. But it was totally worth it.

About a month after I sent everything, I received a personal letter from the President's Chief of Staff - Andy Card. The letter had the name of a couple of people he wanted me to speak to. Within 1 year, we went from $1 million in revenue to just over $11 million because *I didn't follow the 'rules.'*

Rules are meant for 80% of all situations. 20% of the time, someone needs to make a judgement call. A human being (typically a leader) needs to get involved and bypass or change the rules to get things done.

This applies to EVERYTHING!

What rules do you need to throw out the window in your business? For many of us, it's as 'simple' as changing your mindset. For others, you need a coach or mentor to help give you a new perspective or a swift kick in the ass. The bottom line is that we often need a wakeup call. Something to smack us in the face and point us in a new direction.

My wakeup call was that if you don't ask, you don't get. So, I began asking and getting. And my life has never been the same.

My hope for you is that reading this book will be a wakeup call. Whether you are new to the market or a seasoned pro, I hope the following episodes are packed with Game Changers that will last you a lifetime.

Thank You to all of Our Authors

In the spirit of asking, I had a crazy idea to put together a Game Changing (pun intended) book with the help of the top minds in government contracting. So, I started asking. Before I knew it, we had twenty-nine authors signed-on for the book.

When I pitched the concept for the book, every author saw the value of rolling up their sleeves and contributing. They did so during the government Q4 spending spree and conference season. This is arguably the toughest time of year to ask anyone for anything. Yet, they all stepped up.

At first glance, you may think that many of us are competitors. In any normal situation, that may be true. However, this book is direct evidence of the willingness of each author to put aside competitiveness and focus on providing value for YOU, the reader. We all share the same mindset. We all want to help you succeed. I can't emphasize enough what this says about the character of every author in this book.

I've gotten to know many of these authors fairly well over the last four years. They've all appeared on our Game Changers podcast (or will shortly). I have to say that they are some of my favorite people in the world. They are generous, caring, and amazing professionals.

With that in mind, I can't express my thanks enough. Words won't do them justice. So, I ask you, the reader, that if you read an episode and find value therein, please drop the corresponding author an email or a note on LinkedIn and say *thank you*. I guarantee every author will greatly appreciate your thanks.

A Special Thanks

Before I continue, I want to take a minute to say a few words about my business partner Joshua Frank. Josh and I have known each other since 2002.

We both learned a lot about government sales and running small companies together in the trenches of what was basically a small tech start-up. Together, Josh and I made that company millions of dollars.

In 2004, I woke up and realized that I was traveling 328 days out of the year. I had made quite a bit of money, but I barely knew my young daughter and had another on the way. So, I walked away to start my own company.

Josh and I stayed in touch over the years and in 2014 he asked me to join him at RSM Federal. Fast forward about a year into our new relationship and Josh makes me a partner in the business.

Josh and I have an interesting relationship. I won't go into the details except to say, it's extremely rare to see two strong (some may call us hardheaded) individuals working together like we do. We always help the other person and we don't care who gets the credit as long as the client and the company get the win.

You build up a lot of trust with someone after knowing them for 18+ years. So much trust that you don't have to second guess their ideas or motives. You just trust that the person you know is working in everyone's best interest. That is what Josh does for me.

I've thrown out a lot of "crazy" ideas over the years. Some we debate, some we shut down, but many are tested to see where they go. Our Game Changers podcast was one of those tests. With quite a bit of pushing, Josh trusted me to give it a go and to know when to shut it down if it didn't work.

Well, it worked! It worked better than either of us thought it would. But it would have never started without Josh's support and I am extremely thankful that he trusted me with running the program.

This book also started out as one of those crazy ideas that I come up with in the middle of the night. This book includes 29 industry thought-leaders and subject matter experts, 33 episodes, and more than 90,000 words to prove that Josh was right in trusting me. This kind of trust is rare in business and I'm extremely grateful for it every day. Thanks Josh!

How this Book is Organized

One thing you will notice right away is that we have replaced *chapters* with '*Episodes.*' There are two reasons we did this. First, this book is based on our podcast, Game Changers for Government Contractors[1]. So, this was a natural fit. The second and more important reason is that each episode stands on its own. You may find yourself reading this book from cover to cover, but you will likely jump around to topics that interest you the most.

As you read through this book, you will find similar thoughts and strategies, but you will also see them from very different points of view. You will see different writing styles and thought processes. That's fairly standard when you have so many different authors. Regardless, I hope that you walk away with several concepts and strategies that are Game Changers for your business.

Because many authors touch on similar topics, we did our best to put each episode in an order that makes sense and creates a flow of sorts. But don't let that stop you from bouncing around.

My advice, before you dig in, is to grab a notebook and start an **ACTION** item list *and* an **IDEA** list. You may also want to grab a highlighter. I would argue that it's not enough to simply read each episode. You must also *APPLY* the concepts in this book to get the most value. Application starts by taking detailed notes. Implementation happens when you take action on your notes.

One last piece of advice. If you haven't already, put the book down and go subscribe to podcast Game Changers for Government Contractors. You can do it on any podcasting app.

Now let's jump in...

Michael LeJeune

---

[1] The Podcast Game Changers for Government Contractors can be found on any number of podcast sites, including iTunes and Soundcloud.

Episode 1.
What it Takes to Win

By Michael LeJeune

Partner at RSM Federal, Federal Access PM, and Podcast Host
for Game Changers for Government Contractors

Time

Government contracting requires a lot of patience. It's not similar to most businesses where you can start a company in the morning and be collecting checks in the evening. I've done that in the B2C and B2B world. Not B2G.[2]

In a B2B market, most decision makers don't have to deal with federal regulation, politics, procedures, and policy. If you make a cold call and reach a decision maker, they can buy your product or service on the spot.

The government doesn't work that way. In fact, if you ask other contractors and industry experts, they will likely tell you that it takes three to five years to learn how to do business with the government.

The Small Business Administration says that more than 50% of all companies will fail in the first five years under normal circumstances. So, if it takes you three to five years to learn this market and half the companies

---

[2] Business to Consumer (B2C), Business to Business (B2B), and Business to Government (B2G)

fail under "normal" conditions, what does that say about your chances to make it as a government contractor? It says many smaller companies won't be around long enough to make a go of it.

You need every advantage that you can get your hands on (such as this book and other resources).

Small contracts can happen pretty fast. When I say small, I'm typically referring to contracts under the simplified acquisition threshold of $250K. The point is, your first contract or two will likely be small. It will get your feet wet and give you an opportunity to prove yourself. You may also win your first several contracts as a subcontractor on a larger project.

The big juicy contracts that you really want often take many months if not years to win. Looking back, I can't think of a single seven figure contract that I've won that didn't take at least six to twelve months to close. That is from the day we discovered the opportunity until the day we had a signed contract in hand. It often took another three to five months to start collecting payments.

So why tell you this? *Because it's the truth and your company needs to have accurate expectations.*

Many people get into government contracting in one of two ways. The first is when a friend tells them how easy it is going to be. They have a friend who works in government contracting and is making a small fortune.

This advice is often given to newer companies who qualify for any of several statuses such as Service-Disabled Veteran Owned Small Business (SDVOSB), Veteran Owned (VOSB), Woman Owned (WOSB), minority and socially disadvantaged (8a), and HUBZone, etc. The advice sounds like this:

"You can qualify as both 8(a) and SDVOSB, in a HUBZone, and the government is ready, right now, to throw money at you (all day long) if you get into government contracting."

Then you get into government contracting and realize that there are thousands of other companies that not only do what you do, but also have the same small business certifications. This is where the hard truth sets in that the government is **NOT** eagerly waiting to throw you money. You have to earn it. But how?

The second way that people get thrust into this business is actually from the inside. They are working for a government contractor (typically a big prime contractor) and they're on-site with a government client. They have a nice cushy lifestyle with benefits and a simple 9 to 5 routine. One day, the government client starts talking to them about how the contract is coming up for recompete and the incumbent probably won't win. They plant a seed that if you started your own company, they would hire you and you could be your own boss.

So, you start your own company and "win" your first contract at your old job. But now what? You are working 40 to 50 hours a week for the government and you *have no clue how to win the next contract.*

I'm not sharing this to scare folks. I share it to open your eyes to what it's really going to take to win. And the first thing it's going to take is a little time.

Earlier, I said that it takes the average company three to five years to learn the government market. My objective for you is to accelerate that timetable so that you can learn everything you really need to know in just three to six MONTHS! Many of the strategies you need are touched-on in this book.

Instead of taking a year or two to win your first contract, I want you to get some small wins in the first six months. You could be winning contracts in 90 to 180 days if you follow the advice in this book. But that will only happen if you apply the lessons that your learn.

Let's kick this off with seven (7) recommendations. It starts with knowledge.

Knowledge

You get knowledge in one of two ways. Slowly and painfully through experience, or by having mentors. That said, please...please...please...be careful when it comes to choosing a mentor. There are a lot of great mentors out there. Quite a few of them are in this book. There are also a bunch of bad options out there. Be wary and do your homework.

When someone calls me and says they don't know where to start or they are struggling and don't know why, I always take them back to the basics of winning a contract.

Step 1 – Find out who buys what you sell. There are a lot of bid-matching and data tools for government contractors, but my current favorite is the Federal Procurement Data System (FPDS.gov). As I write this, the FPDS website is being rolled into SAM.gov. My heart actually sank a bit as I typed that because FPDS has been so valuable for us over the years. The data is amazing and if the site is still up when you read this, take advantage of it.

You can search FPDS in many different ways. The most popular is searching by NAICS code and keywords. Other popular search strings include the DUNS/SAMMI number and Contracting Office IDs to name a few. Once you hit the search button, you will instantly get back hundreds if not thousands of contract actions (records). You will also get a list of the top agencies and government vendors. This will tell you who your potential clients are as well as your competitors / potential teaming partners.

Step 2 – Get your ducks in order. You need a capability statement (You can get a couple of FREE templates with a free account on Federal Access (https://federal-access.com). You will also need a website and government landing page, business cards, and a professional email domain (no @aol, @gmail, @yahoo accounts). Those are the basics for your marketing.

Step 3 – It's time to start talking to contracting officers. These are the folks that are typically making the purchasing decisions for your products/services. You can get their contact info from FPDS, agency websites, and at the bottom of every RFP in SAM.gov.

When you talk to a contracting officer, your number one priority is gathering intelligence and information that will ultimately help you win a current contract or future opportunity. There are many pieces to this puzzle. You want to ask questions that will help you find more pieces so you can solve the puzzle.

Here's an example of what your first call might look like.

You – *"This is Mike from RSM Federal, I'm new to working with your organization and was wondering if you could help point me in the right direction?"*

[Notice that I haven't even told them what I do at this point]

CO – "Sure, how can I help?"

You – *"Awesome! Thank you. **I'm not calling about anything currently in acquisition.** I was doing some research and noticed that your organization buys (insert product or service) and I was curious how you normally go about purchasing this."*

The CO will either start spilling their guts OR they will ask you to clarify what you are asking. You want to know several things. Do they normally buy via a traditional acquisition such as an RFP or RFQ? Do they use simplified acquisition procedures (SAP)? Do they tend to use specific contract vehicles, GSA Schedules, etc. to purchase these products/services? Does the organization usually hit its small business goals (if you are a small business)? These are just several of the items you want to get answers to.

Before you get off the call, ask the CO this very important question. *"If you were me, is there anyone else you would call? Such as a possible teaming partner or a counterpart of yours in another office?"*

When you finish the call, look up the small business office for that organization, call them up, and ask the same questions.

Step 4 – Find a teaming partner. Now that you have a little intelligence, it's time to reach out to some potential teaming partners. You can find a list of these with FPDS/SAM.gov. However, a better way to finding potential teaming partners is to *ask the contracting officer and small business office if there is someone they would recommend.* You are looking for someone who is already working with your prospect.

When you call a potential teaming partner, it's best to have some intelligence to barter with. Here's an example of how to get past the gatekeeper and to the right person.

"Hi Bob, this is Mike LeJeune over at RSM Federal. I've been talking with (customer name) about an upcoming opportunity. Jan thought I should give you a call to discuss. I think we would make your team extremely competitive."

Do you see how powerful that intro is? If not, here's an example of what the average person would normally say. *"Hi Bob, we are an SDVOSB and we would like to partner with you."* See the difference?

Building Your Pipeline

From this point on, your focus needs to be prospecting to fill your pipeline. Nothing beats old fashioned rolling up your sleeves and making calls, talking to people, and gathering information.

You need to repeat steps 3 (talk to COs) and 4 (find teaming partners) over and over and over again... you get the picture. Remember, you are putting together a puzzle one piece at a time. There might be some quick wins, but ultimately, you need to be playing the long game.

As I said earlier, my largest contracts (the seven figure ones) came from months of hard work. This included on-site visits with the customer, talking to their staff, sitting in on planning and strategy meetings, responding to requests for information and sources sought, and lot of other work. A lot of that work came at our own expense. It was simply the cost of doing business.

One of the ways to build your pipeline is to always ask your client about the future. Sometimes, that's in the form of a forecast, a strategic plan, word of mouth/rumors, and even the President's budget. In terms of forecasts, many agencies update their forecasts on a somewhat regular basis. Quickly take a look and see if the forecasts for the agencies you're targeting actually provide value for what you sell.

I advise asking your prospect. *"Hey there prospect, what are your goals for the next 12 to 24 months? Are there any big projects on the horizon that I should know about? Any big problems that you need to solve? Any big RFP's about to hit the street?"*

Your goal is to build up a healthy mix of small opportunities that will easily keep the lights on (contracts closing in the next 90 days) while also hunting some of those unicorn opportunities that are going to catapult you to the next level.

Most people would advise that your pipeline should be an 80/20 mix of short/long term revenue. My advice is a little different. What I want you to do is look at your corporate expenses. Calculate what type of revenue you need to generate to sustain your government business. Once you have that number, multiply it by ten. That's how large your short-term pipeline needs to be.

Your long-term pipeline can be just about any number. That is going to determine your potential for massive growth. Your short-term pipeline is what keeps you in business while you work the larger opportunities.

Here's something else that most people don't understand about pipelines. They are always optimistic. A pipeline is a best-case scenario IF all the stars align and everything closes. The reality is that everything won't close. Over time, you will start to notice an overall closing percentage. That's your conversion rate. It's also called your win rate. That number is helpful in several ways.

If you know that you win three out of every ten contract opportunities, that means you have a 30% conversion rate or win rate. You can start to look at your pipeline from a percentage point of view. For example, if you have $100K in your short-term pipeline, you can safely say that $30K of that is going to close.

Here's another secret. Let's say you have ten opportunities in your pipeline and you close three of them. Now you have seven in your pipeline. How many opportunities do you need to ADD back to your pipeline in order to ensure that you continue to hit your numbers?

Most people would answer three. Ten minus seven is three. BUT, if your win rate is 30% and you just closed three contracts, the odds are you won't close the other seven. At a minimum, they could get delayed. So, the correct answer is that you need to add ten more opportunities to your pipeline. If you don't follow this formula, you will likely start missing your numbers and think that your conversion rate is slipping. That's not the problem. The problem is that you aren't refreshing your pipeline with enough opportunities.

Persistence

How many phone calls does it take to win a contract? As many as it takes…

How long does it take to win a contract? A long as it takes…

The government works at its own pace. Yes, you can manipulate parts of their acquisition strategy but the government doesn't operate the same way as corporate America. HOWEVER, you can follow-up like crazy and stay in the loop.

You have to remember that your contract is probably one of dozens if not hundreds that a contracting officer is working on. So yes, it helps to jog their memory from time to time.

You will also be told no or not at this time A LOT! That doesn't mean you stop trying. In fact, I always ask *"would it be ok to follow-up with you in 90-days or so?"* The worst they can say is no.

Here's a game changer that our clients often use. If you are getting the cold shoulder over the phone, ask for a face-to-face. Clients will often tell you things in person that they wouldn't dare say over the phone. It's just human nature.

If you are having trouble getting a client to set a date for you to drop by, try the following. Call or email them and say *"I'm going to be in your area on (date/s) and would like to stop by and put a face to a name. Which day works best for you?"* Prospects and clients almost always respond to that. No one wants someone dropping in. They will either pick one of your days or suggest a different one.

Research Skills

If you are going to win contracts, you need to be a research ninja. You need to know how to find information and how to use one bit of information to look for another.

One thing you will always need is contact information. Google is your friend here. I always start with a simple search like "contracting officer Ft. Hood" and see what that gets me. If may give you several names. It may give you one. If you only get one and it's not the one you want, you can still call that contracting officer (CO) and tell them who you are looking for. They will likely be able to direct you.

If you strike out with that CO or get voicemail, go back to Google. This time search "contracting officer Ft. hood LinkedIn." Often adding the word 'LinkedIn' to your search will get you what you need.

But guess what? You find the CO you are looking for on LinkedIn, but you aren't connected. Now what? Send them an invite to connect. In the meantime, now you have a name. Search "Bob Smith contracting officer Ft. Hood" in Google. Now that Google has a name for the CO, it will likely give you more information.

See where I'm going with this? We need the CO's contact info. A few minutes ago, we didn't even have Bob's name. Now we are using his name and position to search for more info.

There's one more stop you should make. Head over to SAM.gov and search Ft. Hood contracting opportunities. If Bob is a CO there, you will likely find his info on an existing RFP. For those of you wondering how to search SAM for all Ft. Hood opportunities, get all the Contracting Office IDs for Ft Hood. Now query SAM by those IDs. To simplify, any opportunity you find for Ft. Hood in SAM will have a solicitation number. The first six digits of that solicitation number is the Contracting Office ID code. So, for that specific contracting division on Ft Hood, just search by the six-digit code in SAM and every active solicitation will be found!

There's no wrong way to search for information like this. You just have to be willing to keep searching until you find what you need. Also, this isn't just limited to contact information. Apply this same thinking to contract vehicles, teaming partners, certifications, you name it. The information is out there just waiting on you to search for it.

What happens if you come up dry? Email me. There's a good chance that I can point you in the right direction because I AM a research ninja!

Writing Skills

Just about anything you do with the government will require at least basic writing skills. You may not be writing 300-page proposals, but you will be writing emails, marketing pieces, briefings, and content for your website and capability statements. (We recommend that you have multiple capability statements to tailor for specific prospects or opportunities).

Some of this writing, such as emails, will take place on a daily basis. When it comes to proposals, you will probably come up with some templates that will only need to be tweaked at proposal time. But the bottom line remains, you need to be able to write. You need to be able to communicate your thoughts in a clear and concise manner.

If you don't feel you are good at writing, I suggest taking a class or two at your local community college. There are tons of courses, webinars, and videos online that you can take for free or for a small fee. One of my favorite tools for writers is ezinearticles.com. If you sign up for free, they will email you a free course to help you learn better writing skills.

At the end of the day, nothing beats writing. The simple exercise of writing will help you more than just about any course on the planet. Start with a simple journal or by blogging. Don't worry about grammar and punctuation at first. Focus on telling your story and communicating it effectively. The rest will come with time.

Speaking / Presentation Skills

People who book speaking events earn 40% more than their colleagues. A mentor once told me that. I tested the theory. I actually found the number to be off quite a bit. When I first started speaking at conferences, I quickly established myself as a subject matter expert (SME) in my niche. When I asked my friends what they were making, I was making double or triple.

So, what's my point? Speaking establishes you as an expert and exposes you to larger audiences.

Get out there and speak at conferences or ask to be a member of a panel and you will grow your company. What are you an expert at? You know much more than you give yourself credit for.

The trick to speaking is not having a $30K sizzle reel of your 'best talk.' The trick is in writing an abstract/overview of the session you want to give and then submitting that to the organization that is hosting the event. Many organizations have an open-call for speakers. That's your opportunity to get your abstract submitted for review.

If you get rejected, ask why. If you missed the call for presentations, ask when they typically do that and if you can be notified next year. Also ask to be added as a backup in case anyone cancels. This sounds a lot like persistence again doesn't it?

When it comes to delivering your message, keep it simple. If you are new to speaking, you will probably want slides as your guide to keep YOU on track. Again, keep them simple. A mentor of mine once taught me, "if you can't or don't want to explain it on the slide, take it off." The idea is that if it's really complicated, it needs to go!

I've been speaking for many years. At first, I hated it. Today, it's probably my favorite activity in business. I'm also fairly natural at. Sometimes I don't even use slides. My trick to speaking without slides is to keep my talk to three or four main bullet points. Three is ideal. If you narrow your message down to just those few highlights, it's easy to fill in the gaps. More importantly, it's fairly easy to remember three points without notes.

Business Coaching

My final tip for this episode is to get a coach. It doesn't have to be one of us. You just need someone in your life who is going to guide you. There is absolutely no reason for you to do this on your own. In fact, I believe the worst thing you can do is to try to do it by yourself.

There are a lot of free resources such as the Procurement Technical Assistance Center (PTAC), SCORE, and friends who might be willing to mentor you for free. Absolutely take advantage of that. But…and this is a HUGE but…at some point, if we want to accelerate our revenue, we need to step up and consider the value of paying for a professional coach.

Free services are great when you are starting out, but most of the free services have limitations. Truthfully, these organizations are more designed for volume and for getting you started. They aren't designed for the level of intimacy that a professional coach provides. A professional coach has a smaller client load and can give you the tailored support that you need and want.

I talk more about this topic in Episode 4 – *How to Grow Fast*. If you are in the market for a coach, go read that before you make any decisions.

After you read Episode 4, if you would like to interview for one of our coaching spots, please visit https://rsmfederal.com/breakthroughcoaching. You'll learn more about how we approach coaching and whether it's the right for you.

*   *   *

Michael LeJeune is a Partner with RSM Federal and Program Manager for the Federal Access Knowledge-Base and Training Platform. He is an award-winning business coach, author, and host of the podcast Game Changers for Government Contractors. He has been consulting and mentoring companies in the government market for twenty years. Michael is also an Army Veteran. Find him at www.linkedin.com/in/michaeljlejeune/

Episode 2.
Finding the Right Revenue Mix

By Chris Bobbitt

Co-Founder and Vice President, Technical Assent

In this episode, we'll talk through some ways to think about finding the right mix of revenue for your government contract's business. In the government service business, revenue really comes in two categories: definitive contracts and contract vehicles. Vehicles solve a type of problem for an agency (or types of problems), whereas definitive contracts (a.k.a. direct work) solves a specific, *defined* problem. You need both to be successful in the long run. You have to build and balance your portfolio of these in parallel and align that portfolio to your business strategy and growth stage. A good portfolio of definitive contracts and contract vehicles will make your business easier to run (and more attractive as an acquisition target, if that's part of the goal).

The Basics

Definitive Contracts procure a definite quantity of a supply or service to be delivered or provided at definite times. Definitive contracts are the only things that come with money attached. Orders on vehicles are in effect definitive contracts.

Vehicles allow the government to order indefinite amounts of a supply or service at any point in a set period of time. Vehicles are what you need so you have an answer when a potential client asks, "So how do I get to you?".

Vehicles come in two main types: indefinite delivery indefinite quantity (**IDIQs**) and blanket purchase agreements (**BPAs**). There are important

21

differences in how the two types function, but these differences aren't important to the concept of vehicles.

At least half of the money the government spends is through vehicles: 52% for the federal government overall for FY2018. For some types of services, as an example, this proportion can be much greater: for Administrative Management and General Management Consulting Services this was 80% in FY18 (NAICS 541611, which includes management consulting, program management); for Computer Systems Design Services it was 95% (NAICS 541512, basically all IT development, digital services).

How to Think About the Mix

First, understand your objectives as a business and where you are in the maturity of the business. If you are just starting out, vehicles are nice, but you need revenue. You are talking to your connections in government and at established firms about their needs and upcoming opportunities, you're looking at SAM.gov for work in your wheelhouse but maybe that you weren't tracking. The only time you should be touching a vehicle at this stage is if you are supporting a task order as a sub or you are scouting the vehicle landscape.

The timeline for vehicles – from conception to first task order award – can be years. This cycle can be so long that putting all your eggs in a vehicle basket without a very long cash runway is a poor choice. You will run out of money before you win enough work to replenish your coffers.

Be clear on your relationships (other smalls, mid/large primes, government clients). It's hard to get someone to bring you onto a team if you don't have very differentiated capabilities and experience, or true intimacy with the government customer.

Don't chase everything. Don't bid on everything you see on SAM.gov with your NAICS code, and don't chase every vehicle. You have to be judicious and a careful steward of your own time and money.

What Vehicles Should You Get On?

There are three basic answers to this question; they are all correct and you should do all of them:

1. GSA Schedule(s) for what you do

2. GWACs for what you do
3. Key vehicles for your target agency / agencies

GSA Schedules

Billions of dollars each year get awarded on these by all agencies. GSA Schedules are an important indicator that you are a bona fide firm with a performance track record, good finances, and fair and reasonable pricing. Agencies create vehicles (BPAs) from these schedules.

If you don't have the time to write that proposal yourself, particularly because the solicitation requirements have changed in the last year, it is absolutely worth the $7,000-$15,000 you will pay someone to write it for you if you do a specific kind of service that's generally applicable in lots of different agencies like program management, CIO support, or software development.

> There is a GSA Schedule for whatever you do:
>
> *   Facilities and Construction
> *   Human Capital
> *   Industrial Products & Services
> *   Information Technology
> *   Medical
> *   Office Management
> *   Professional Services
> *   Security & Protection
> *   Travel, Transportation, and Logistics

GWACs for What You Do[3]

Government-Wide Acquisition Contracts are in many senses the way of the future for the products and services that every agency buys. With the push toward Category Management across the federal government and the very strong preference for agencies to use vehicles with a "Best in Class" designation (BICs), you'll see more and more work come out on GWACs like OASIS, VETS2, Alliant 2, and 8(a) STARS II / III. These have low fees, audit procedures are easy, and ordering is straightforward. And again, it

---

[3] Government-Wide Acquisition Contracts (GWAC) are specific to information technology (IT) services. Multiple Award Contracts (MAC) are IDIQs for all industries. GWACs are simply one form of a MAC.

conveys an element of legitimacy and sophistication about you as a business. You aren't shut out if you aren't on these, but they make a big difference when a client asks, "So how do I get to you?"

Key Vehicles for Your Target Agencies

I believe these are the best paths to revenue, but they don't have rolling on-ramps and can be competitive. Customer relationships and timing are essential.

You are looking for on-ramps to vehicles that clients in the market like to use, follow-ons to those kinds of vehicles, and vehicles that are going to be strategic vehicles for that agency for the next 5-10 years.

Every agency is going to have their own specific vehicles just for them for strategic pockets of support. I normally avoid telling people to go to the Office of Small and Disadvantaged Business Utilization (OSDBU), but a very focused question like "what are the big vehicles at this agency?" is really helpful because then you can take that information, go find out who the primes are, and start to pitch your value proposition as a prospective team member. Then you can use that to target the customers within the agency you're actually ordering on these vehicles. Free tools like USASpending or pay services like GovTribe or Bloomberg Government are great for this.

Should I Be On This Vehicle?

When evaluating vehicles, you should ask yourself a few questions:

- Is it an important vehicle for an important customer?
- Is it a follow on to a vehicle that we've been on before?
- Does it constitute a significant amount of the kind of work that we do?
- Am I a credible prime?
- If not, can we be a significant contributor to it as a subcontractor?

If you don't know the competitive landscape in the agency for that vehicle, you are likely not a competitive prime, so you should focus on finding a competitive team to join as a key subcontractor.

What Happens After I Get the Vehicle?

Once you win a vehicle such as ADVISOR or even a GSA schedule, you might be tempted to think money will just rain down from the heavens.

I think of vehicles and direct contracts, a lot like farming and hunting. Just because you've cleared the plot of farmland, that's your vehicle. You actually have to plow the field, sow the seeds. Water your field. And then eventually harvest. So just because you've won a spot on the vehicle just means that you're in a smaller pool to compete. This means that you need to continue to run a tight proposal shop. You need to continue to demonstrate value. You need to always be sharp on your pricing and you need to go out and market the vehicle to prospective customers.

Ultimately, obviously, the choice of what vehicle to use if you're going to use a vehicle is the purview of the contracting officer exclusively. But if you're customer doesn't have a preferred contracting method and you know that, you can steer their work to your vehicle or help them do that. That's the kind of information that's useful in a program. Program managers love to work with contracting officers who understand their needs and who can help them get the support they need in a timely way, provided, of course, that the program office is responsible and thorough in their own requirements, documentation and things like that.

You still have to sell. It's just a lot easier than if you didn't have the vehicle already. There are things that you don't have to do, like demonstrate that your pricing is fair and reasonable. Sometimes you don't have to submit past performance questionnaires anymore, although I've seen some agencies start to require that after 18 months or two years on a five-year vehicle and the ordering procedures can be more straightforward. So instead of taking 120 to 180 days or even a year to get some kind of direct work, even a big task order ($10-$30 million) can take less than 60 days from the time your client gives the contracting office money to the time that you get an award.

Don't Forget About Definitive Contracts

Many people are taught that, when you get a contract vehicle, you've bought a field that's already been plowed, it's already been planted, it's already been watered. It's literally ready for harvest. And I think that's the perception most people have. They think they've bought the harvest table instead of ground they have to work in. What you've really won is a license to hunt on a game preserve; as opposed to just wandering the wilderness with no boundaries.

Another challenge that people have is once you have a few vehicles under your belt, it's really easy to ignore these outside opportunities. You almost wind up treating the vehicle itself as your security blanket and burying your head in the sand. You have to balance staying focused on the task orders that are coming down from your contract vehicles while also continuing to look for additional outside opportunities.

A great way to keep this balanced focus is to work backwards from a growth target. If you have a certain revenue goal, you want to achieve a given run rate, and you want to achieve it by a certain point in time. You can know what the average size proposal that you'll need to bid is. You can work backwards from your average win rate into how many proposals you need to submit. Once you know how your pipeline works, you know how many opportunities you have to identify and qualify before you actually get to ones that you're ready to bid.

And so, if you need to win, say, six proposals for six $1 million opportunities at some point in the year, you probably need to look at 100-150 deals throughout the year in order to really fill that pipeline. One way to think about looking at what comes out in a vehicle versus direct opportunities is to add them into your pipeline.

Just because it's not a vehicle doesn't mean it's not good. Lots of definitive contracts have a base year and three or four option years. These are still good, stable, long-term work. The great thing about this is you're not hamstrung or tied up based on the rates you've built on a vehicle three years ago. If the market's gone in a different direction, you have the flexibility to propose different labor categories, different skill mixes, different rate mixes that better reflect the realities of today's market. You can then use that to justify rate changes on your GSA schedule or to substantiate your pricing on future vehicles.

Remember, getting a new vehicle is just clearing a field or buying a hunting license. Getting direct work is that animal you're tracking today. That's how you will know if you're successful: you will hire staff, either for that work or to replace staff that you've transitioned over. Definitive contracts give you past performance. You will start collecting revenue, which at the end of the day is the only thing that turns into cash and earnings. And those are what matters in the business.

The Right Revenue Mix Can Make It Easier to Sell Your Business

(if you want to)

Getting the right mix of definitive contracts and contract vehicles isn't just about making your business easier to run – this can also make your business easier to sell. Selling is the ultimate end-game for many founders in the government services space. Revenue mix impacts both your valuation (how much money you might get) and the number of potential buyers (how easy it would be to sell).

The valuation of a business can be based on earnings before interest, taxes, depreciation and amortization (EBITDA) – *not revenue*. A more complex business might have more depreciation and amortization on the income statement than a straightforward professional services firm.

My co-founder at Technical Assent and I sold another company before we started this one, and we've looked at maybe a dozen acquisition opportunities over the last two years. Valuations can range from 3X – 8X earnings depending mostly on four factors:

1. Prime vs. Sub
2. Full & Open vs. Set-aside
3. Vehicle vs. Definitive Contracts
4. Cleared vs. Unclassified

Prime vs. Sub

Prime contracts are always more valuable than work as a subcontractor. If you're earnings are all from prime contracts, that's viewed as more stable, more within your control, and therefore more valuable to an acquirer.

Full & Open vs. Set-aside

Contracts won through full and open competition are always more valuable than set-aside work. Set-aside programs are great "hand-ups" to get a business on its feet and get some great past performance. But if you want to really sell, you've got to shift the revenue mix toward full and open.

Vehicle vs. Definitive Contracts

Vehicles are more valuable than one-offs because vehicles are umbrellas for one-offs. Vehicles make it easier to get a tighter return on your bid and proposal dollars because it doesn't take as much effort to respond to a task order request as it does to do a completely new proposal for a full and open one or a direct award solicitation.

Cleared vs. Unclassified

Cleared work is always better than unclassified work. This means the contract has a DD Form 254 Contract Security Classification Specification attached to it, not that the existence of the contract is a classified national security secret. This means your company must have a Facility Clearance. This is a significant barrier to entry and limits the pool of competition. As a rule of thumb, higher classification is better, but not every type of firm is going to specialize in analytical support at the Top Secret / SCI level to the CIA.

To recap, you want contracts and vehicles that are more prime than sub, more full and open than set-aside, more work won on vehicles than one-off contracts, and a facility clearance, if applicable for your market.

A Few Final Thoughts

If you're a business owner, either partial or total, there are really a handful of things you have to keep in mind.

Understand your objectives as a business and where you are in the maturity of the business.

You have to understand "What's your objective?" This is business. But if you're trying to have a lifestyle business, then maybe you don't care so much about whether you're closer to 3X to 8X valuation. But if you're really trying to build and sell, you've really got to start to understand where you are in the maturity level or are you a true startup? Are you still proving a concept? Are you small but sustainable? Are you a mature small business that's on the cusp of transitioning to the majority prime track and more full-and-open work?

This drives how much of your time as a leader is spent doing sales and how much of your business development and capture function is being executed organically, either by a dedicated staff or by a mix of dedicated staff and your delivery side leaders.

Understand your current cash and cash flow position.

You really have to understand what's going on with cash and cash flow in your business. And you have to compare that to the government sales cycle. This cycle can be so long that putting all your eggs in a vehicle basket without a very long cash runway is a poor choice. You will run out of money before you win enough work to replenish your coffers. This underscores the value of these direct work opportunities outside of vehicle task orders because they build your cash position, which allows you to be strategic and make pursuits and investments in vehicles.

Be clear on your relationships
(other smalls, mid/large primes, government clients).

You need to know where your relationships are. This ties back-in to how you pick the vehicles that you're going to go after. If you've got lots of relationship to other smalls, that points you in the direction of smaller vehicles, set-aside vehicles. If you're focused on a lot of relationships with midsize and larger prime contractors, that may push you into a different vehicle set, both as sub and sometimes as a prime. But you've got tons of specific government client relationships and special status or something like that, maybe that points you in a different direction in terms of what vehicles you might compete on, how competitive you'll be, and even possibly having a client create a vehicle specifically *for* you.

Understand if you're better at selling in person or writing proposals.

This will drive how you spend your time. Bring on a partner or hire someone who complements and balances you.

Put it all together - and don't bankrupt the business!

Remember that you're in this business to grow it. Don't make investments that send you into cash-flow negative. As you're evaluating vehicles, ask the questions: Are we really going to be able to capture what we need out of this, given the cost? What's it going to cost us to act to potentially acquire it? Or is it too risky? And should we focus on either smaller vehicles or waiting until the kinds of vehicles that we really want come up for recompete in two or three years? In the meantime, pursue partnerships with folks who are on those vehicles and direct work with clients that you already know and can add value to their mission.

*   *   *

Chris Bobbitt co-founded Technical Assent to help government improve performance by using Customer Experience as the primary driver for change. A pioneer in using human-centered design to tackle complex government challenges, Chris leads solutions for strategy execution, service management, and program management for Technical Assent.

He has executive experience in several government consulting firms including Kickstand LLC where he served as a founding member and Director until its acquisition in 2012. His federal government experience includes Defense, Healthcare, Veterans, Intelligence, and Homeland Security. His industry expertise includes the national security, energy, capital markets, and banking sectors.

Chris received the Secretary of Defense's Global War on Terrorism Medal in recognition of his service in Iraq. He holds a B.A. from Georgetown University in Economics and in History and resides in Washington, DC. Find him at https://www.linkedin.com/in/cbobbitt/

Episode 3.
How to Communicate Your Past Performance

By Joshua Frank

Managing Partner, RSM Federal

The strategies we use to grow our companies are constantly changing. If you're consistently changing how you market your company, you're likely having trouble communicating not only what you do, but the value that your company provides. I've been training companies for more than a decade. Without reservation, this is the number one challenge faced by companies of all sizes. I've worked with startups, small businesses, mid-tier and large companies. Understanding how to best position and communicate your experience and past performance is a common challenge.

For this episode, I want to expand on several chapters from my book *"An Insider's Guide To Winning Government Contracts" (An Amazon bestseller)* and provide you with a real-world case study that may open your eyes to new concepts and strategies. As with all of my coaching and training, I want you to be able to immediately shift *how* you communicate your value and expertise.

No two companies are alike. No two companies operate the same way. While some companies will be able to implement these concepts, some will not. If you need help, you'll find me on LinkedIn. Speaking of which, I'm fairly active on LinkedIn and often share key market updates. So, before you read any further, take out your phone and connect with me.

Okay, let's get down to business. Done correctly, these simple yet highly effective tactics will help you see the "forest through the trees." When done correctly, most companies are able to communicate a more mature position in the market and increase revenue. Sound simple enough? You may want to grab a highlighter or pen.

So, how do you improve *how you communicate your past performance*?

It starts with value. It ends with quantifiable and qualifiable metrics, numbers and percentages.

The Forest Through the Trees

When I speak at events, I discuss the difference between a government sales strategy and basic business strategy. I often say, "Trust your gut! No matter what you hear or what you're told to do, a government sales strategy should never be developed without a foundation in general business strategy.

Sounds obvious, right? But sometimes it's not that simple.

For example, government contractors are given dozens of recommendations on how to sell to the government. You're educated on federal procurement. You're told that you have to get certified by the Department of Veterans Affairs (VA) or the Small Business Administration (SBA). You're told to speak with small business offices and government buyers. At some point, every company throws their hands-up, rolls their eyes, and says, "Oh, for heaven's sake! I'm doing what everyone told me to do but everyone has a different way of doing it. I'm not winning as many contracts as I want. I really don't know if I'm doing what I'm supposed to be doing!"

Another way of looking at it: If you're a small business, what's the absolute most common question that you're asked by government buyers and potential teaming partners?

Correct, your business size and certifications for socio-economic status. Are you a small business? Are you certified minority, woman, HUBZone, or Veteran?

Many tell you to lead with your socio-economic status, your certifications. If you don't have any but you're a small business, they tell you to lead with being a small business. From the perspective of a *government sales strategy*, it makes sense! The government must spend 23% of all dollars with small businesses which includes 5% to women, 5% to minority and socially disadvantaged, 3% to HUBZone, and 3% to service disabled veterans. As a result, many small business professionals inside and outside the government tell you to focus on status. Why not? We're talking more than $270 Billion in contracts! The government is federally mandated to use companies just like yours.

So, for a government sales strategy, it makes perfect sense to focus on your size and status.

Right?

Wrong.

From a business perspective, not only is it a bad strategy, you won't win many, if any contracts. I go into extensive detail on this and how to market your certifications in the *Insider's Guide To Winning Government Contracts*.

If you're a member of the Federal Access Knowledge-Base, one of our coaching clients, or seen me present at training events or conferences, I don't have to sell you on this. You already get it. But if not, I want you to answer one question:

Answer One Question

When you are face to face with a government buyer and you have to communicate the value that your company provides, how do you describe that value?

If you're a small business - go back and read that again. What *value* does your company provide? When I ask this question, not a single person ever says, "Well gee! Our value is that we're small and woman owned."

But there's something odd here. When I look at their website, their capability statement, their proposals, and how they communicate with the government and teaming partners... they market as if their value is their size and status.

Many small business professionals introduce themselves with, "Hi! My name is Jack and we're a woman-owned small business that sells / provides these products or services."

At this point, you know where I'm going with this. In this example, Jack is saying, "The value we provide is that we're small and woman-owned." He's implying that there are federally mandated set-aside percentages that his company can help fulfill.

This is what most companies are taught. This type of introduction perfectly aligns with the most common recommendations given by government buyers, small business offices, and yes, even consultants.

There's just one problem. *Leading with your size and certifications violates general business strategy.*

Whether commercial sales or government sales, people buy your products or services because of the value that your product or service provides *to your other customers*. It's one of the strangest things I've seen in business. Many companies have this challenge and when you finally recognize that your certifications will not win you a contract, the shift in your sales strategy becomes a **Game Changer**.

Give me one more opportunity to prove my point. The Department of Commerce releases a Request for Proposal (RFP) and it is being set-aside for woman-owned small businesses (WOSB). Twenty companies respond to the bid. What do all twenty companies have in common?

I'm chuckling as I write this because I'm pretty sure there will be no shortage of readers who start yelling at the book about asking dumb questions. Yes…all the companies are woman-owned.

So why do so many spend so much time and energy on making their size and status clear in their proposal? The company that wins will not win because they are woman-owned. It doesn't matter which company is awarded the contract. Whoever wins… will be woman-owned.

The winning contractor won because they had a stronger proposal that communicated superior value. (Unless it's a Low Price Technically Acceptable (LPTA) acquisition.)

Your value is not your status! You will **NOT** win government contracts because you are woman, veteran, or minority-owned.

Think *business strategy*.

Mapping Your Past Performance to Communicate Value

At this point, you're thinking, "Okay. Got it. Value is not my size or socio-economic status."

If you're new to government sales, past performance is just another way of saying your past work, your experience, your past contracts.

So, let's talk about your expertise and past performance. I want to provide you with several concepts and strategies that will make you perceptually more mature. While these concepts provide exceptional value to small businesses, from working with many mid-market and large companies, this applies to them as well. These concepts will put your marketing and positioning on a higher level:

- Website government landing page
- Capability statement and / or marketing collateral
- Elevator pitch in face to face meetings (buyers and teaming partners)
- Bids and proposals

The reality is that every company is going to approach this process differently. We all have different products and services. Even if we have the same solutions, we run our companies differently. We also have different teaming partners and clients. This leads us to the concept of competency-mapping which is the core theme for the rest of this episode.

Competency-Mapping™

Competency-Mapping is a method that forces you to evaluate and map the value and benefits of your products or services and differentiate them based on a specific prospect, that prospect's unique problems or challenges, and/or a specific opportunity."

The objective of competency-mapping is to realign how you communicate with prospects and customers by improving the positioning of proposals, call plans, prospect meetings, and how you communicate at conferences and trade shows. It helps improve how you shape your core competencies in response to new opportunities.

It doesn't matter if you've been in business for one year or thirty years. It doesn't matter if you have four clients or one hundred. It doesn't matter what you sell. Every company needs to go through a competency-mapping exercise. By the way, it's an *iterative process* that you perform and update after you win every new contract. I've taught this process to thousands of companies.

Explosive Acceleration

*Every one of our Clients and Federal Access Members are taken through Competency-Mapping and it **quickly redefines how they position in the market**.*

Now, before we jump into competency-mapping and a step-by-step example, I want to provide a couple real-world outcomes from this strategy.

In 2009, I worked with an information technology staffing company in Dallas, Texas. They wanted to go beyond staffing and start bidding on their own contracts. They wanted to prime. They were staffing positions for a couple dozen companies with three or four contracts providing most of their revenue.

My competency-mapping strategy had just been developed and documented. The staffing firm was the first company I took through the process. We selected twelve contracts, current and completed, and started reviewing (mapping) the statement of work, systems touched, organization's directly and indirectly supported, who was impacted, and other pieces.

The first step in this process was interviewing their employees. Sounds simple enough, right? Many companies have no idea what their employees are really doing on their contracts. Think about that for a moment. If your company provides services, do you really know what your employees are doing on a *daily* basis? Many companies think they know but really don't.

About a week after they started interviewing their employees, I received a call from one of the business developers. "Hey Josh, we just obtained some strange answers from one of our full-time employees (FTEs). We've received a response that is clearly outside the scope of their contract. We're not sure what we should do next?" The FTE in question was a software developer staffed-out to another company.

After asking several questions, I asked them to schedule a call with this employee.

We completed the call and I walked into the CEO's office. I looked at the CEO and said, "You have an employee, a software developer at Express Scripts. You staffed them to provide application development for a human resources project. Did you know that a Director in another department is using your employee to build a new system?"

At first, all the CEO could focus on was the fact that an employee was doing something out of scope.

So I looked at him and said, *"You have an FTE that is currently developing the next-generation account payable system for a Fortune 25 company."*

He was stunned. Then he considered the value this provided to his company. I told him to capture the story of what his employee was doing on the project.

This is clearly an example in the extreme. But this result happens, **on some level**, with *every company* that maps their current contracts and past performance.

Can you imagine if this had been your employee? Think of how you could market this! Think of how much more mature your company and solutions would be perceived in the market.

In early 2019, I received a call from a company in Bethesda, Maryland that wanted help with the acquisition of an $8 million company. They listened to Game Changers Episode 62 on Growth Through Acquisition with guest Erin Andrew of Live Oak Bank. Now, I'm not an expert in the legal aspects of M&A but this company needed help integrating the sales capabilities and resources of two companies.

Unbeknownst to my team, they had joined the Federal Access Knowledge-Base and had become die-hard fans of our tactics and strategies. Later in 2019, I received a call from the CEO and he recognized the value of competency-mapping but needed help keeping on task, maintaining focus, and having someone brain-storm with a whiteboard.

Fully grasping the value of this process, he personally interviewed every employee. When finished, he excitedly called me and said the new company he acquired had past performance in two agencies, NSA and NASA. He wasn't aware of this when he acquired the company!

Some of you are thinking, "How is that possible?" Again, whether it's one of your FTEs or a company recently acquired... you'll be amazed at what you'll find if you simply interview your employees and ask questions. If you're a product company, do you really know how your customers are using your products? Don't assume! You'll be amazed at what you'll discover if you simply ask the right questions. Don't just sell your products. Understand how they are being used.

Let's move to a case study.

I'm going to walk through this process using a real-world company that my team recently worked with. For more mature companies, your company might be ten years old with more than a dozen active contracts. But, if you're having problems communicating the value and benefit (not the capabilities) that you provide to your customers, then you are impacting your ability to increase future revenue - with both current and future clients. You need to not only collect highly detailed information on your current and past contracts, but have a formal process to capture, document, and file information with easy retrieval.

Now, let's jump into a case study that will help you better understand how this process works.

The Lubricant and Penetrating Solution

I recently worked with a small business on the East coast. They have four (4) full-time employees, two (2) part-time employees, and an annual revenue of $350,000. They sell a multi-use lubricant and penetrating solution. Think WD-40. Think hinges on squeaky doors. Think lubrication for weapons. Their revenue comes from primarily two sources. One is a hospital and the second is a recent agreement with Home Depot, the world's largest home improvement retailer.

They have commercial contracts but nothing on the government side. While they've been in business for more than five years, they're still in the go-to-market phase. They wanted help not only entering the government market, but overall positioning in the commercial space as well.

One of the awesome results of mapping your past contracts is that the results are industry and market agnostic. Whereas the podcast Game Changers for Government Contractors is focused on government sales, you'll find that most of the recommendations from our guests are just as applicable to the commercial market as they are for the government. So, mapping your past contracts will not only better position you to win government work, it will also help you win more commercial work as well!

The Status Quo

Like most companies, they were focusing on direct differentiators. For example, their multi-use lubricant easily cleans-up with soap and water. It's odorless, non-toxic, non-flammable, and can be purchased in both aerosol and liquid form.

These are all good. Their elevator / sales pitch was similar to how other companies position in the market.

Their Elevator Pitch
"We sell lubricants"
We have two contracts, one with a hospital AND we're carried by Home Depot.

We're a certified woman-owned small business. Our products work all the way down to -10ºF so we're much stronger than WD-40 in cold weather. Our lubricants are odorless, non-toxic, non-flammable, and clean up with just soap and water.

So what do you use for lubricants?
Who are the buyers for your agency?"

An accurate pitch. It clearly identifies what they sell and the features of their products.

But it doesn't really differentiate them from their competition, does it? Now think about your company and the products or services you sell. You're probably thinking, "That's similar to how we market," or "I get it but what are some strategies to making our pitch stronger?"

Mapping Your Past Performance

Let's better understand these two contracts. First, with $350,000 in revenue, what was the average sale? We'll call it the manufacturer suggested retail price (MSRP). Their MSRP was $9.95. At that price point, the company sold 35,500 units.

The first contract was for a hospital called St. Johns Mercy Medical. They had one buyer that made repeat buys. Month after month, they sold thousands of units to St. Johns. In their mind, they had one client at the hospital.

That's a mistake.

When we discussed the contract, I asked them to think beyond the dollars and cents. I asked if they had ever asked the buyer *where their product was being used*. They said no. They were simply interested in selling more to that specific buyer. When pushed, they called the buyer and found that their product was being distributed across the entire medical system.

Medical System.

We discussed the fact that St. Johns is not just a hospital, but a complete medical system. It's comprised of seventeen (17) hospitals located in five (5) states including Missouri, Kansas, Arkansas, Louisiana, and Oklahoma. Across five states there are 1,537 hospital, clinic, and outpatient locations. There are also 44,000 employees across the entire system that provide medical services to *more than one million patients each year*.

Then we looked at Home Depot. They had recently signed an agreement with the world's largest home improvement retailer. Like many large companies, Home Depot carries the goods of local small businesses. This was the case with lubricants. Three stores in their local region carried their product. *That was their focus*. But when we dug deeper, although they didn't have sales with any other stores, they dropped a nugget of information - that all 2,200 Home Depot stores had access to their products. These included stores not only in the United States, but also Canada and Mexico.

I should point out that the best way to work through this strategy is on a whiteboard with the whole team. The facts and figures I've listed above are just a fraction of the information we collected. At the conclusion of the exercise, we updated their elevator pitch.

Before you read the updated pitch below, I recommend first going back a couple pages to look at their original pitch.

Updated Elevator Pitch
*"We provide an environmentally safe, non-toxic, and non-flammable lubricant and penetration solution that is strong enough for **military-grade** applications, but safe enough for children.*

*We support more than **1,500 medical clinics** for **17 hospitals** in **5 states** where our lubricants are used by more than **44,000 professionals** supporting more than **1M end-users**.*

*Our lubricants are also carried by Home Depot, brick-n-mortar and online, supporting more than **2,200 stores** in the **US, Canada, and Mexico**.*

*What differentiates our lubricants is the fact that they are **odorless**, **non-toxic**, **non-flammable**, and work down to -10ºF.*

*In just the last year, we've sold more than **35,000 units** both **CONUS** and **OCONUS**.*

Many readers will look at this and smile. You're probably thinking, "This looks so simple!" Well, it is… and it's not. If nothing else, it may just be a different way of looking at your past performance. It's mapping multiple data points to create a much stronger perception of capability, value, and past performance.

Recognizing that this was for the government market, notice how we used Continental United States (CONUS) and Outside Continental United States (OCONUS) instead of just the U.S., Canada, and Mexico. We're using the government's language.

Now It's Your Turn

It doesn't matter what you sell, product or service. Think quantifiable and qualifiable metrics. No matter what you sell, mapping your past performance makes you perceptually stronger, more mature, more capable, and more attractive to commercial and government prospects and teaming partners.

If you're a technology company that provides software development, don't just focus on the system your employees are building. Here's a question, as part of that software project...how many other technology systems do you have to *touch from an integration perspective*? What are the names of those systems? Are they logistics systems? Human Resource (HR) systems? Tactical systems? Internal intranet systems? How many employees access EACH of these systems? Are any of these systems public-facing?

See where I'm going? The value is so much more than you think.

What if you're a security company? Let's say you install closed circuit television cameras (CCTV) as well as intrusion detection systems (IDS). What do most of these company focus on? They focus on the number of cameras and systems. Some, smartly, focus on the geographical dispersion of buildings on their contracts. This can be used to ghost maturity and capability while barring entry to competition.

For more information and strategies on ghosting your strengths and the weakness of your competition in order to influence procurements, grab a copy of the Insider's Guide To Winning Government Contracts on Amazon.

For the security company, we ran competency-mapping on a whiteboard. I asked them about the wiring, conduit, and cabling. Surprising them completely, we calculated that they had run and installed more than 100,000 feet of cabling, another strong metric that provides for perceived maturity and capability.

No matter what you sell, if you want to accelerate in the market, any market, you must perform competency-mapping. What I've provided in this episode is enough to get you started. All of the basics of this strategy are spelled out in the previous examples. Once you go through the basics, then you can move to more advanced mapping strategies.

Now, here's where it gets exciting! Think about your website, your capability statement, your marketing collateral, your teaming collateral, your 45 second pitch, introducing yourself at conferences... and writing proposals. When you go through this process, you will end up updating all of these!

Have you taken your company through this process?

What is your first step?

Something to think about.

*   *   *

Award-winning business coach, professional speaker, and #1 bestselling author, Joshua Frank is a nationally recognized authority on government sales and business acceleration. With 30 years in the government market, he speaks nationally on federal acquisition and business strategy. He specializes in the development and implementation of tactics and strategies required to differentiate, position for, and win government contracts.

Mr. Frank's coaching has helped companies win more than $2.6 Billion in government contracts. Managing Partner at RSM Federal, Mr. Frank is author of The Government Sales Manual and Amazon's #1 bestseller An Insider's Guide To Winning Government Contracts.

Mr. Frank serves as Chairman of the Board for the Midwest Veterans Advocacy Foundation (VAF). An avid outdoor enthusiast, Girl Scout and Boy Scout leader, Mr. Frank lives in St. Louis, Missouri with his wife, daughter, and son.

He is a former military intelligence officer with an undergraduate degree in English, a Masters in Management Information Systems (MIS), and a Master's in Business Administration (MBA). Find him at www.linkedin.com/in/joshuapfrank/

Episode 4.
How to Grow Fast

By Michael LeJeune

Partner at RSM Federal, Federal Access PM, and Podcast Host
for Game Changers for Government Contractors

Most books about government contracting are typically niche books. What do I mean by that? They tend to focus exclusively on government contracting skills. I think this is a mistake. Let me provide a little insight.

If you want to jump into the government market, the barrier to entry is actually very low. It doesn't take a ton of effort or skill to get lucky and win a contract. I'm sure a lot of people reading this just rolled their eyes. Just stay with me for a second. Your first contract win isn't typically the hardest. In fact, many people get into government contracting because a connection helps them win a contract. But this is where the problems often start.

Once you win your first contract, you believe it's always going to be this easy. And that's just not the case. It DOES take a lot of skill and a massive amount of effort to win more contracts.

I believe that regardless of how you enter this market, one common challenge for people is that the market can be intimidating. After all, you are working with the government. It can be confusing and frustrating to learn the jargon and how to navigate all the red-tape. With that in mind, most of the books you pick up on government contracting tend to play off this fear and only focus on government fundamentals like proposal writing, prospecting, bid-matching, capability statements; that sort of thing.

Let me be clear. There's a time and place for all those books. They are great resources for helping you learn about the government market. However, at the end of the day, you are running a business and it is a disservice to only focus on government systems and never talk about the *fundamentals of business*. One thing I can assure you is that the business fundamentals will save your butt over and over again.

The Law of Fundamentals

When times get tough or you don't know what to do, you can always count on business fundamentals to point you in the right direction.

The two most common stages of business are start-up and what we affectionately refer to as "the plateau." Regardless of which stage you are in; the fundamentals have the potential to provide the real game-changing ideas that you need. If you happen to be in serious growth mode, these fundamentals will also serve you well. In fact, if you are in growth mode, this episode is probably one of the more valuable episodes.

Mario Burgos, one of our recent podcast guests said, "nothing eats up cash like growth." I like to say, "ignorance is the only thing that eats up cash faster." That's why it's so important to understand the concepts below.

There are dozens of fundamentals, but for this episode, I decided to zero-in on three major concepts that apply to every stage of business. These three concepts have been the ultimate game changers for me over the last twenty years. When I get stuck, I refer back to them.

I want to caution you before you continue reading. It's very easy to dismiss the value of these concepts. But I am living proof that these concepts can be the pillars of your success. In fact, over the first four years of hosting the Game Changers podcast, I asked every guest about these concepts. Guess what? Every single subject matter expert agreed that these concepts are, without a doubt, critical to your success. So, buckle up and let's dive in.

Fundamental #1 – Get Your Head in the Game

Let me start by asking you a few questions. How dialed-in are you? Do you feel like everything is "clicking" right now or do you feel disjointed? Do you feel overwhelmed? Do you feel lost or scattered? Do you know what to do next? Are you working more IN your business or ON it?

When I interview new coaching clients, I always wind up saying the same thing. "It sounds like we need to hit the pause button and take a step back. Would you agree with that"? The answer is almost always yes.

Here's the reason - you are neck deep in your business. I'm on the outside looking in. Your challenge is usually just a symptom of a problem and not the actual problem. My job is to help you zoom-out and look at the bigger picture.

We can't cure the symptoms without addressing the root causes. And you can't write a prescription for a root cause if you haven't identified it.

One of the most popular strategies for starting this process is simply take a break from the business to clear your head. It could be as simple as leaving the office and going to a movie. The key is to get out of your normal work environment and into a fresh location that you don't spend a lot of time in. Fresh locations allow our brain to take a break.

If you read a lot of self-help books, you have probably come across the concept of 'sharpening the saw.' Stephen Covey is usually credited for this one. The concept is very simple. You are your greatest asset. You should spend more time on you than anything else. You need rest, sleep, fun, excitement, love, etc. You need these to be a better you. The better you get; the easier life and business will be.

Often, when someone is focusing on a problem, they tend to put blinders between themselves and possible solutions. It's easy to want to get the job done. Especially if there's a deadline. But we don't realize how effective a break can be as a way of accelerating your answer to a problem.

When I get stuck, I will often go out for an early lunch or take a shower. It just depends on my mood and the weather. One benefit of something simple like a shower is that you can't take your phone in the shower. It's a great, simple, and free way to isolate yourself for a few minutes.

Did you know there are several studies on why we get some of our best ideas in the shower? They all conclude that the simple task of taking a shower is a distraction for your conscious mind and allows your subconscious (that has been working on this problem all along) to inject new ideas into your process. There's more science behind it, but take my word for it that something as simple as a shower in the middle of the day can be a great way to unblock your mind and a solve a problem.

The argument against taking a break is that you are on a deadline or "how is that working on the problem?" Here's the deal - what good is it to stare at your computer for four hours with no solution? It's not. How awesome would it be if you could step away for half an hour and solve the problem? It's worth the break for your sanity if nothing else.

Will taking a shower or going to a movie help with all your challenges? Of course not. If you are struggling with major challenges or something major such as the direction of your company, a small break isn't going to cut it. What you really need is a retreat or a vacation.

I try to get away for a retreat several times a year. Sometimes I bring my family and sometimes I go by myself. My partner Josh and I get out of the business three or four times a year and meet at a hotel just to talk about the future. These little getaways are critical to refilling your tank with energy and enthusiasm so you can attack your business with everything you've got.

Before I go on a retreat of any kind, I sit down and create a list of things I want to work on. During my last retreat, I had two major tasks that I wanted to work on. The first was the outline for this book and the episodes I wanted to write. The second was my content plan for the upcoming year.

I went to Lake Geneva for my last retreat. I had never been there before. I had a deluxe hotel suite with a desk right by the fireplace. My room overlooked the golf course. Beyond the golf course were trees for miles. This kind of setting is a writer's dream. I loved it.

I stocked up on a few groceries and settled in for an upcoming snowstorm. I mentally laid out the next four days of writing and planning and all that I needed to do. I knew going in that I had about two weeks' worth of work that I wanted to complete in four days.

I woke up around 4:30 am the first morning. I don't always get up that early, but I was ready to go. I hit the ground running. When I took a break at lunch, I did a quick review to see how much I had left for the day. I was actually halfway through my entire list for the week. By breakfast the next morning I was done with my entire list. I had accomplished more in 24 hours than I thought I could accomplish in two weeks.

There's a lot of power in getting out of your office and clearing your mind. Smaller challenges require small breaks. The big stuff deserves more of your time.

Here's a tip. You don't have to solve the world's problems every time. You just need progress. A little progress here and there will do wonders for your attitude and motivation. And a little progress every day will compound over time and that's how you drive massive results.

Fundamental #2 – Getting a Grip on Your Numbers

Numbers don't lie. Numbers act as a scoreboard to tell if you are winning or losing the game of business. Numbers tell you exactly what's working and what is not.

Numbers highlight trends!

Numbers don't care about your emotions. They care about the facts. And you need facts to guide your decisions.

Before I go further, I want to make a point. If you don't look at the various numbers in your business, you will never reach your full potential. You may *accidently* have success, but that will likely only happen if you put in an insane amount of hard work. I don't want to downplay hard work, but I do want to emphasize SMART work. And that requires numbers.

The first step to getting a grip on your numbers is understanding your Key Performance Indicators or KPI's. These are the important numbers that drive your business. Some common KPI's that we track are number of customers by type, conversion rates, average dollar sale, retention rate, monthly revenue, pipeline size, and percent of revenue by product or service.

When you think about the important numbers in your business, think about the decisions you need to make and what information would be helpful for those decisions. One way to think about KPI's is by department.

Every department and every position in the company should have numbers that are associated with performance. It's a quick way to tell if departments and individuals are being productive.

Once you identify your KPI's, you need to build a dashboard. Your KPI dashboard should be simple and allow you to see at a glance exactly what's going on in your business. I personally like Excel for building dashboards. Everyone has access to Excel and it's extremely easy to use. If you don't know how to create formulas, there are tons of video tutorials on YouTube.

KPI Dashboards
Whether you are a large or small business, EVERY company needs a KPI dashboard.

If you are already a Federal Access[4] member, you can watch a training seminar on KPI dashboards. It's in the on-demand webinar section. Just search for 'KPI dashboards' and it will pop up for you.

When you build your dashboard, think about the type of data you need. Do you need daily, weekly, or monthly data? Can you combine departments or do you need to have a separate tab for each one? How granular do you want to get?

In the beginning, you just need an overview. No matter where you start, your dashboard is bound to evolve over time. That's natural. As time goes on, you are going to want different information and thus your dashboard will evolve and get more complex. But you need to start right now! Don't wait to get moving on this.

One of the greatest benefits to creating a KPI dashboard is being able to clearly see where you need to put your focus and energy. It's very easy to think you know what's broken and it's even easier to try changing things in the hopes of fixing your problems. But if you aren't using data to make that decision, you may be making things worse.

---

[4] https://federal-access.com

A few years ago, I had a client that kept losing salespeople. He was getting ready to fire his last salesperson and start over when we met. I asked why he kept losing salespeople and his answer was scary. He said, "I have no idea." He just knew that no one seemed to be able to successfully sell their software.

I asked him to hold off firing the last salesperson for a week and to let me do a little research. I called up the remaining salesperson and bluntly asked, "what's going on?" The salesperson told me that he was crushing his sales quotas but every time he closed a deal the customer support team screwed it up. He told me that there was a broken process. The owner's dad was on the customer support team and every time sales submitted a new order, he failed to fulfill on time, according to the contract, or he was doing it wrong. Customers were cancelling their order more than 50% of the time.

When I went back to the owner, he didn't believe me. He was convinced that the sales people just couldn't close a deal.

I said, "prove it!" Let's put some KPI's in place for the customer support team and find out the truth. So we did. And the sales person was wrong! Customer support was actually *losing 73%* of all new customers - not 50%.

When it comes to your business, be sure that you are working on the areas of the business that need fixing and not messing with something that is already working. Sure, you can optimize every aspect of your business, but broken pieces often need priority over optimization.

If you are having trouble with creating KPI's, I often find that flowcharting a process is an easy way to figure out what to measure. Everything has a process. Some activities have twenty-five steps and some have three. But everything has a process. Map it out and use that information to determine the numbers you need to measure.

One final word on numbers. You can't improve something that you don't measure. The simple exercise of measuring everything is actually a growth strategy. Good things happen when you diligently watch over your business.

Fundamental #3 – Business Coaches Accelerate Time and Experience

As you exhaust your knowledge, you begin to slow down. So how do you get more knowledge? The two most common ways are time and experience. Both of these are costly. The third and stronger option is a coach. Someone out there has the knowledge that you need. That person also has perspective that you don't have. Together, you can go farther, faster!

A great coach will accelerate your growth but the real value of a coach comes over time. Month after month, year after year. The better they get to know you and your business, the better their advice will be. Over time, you will both become more invested in the success of the other. This takes time, but is proven to accelerate the growth of your company.

Three major benefits of a coach.

#1 Wisdom – Wisdom is information, experience, and knowledge gathered over time and put to good use. Wisdom stops an adult from sticking a butter knife in a light socket. In business, wisdom stops you from making hasty hiring decisions because you feel the need to fill a role. Wisdom will often sound like a quiet voice in the back of your head that says you need to slow down or speed up or take a step back. Wisdom is a feeling in your gut that's backed by logic. Your emotions "know something," but your mind can't quantify it so you think through it.

The challenge with wisdom is that turning experience into wisdom can be painful and based heavily on trial and error. A coach can help you bypass a lot of pain by pointing you in the right direction. I often do this with my clients without them asking. It usually starts off with the question, "have you thought about…?"

The other great thing about wisdom is that over time, you learn to see things before they happen. As a business coach, I can often tell if a company is in trouble by the actions I see them taking. Even if they have decent cash flow, I can see the storm brewing.

A few years ago, a client came to me and said all the wrong things. Their focus was on hiring, building out their website, and a few other areas that I consider "fun stuff" versus core activities. I put the brakes on and asked about their sales pipeline. They didn't have one. They assured me it was OK.

My response to "it's all going to be OK" was, "Bullshit! You will be broke and living off credit cards in six months. If you aren't willing to work on your pipeline, I can't help you." The conversation went as you would expect. They were defensive, but I was firm. I had seen this type of behavior many times.

So, we started working on their pipeline. Very quickly the client saw the value of properly managing a pipeline and began to focus more and more on it. Fast forward nine months. At the end of one of our calls the client said, "we have a problem." He said that sales were barely enough for the company to survive. Then he paused and said, "but we are going to make it because nine months ago you made me properly manage my pipeline. If we hadn't done that, I would have lost everything by now.

It's very humbling to be in a situation like that. It's also a reminder that we don't know everything. It's always good to have someone who cares about you looking over your shoulder.

#2 Speed - I'll keep this brief. A coach will teach you shortcuts. One of the biggest reasons people hire a coach is because they want to go faster.

In order to go faster, you sometimes have to slow down on the front end. I know it sounds counterintuitive, but you can make quite a few unnecessary mistakes when you go too fast in the wrong direction.

I often think of the movie *Dumb and Dumber*. Early in their cross-country trek they miss a critical exit in the middle of the night. They drive hours in the wrong direction. Businesses do this all the time. They don't always think things through before diving-in head first. I'm all about leaping and learning, but I save those kinds of jumps for uncharted territory. When I'm pioneering an idea, there's no roadmap. So, I jump and you learn.

When you are following a common business model or trying to market your company, there's no need to jump without doing a little research and planning. Once your planning and research are done, then you go fast.

#3 Profitability – My business partner Joshua Frank often says, "*it's not about the money,* ***it's about the money.***" Yes, you read that right. I've read many times that money isn't everything. I can tell you, without a doubt, that having money is way more fun than not having it. You need someone in your life (besides your family and employees) that is driving you and helping you to achieve profitability.

In its simplest form, profit equals revenue minus expenses. You increase profit by increasing revenue and managing expenses. Notice that I didn't say cutting expenses. The old saying that you have to spend money to make money is true. You either spend it on labor, marketing, cost of goods, or other overhead costs like utilities, insurance, etc.

Profitability ties directly with creating KPI's (fundamental #2). Profit is driven by your ability to track everything. A key example of this is your marketing efforts. Marketing costs can be outrageous depending on the methods that you choose. You need to quickly be able to determine if a strategy or campaign is working and if its profitable. Coaching clients will often hear me talk about acquisition cost versus lifetime value. You need to know how to calculate this and how to make decisions that decrease acquisitions cost and increase lifetime value.

A very simple way to calculate acquisition cost is to look at what you spent to get a new customer via a specific method. For simplicity sake, let's say you spent $1,000 on LinkedIn advertising, received 100 leads, and 20 of those leads turned into new customers. Your acquisition cost per LEAD is $10 (1000/100). Your acquisition cost per CUSTOMER is $50 (1000/20).

Lifetime value is measured over time. To do this, you need a strong Customer Relationship Management (CRM) system that will help you track start and end dates for clients as well as how much they spend while they are a client. You can then compare that to the marketing method used to identify if the client's lifetime value outweighs the acquisition cost. If you need help with this, send me a note on LinkedIn.

What to look for in a coach?

- Someone you respect
- Someone with broad knowledge
- They need to be a great listener
- They need to ask great questions
- Someone who pushes you
- Someone you trust

Notice that I didn't say you need someone from your industry, someone that has a hundred clients, or someone that has fifty employees. None of that matters. You will likely be dealing with them one-on-one and that relationship is the most important factor.

What you should expect to pay for a coach.

One-on-one coaching options vary greatly, but you can expect to pay a minimum of $1,000 up to several thousand a month for one-on-one coaching (depending on your needs and the demand for the coach).

Most coaches have three or four support levels to choose from. Be sure to choose a level or program that provides basic support outside of scheduled calls. Things always pop-up outside of regular calls. You need to be able to reach out with questions and not have to wait days or weeks for an answer. Many clients are fine with email support, but if you prefer phone support, be sure to ask for it.

* * *

Michael LeJeune is a Partner with RSM Federal and Program Manager for the Federal Access Knowledge-Base and Training Platform. He is an award-winning business coach, author, and host of the podcast Game Changers for Government Contractors. He has been consulting and mentoring companies in the government market for twenty years. Michael is also an Army Veteran. Find him at www.linkedin.com/in/michaeljlejeune/

Episode 5.
The Basic Fundamentals of Business

By Dr. Russ Barnes

CEO, Systro Solutions

The path to doing business with the government starts with doing good business. Many business owners are masters of their craft, but struggle with the complexity of business activities, often feeling overwhelmed, frustrated, and angry. They exist in a condition I now describe as entrepreneurial poverty. It's a situation where people are in business but are not generating enough income to have the lifestyle they envisioned when they started. If this is what you're experiencing, you're doing way too much for a fraction of the outcomes you desire. Unfocused effort wastes time, energy and money. *You can do business better.*

Knowing what to do and when to do it seems like a simple concept, but it is not easy to execute. A normal tendency is to rely on trial and error which seems to be the best option for working through complicated business issues. Persistence and luck appear to be the only path to prosperity. Fortunately, that is not the case and what you learn from reading this episode will show you how to do business better. You will realize that success in business is within your control. It takes work but, done right, actually takes less work than you're doing now.

In my youth, the sport most people played in my community was basketball. When I first began playing the game in my back yard, I spent a lot of time launching the basketball at the hoop. I called it shooting, but I missed so regularly that my brothers called it "chucking." After reaching a point of frustration at not being able to consistently make baskets, I set out to find a better way. I chose a book from the library titled *The Fundamentals of Basketball* and studied the basics of shooting a basketball. After mastering the fundamentals, I was able to make shots more consistently and improve to the point where I played basketball in high school and college. Most importantly, when I wasn't playing well, I could fix what was wrong by focusing on the fundamentals.

In any skill-based activity, if you don't master the fundamentals, you will never be able to reach the heights of success. The fundamentals are the basic skills that enable you to participate in the activity and to eventually excel. In music, the fundamentals are the scales. In basketball the fundamentals are dribbling, passing and shooting. To be an accountant requires a foundation in math. An attorney must know the fundamentals of law. A doctor learns anatomy and physiology. In every skill-based activity fundamentals must be learned, mastered and practiced.

Business growth is also a skill-based activity. Stop for a moment and picture me chucking a basketball. If you are "chucking it" in business you are wasting energy and having no meaningful impact on the community or your bottom line.

In 2012, I began a journey to find a solution to this condition called entrepreneurial poverty. For the next four years, I worked with small business owners to determine whether this problem existed only in my imagination or if it was a real-world problem with wide ranging implications for society. I wanted to know why existing solutions had not moved the needle on the "failure to succeed" statistics.

In 2016, after validating the magnitude of the problem and attempting to solve it in various ways with less than satisfactory results, I started a course of study to get help with crafting an effective solution. I was accepted into the PhD program at Benedictine University and over the next three years, I completed a research project that resulted in my dissertation titled *Organization Design for Small Business: A Discovery of Business Fundamentals for Executing a Purposeful Path to Profitability.*

Having put in a tremendous amount of work to come up with a solution on my own, I started the PhD program with a certain set of ideas that I intended to validate, but over the course I realized that some foundational insights regarding how to succeed in business were missing. The most significant gap was a lack of consensus on the basic fundamentals that business owners must master in order to become purposeful in leading a company to prosperity.

Given my history with games, as both an athlete and a coach, this lack of consensus struck me as odd, because everything that applies to a game also applies to business. There are rules, there is competition, there is a way to keep score and there are winners and losers. There is strategy, there are coaches and there are players. The game of business is not new. It has been played for centuries. Therefore, it seemed logical that basic fundamentals for playing the game of business would be evident, but that is clearly not the case. If you ask ten business owners to list the business fundamentals, you will get twenty distinctly different answers. With that realization, I focused my research on finding fundamentals that frame the game of business.

Small Business Administration statistics show that 50% of small businesses fail within five years. I wanted to know what the 50% who succeed know and do that the 50% who fail do not know and do. Therefore, my study sample consisted of 75 business owners who succeeded in building businesses from zero to $100 million in annual revenue. I concentrated on the pre-profitability stage to learn what they did, when they had no resources, to position their company for the success that came later.

To qualify as a basic business fundamental, within the context of my study, activities had to meet specific criteria:

- They had to have a direct connection to growth and profitability
- They had to be common sense and logical
- They had to be learnable and teachable
- They had to have been implemented by each of the seventy-five business owners in the discovery group

My study revealed three basic fundamentals – Selling, Cultivating Relationships and Research. Let's break them down one at a time.

Business Fundamental #1 – Selling

Nothing happens in business until someone buys something, but many small business owners attempt to circumvent the process of selling their product or service. There are several reasons.

1) None of us like to be sold to although we all enjoy buying what we want. So, we understand why our sales calls are rejected but we don't know what to do about it. Rejection seems reasonable, rational and unavoidable.

2) Employing high pressure closing techniques feels manipulative.

3) Selling to one customer at a time doesn't seem to be a good way to grow a company.

Let's define "selling." Contrary to what many people believe, it's not persuading someone to make a purchase that they would not otherwise make or to "hard sell" someone by not taking no for an answer. It's not about facing down rejection, the ABCs of closing, or numbers, numbers, numbers. It is about identifying the painful problem that a person is experiencing, determining whether your product or service is a suitable solution, setting the price and signing a contract. It's a personal interaction aimed at *helping* a person make a purchase. To qualify as a sale, money must change hands. Repeat sales come from delivering a satisfactory experience.

My research revealed that seventy-five out of the seventy-five entrepreneurs in my study engaged in some sort selling activity early in the process. Selling served to do more than just acquire a few dollars. It provided the feedback that let them know they were solving a problem in a way for which people were willing to pay.

The direct sales process brings as much value in terms of customer information and insights as it does revenue. When someone makes a decision to forgo a purchase, there are rational reasons for that decision. Perhaps they don't need it. Why buy a hammer if you never plan to build anything? Perhaps they don't want it. Why buy a hammer when the type of work you do can be accomplished with the heel of a shoe? Perhaps the price is too high or the quality is too low. Maybe the timing is not right. If you walk away from a prospect without addressing these questions, you have missed a golden opportunity to understand your customer.

Once you have paying customers, you can identify the patterns of the people who purchase. This information will help you target your marketing. If you attempt to pay for marketing before you can describe your ideal customer, you risk running out of money before you find the group of people who are most likely to purchase your products or services.

Business Fundamental #2 – Cultivating Relationships

As a business fundamental, cultivating relationships includes both internal and external relationships. It involves more than going to networking events and collecting business cards. Cultivating relationships means understanding where you need assistance and identifying people who have the skills you lack. It means building relationships with people before you need their help, but also getting help from the right people when your back is against the wall.

Cultivating relationships includes learning the strengths of the people around you. When you need help, ask people to do what they do best. They will be happier to help and will get the task done quickly and well. Some people have specialized knowledge in some area and can help you when you need that expertise. Some people will serve as a support structure for you. They encourage you, inspire you, and lift you up when you're down; and some people will promote you and connect you to others who can help you.

Few individuals are experts at every aspect of business. Some people have the ability to invent, innovate and create. Others have the ability to take an idea and turn it into money. Some can take a profitable enterprise and scale it. Elon Musk is an example of someone who has proven he can do all three. His engineering skills and ability to see what needs to exist in the world combined with his ability to build a company has enabled him to grow Tesla, SpaceX, Solar City and other game changing companies. For those who can't do it all, it's important to be intentional in connecting with people who bring complementary capabilities to the company.

To effectively cultivate relationships, you must establish criteria to identify who you need to know. The next step is to identify the sources through which you can find them. You can hire an agency to do a search, but if you're short on money, you can use social media platforms to perform your own search. Different platforms will reveal different types of information, so consider carefully what you need to know about a person and why it will be useful to know it. Having criteria will help you assess what you find on their profiles prior to meeting them in person.

As the CEO of your company you must always be on the lookout for talent. Talent management includes talent identification, talent acquisition, talent development and talent retention. Talented people have the ability to perform at a high level in a particular area using natural skill. The best ones are those who love what they do and have worked hard to develop their talent.

Your business is powered by your people. If you take care of them, they will take care of your customers. Employees who are invested in the success of the company will contribute not only their labor, but their intellect, to the growth of the organization.

Business Fundamental #3 - Research

All business owners periodically hit a wall where they don't know what to do next. Research skills gets them past that obstacle. Once they have mastered the skill of research, they know how to define the problem, gather information, identify a solution, test alternatives and repeat. They know how to use sources and contacts to gain an understanding of the things they don't know. Research skill is critical for every business owner.

A key benefit gained from research is resourcefulness, which is simply stated as the ability to figure things out. Figuring things out means taking an intentional, maybe even scientific, approach to evaluating viable options to find the ones that have the best chance of succeeding. A trial and error approach is not out of the question if each trial eliminates an error that brings the next trial one step closer to a solution. Thomas Edison went through thousands of trials on his way to making a successful filament for the lightbulb.

Through data analysis, research becomes a way of finding answers that are not obvious. At a point, you will know so much about a subject that solutions seem to come out of nowhere. The most successful business owners use the research skill to move forward with the confidence that, when an obstacle appears in their path, they can figure out how to overcome it.

Research comes in many forms from the Socratic Method to the Scientific Method. Research can be qualitative or quantitative. It can be short term or long term. Research involves your eyes and your ears. It's conducted through reading, watching and listening. Sources include trade journals, videos, books, magazines and online articles. The most valuable research of all is what can be learned from people by using tools such as interviews, surveys and focus groups.

To have an effective research process, tracking and documentation are critical. Each additional bit of information leads to insights that reveal the next important step. Without tracking and documentation all new knowledge is lost and those flashes of insight are less likely to happen.

Research is best accomplished by igniting your curiosity. Search relentlessly for answers. Be ecstatic when you actually come up with more questions. Incorporate research into the routine of running your company. The results will speak for themselves.

Conclusion

How do you survive, thrive and win in the game of business? First things first – master and apply the fundamentals. The growth of your company accelerates when you rely on fundamentals. Chaos and crisis are common in commerce, but can be conquered with consistency.

The good news is you don't need to pause your current business activities and go back to school for formal and costly education before you can get started. Applying fundamentals contributes directly to your ability to successfully play the game of business. You simply need to make a subtle shift from depending on trial and error to focusing on fundamentals.

When the going gets tough, you won't get confused if you take the following steps:

- **Apply Business Fundamental #1**: Ask yourself…What am I selling? Am I still solving a painful problem with a solution for which people are willing to pay?

- **Apply Business Fundamental #2**: Ask yourself…Do I have the right people on my team, doing what they do best?

- **Apply Business Fundamental #3**: Ask yourself…How do I frame the problem, gather the information I need, and identify a way to overcome this obstacle?

It is true, as they say, that if you always do what you've always done, you'll always get what you've always gotten, and of course, insanity is defined as doing the same thing over and over and expecting a different result.

From today forward, do something differently in your business. Focus on the fundamentals.

* * *

Colonel (retired) Russ Barnes is the CEO and Senior Business Advisor to Entrepreneurs and Executives at Systro, an organization design firm specializing in small business development. His 30+ years of experience in organization development is drawn from military service, franchise ownership, academic programs, and strategy consulting, specifically with small businesses.

After retirement from the military, Russ grew a franchise territory from zero to profitability in less than three years. His growth was based on a clear vision, building an effective network, consistently delivering a quality product and maintaining a relentless focus on customer service.

Russ is a graduate of the Referral Institute Certified Networker program where he received extensive training in referral marketing. He received his Bachelor's Degree from Manhattan College (NY), his MBA from Embry-Riddle Aeronautical University, and his Master of Science degree in Strategic Studies from Air University. He is currently earning a PhD in Organization Development at Benedictine University. Find him at www.linkedin.com/in/rcbarnes/

Episode 6.
Top 10 Veteran Owned Business
Must Dos for Success

By Eric "Doc" Wright

CEO, Vets2PM

Over the past two decades, I have collected dozens of pages of lessons learned about how to successfully start and grow a business. These lessons come from taking private companies public; teaching business at university; mentoring dozens of Veteran-owned businesses; and starting three successful businesses and one non-profit organization myself.

Some of the lessons represent things that worked and some represent things that didn't. This duality produced an amalgamation of things Veteran business owners (VBO) should consider for achieving business success and longevity.

However, it should be noted that this Top 10 item list is not exhaustive. It only represents those items that either contributed the most benefit or proved the most painful in the pursuit of business success and longevity; both for myself and dozens of VBOs I have worked with over the years. In fact, I have presented these items in multiple VBO-attended forums, and audiences across the country have reinforced through their reaction and feedback that they do indeed consider these items essential.

Additionally, many of the items are connected with each other, which can produce synergy.

Finally, the list is in no particular order of precedence, so I encourage you to consider all of them.

Please enjoy, and "Cheers!" to your business success!

Small Business

The U.S. Small Business Administration reports there are 27.9 million (M) small business in the U.S. and defines them as having less than 500 employees, any for-profit business legal structure, independently owned and operated, not nationally dominant in its field, and physically located and operated in the U.S. or its territories.

Additionally, Fundera.com reports that 89.6% of all U.S. small businesses have fewer than 20 employees; 23M of them actually have no employees at all, just the owner, and Veteran-owned businesses number 3.7M with average [annual] receipts of $450,000.

That's what I specialize in - helping military Veterans achieve meaningful, lucrative post-Service careers as intrapreneurial[5] managers or as entrepreneurs. As such, that is what I spend a great deal of my time talking and writing about.

The following lessons I share are applicable across all small businesses. That's because combined, we all sell a lot, hire the most, hustle the hardest, and share many things in common with mid and big-sized businesses. Generating sales, finding and retaining customers and talented employees, complying with internal policy and procedures and external laws and regulations, and turning revenue into profits and cash are some key examples.

---

[5] Intrapreneurship is the act of behaving like an entrepreneur while working within a large organization. Intrapreneurship is known as the practice of a corporate management style that integrates risk-taking and innovation approaches, as well as the reward and motivational techniques, that are more traditionally thought of as being the province of entrepreneurship. Wikipedia, https://en.wikipedia.org/wiki/Intrapreneurship

The rub, however, is that many Veteran Business Owners (VBO) do not know this because they do not have access to lessons learned and mentorship from mid to big-sized businesses. This episode provides a bit of that insight.

#10 - Have a Compelling Story!

In spite of all of our modern trappings and technology, the old maxim "no one cares how much you know until they know how much you care" still holds true. Your customers will enter into an economic relationship with you if they trust you to help them either solve a problem they have (need) or achieve something they want (desire). It's human psychology to avoid pain and seek pleasure.

The next two Top 10 items relate to this one as they are all about connecting with the customer and conveying clearly, concisely, convincingly, and authentically that you can and will help them. To do that, you have to: Identify who they are; Understand what they want or need and why; So you can create a story that connects with them and compels them to act on the trust they build with you through your story and actions serving their needs and desires. Your story is the touchpoint between you and them; it is the foundation of your relationship of trust.

Your story's format is what I call a Value Proposition Statement (VPS). Your VPS answers: 1. Who are you; 2. What can you do for whom; and 3. What is the value they get from a relationship with you? I'll use my VPS to illustrate: *I am a two-Service, two-Era Military Veteran that endured a long, arduous, dark transition from military Service to the civilian workforce, i.e. the CIVDIV (civilian division), to project manager, to general manager, and finally to entrepreneur, founding multiple successful organizations. My professional mission is to help other transitioning military Service Members, Veterans, and Spouses do the same; achieve meaningful, lucrative post-Service careers as intrapreneurs or entrepreneurs.*

If you are a transitioning military Service Member, Veteran, or Spouse, and/or you desire a meaningful, lucrative career, as defined by you, you'll reach out to me to see how I can help you achieve success. It's my story, but it's not for me, it's for my specific constituency of customers: 1. Transitioning military Service Members; 2. Military Veterans; 3. Military Service Member or Veteran Spouses; and 4. Companies that need Veteran talent, and they can see themselves in it.

If they do, they'll reach out to me; i.e. extend to me an opportunity to build trust with them, which they do. My company's word-of-mouth rate is about 48%.

#9 - Make Your Business and Story About Others First!

It is often said that 'business is built on relationships, and relationships are built on trust'. When you make your story and business about serving others first, your well-defined customer constituency, they reach out to you for help. This provides you an opportunity to build trust with them by doing what you said you'd do, helping them, which means they come first in the transaction!

This means we're using a bit more human psychology to help us when we set the relationship up this way. We're tapping into *reciprocity* and *fairness* by ensuring they get their good deal first. Why? Because as humans, we're social critters, which means we can intuitively sense fairness. We don't mind if someone else gets a good deal, we'd just like one too, and if someone provides something of value to us first, we feel a bit of obligation to repay them when we can.

Therefore, when you set your business up so that it's clear your customers' satisfaction and success hinges on them getting what they want before you get what you want, they feel comfortable buying from you. Especially over competitors who either don't do this explicitly, or don't do it at all.

#8 - Always Under Promise and Over Deliver!

To do this well, you must understand your customer constituency deeply! You have to know what they expect, and why, so that you can meet and when possible, exceed their expectations; the ones you help them set with your VPS! This item relates to the previous Top 10 items ten and nine.

Meeting and exceeding expectations deepens the trust and drives product-market fit, revenue generation, loyalty, and advocacy. Plus, if you're not meeting their needs as advertised, savvy customers can use the always-on Internet and find substitutes in minutes, and you'll never even know it. Furthermore, it typically costs less to sustain existing customers than to acquire new ones. You save money on customer acquisition and advertising costs!

#7 - Get Really Good with LinkedIn!

Why? Because it's the gig economy's marketing silver bullet!

Once you have a compelling story, you have to tell it as far and as wide as you possibly can! LinkedIn is that bull horn. There are over 562M members on LinkedIn. 91% of executive's rate LinkedIn as their #1 choice for professionally relevant content. 64% of social referrals to corporate websites come from LinkedIn. 61M LinkedIn users are senior-level influencers, and 40M users are in decision-making positions. The platform drives 80% of B2B leads, and 86% of Americans say business transparency is more important today than ever before. Finally, the Foundation states "Every single week, content in the LinkedIn feed is seen 9 billion times, [totaling] about 36 billion impressions per month and 468 billion per year".

As you can see, if you aren't using LinkedIn, you're missing a huge competitive advantage to reach, educate and entertain, or as I like to say "edutain", and serve your customer constituency. *Learning to use LinkedIn well can really level the playing field with your larger competitors.*

So, what does "get really good with LinkedIn" mean? Well, having used it to successfully start and grow three organizations, and having not used it in one failed business, to me it means: Content, Engagement, and Resolve.

Content: Deliver your story, set expectations, edutain your audience to create demand and trust, and consistently deliver reinforcing bits of your message by writing the occasional long article on LinkedIn, and by posting weekly short articles and/or videos on LinkedIn.

Engagement: The real magic is not your content, but the engagement it creates! This is what drives visibility on LinkedIn. When you post your content, people will *Like* it, *React* to it, and *Comment* on it. Every other day, thank all of the folks commenting on your content, and engage them through the comments and observations about what they said to deepen the conversation. This interaction deepens your connection with your customer constituency because it's highly personal. People like to feel valued and heard! Yep, more psychology!

Resolve: Stay resolved to serve your customer constituency! Cross the bridge to Successville and ignore all of the trolls under it! They will be there trying to derail you. If they're customers, help them solve their issues publicly so they and your customer constituency see your commitment to their success. You're building trust in the open! If they're competitors, ignore them! Arguing with them brings no value to your customer constituency, brand, or message, and everyone can see and judge for themselves the troll's posts for what they are: distracting and non-value adding.

#6 - Assemble Your Team of Experts!

Along with cash flow, which we discuss next, not having experts assembled around the business is one of the top four reasons small businesses fail within the first five years.

Get a good accountant, attorney, insurance professional, and owner/CEO peer group for on-going mentorship and fellowship. It's empowering and encouraging to learn your business problems are the same as everyone else's; just the scale is different!

Also screen your team members for intangibles like ownership mindset, resiliency, and critical thinking. They need to treat the business like you do so they can make decisions, steward resources, and take care of customers the way you would when you're not around or not looking.

The following lesson learned directly supports this sixth Top 10 VBO Must Do...

#5 - Watch the Cash!

The non-profit Service Corps of Retired Executives (SCORE) states that 82% of the small businesses that fail within the first five years fail because of cash flow issues. That's because revenue and cash are two very different things! You can have tons of revenue from goods and services sold, but not have the actual cash from delivery. However, until you receive payment, you'll need cash on hand to pay bills, employees, and the experts we mentioned in Top 10 item six.

I check my cash-on-hand balance every other day!

#4 - Clearly Communicate Your Culture to Everyone Often!

It is the foundation for everything else you do, and it must permeate your business!

For example, at Vets2PM, our culture is the backbone of everything we do, from services delivery, to decision-making, to expectation setting, and to hiring, assessing, and firing, all of it!

Our corporate culture is the result of our deep conviction for and commitment to our Mission, Process, Values, Standards; our Veteran Clients and Corporate America Customers; and our great Nation and her precious defenders.

Here's what I mean:

Mission: *We help Military Veterans become Project Managers;*

Process: *Using our knowledge, skills, and decades of experience to: 1. Inspire them with a clear, meaningful, lucrative end-state as a career Project Manager; 2. Train them to deliver project success and obtain project management credentials; 3. Prepare them for CIVDIV reintegration with professional resumes, interview skills, and social media savvy; and 4. Place them into meaningful, lucrative project management careers (to include project, program, and general management);*

Values: With integrity, commitment, and excellence in everything we do:

Standards: Integrity: *our communications and interactions with others are always truthful, transparent, and clear;*

Commitment: *we always keep our commitments to our clients, customers, teammates, processes and systems, and company image and culture;*

Excellence: *we constantly demonstrate responsibility, accountability, and ownership for all timely, accurate work products we produce.*

#3 - Hire Slow and Fire Fast!

Your culture will go a long way in helping you hire great employees, customers, vendors, and partners, and in firing them as well, when warranted, and when at last resort.

Frankly, every day you delay in firing fast someone that you have tried to help rise to the occasion or that doesn't want to be all-in on the team, it costs you time, money, effort, distress, and morale. Therefore, you owe it to your team, business, and customers to focus on those adding value, and jettisoning those that don't. Quickly.

#2 - Don't Race any Other Company to the Pricing Bottom!

If you're providing value at or above expectations, and your goods and services are priced honestly and accurately, your price is simply a reflection of that! However, when you discount it here, there, and everywhere, you signal to your market that your advertised price isn't really your price at all! Your price is really whatever price people are paying! You're potentially leaving brand equity and revenue on the table.

Think of a steakhouse…are you a Morton's, or are you a Golden Corral? Both are viable models for steakhouses, but you have to decide which one you want to be!

#1 - Keep Your Project Management Mindset Sharp!

You developed one in the military while leading missions and exercises. Since missions and exercises have specific start and stop dates and unique expected outcomes, they meet the definition of projects in the CIVDIV! Additionally, projects are accomplished through small, high-performing teams and undertaken to make the organization better; both of which are also similar to military missions and exercises. In small businesses, especially start-ups, you'll use your project management mindset in every aspect of your business, every day!

* * *

Eric "Doc" Wright, PhD is a dual-Service, dual-Era Military Veteran, Founder of Vets2PM, LLC, Vet Stone, LLC, and co-founder of The Veteran Project Managers Mentor Alliance, a non-profit. He is also a successful Project Manager, PMI Chapter-recognized mentor, and an edutaining (entertaining + educational) public speaker on: 1. project management workforce optimization; using LinkedIn for business success; Veteran entrepreneurship; and project manager development. Eric's passion and purpose stem from his own rough transitions from military to project management to entrepreneurship; he *helps transitioning military Service Members, Veterans, and qualifying Spouses achieve meaningful, lucrative post-Service careers.* Find him at www.linkedin.com/in/docwright2012.

Episode 7.
GovCon Small Business Growth Model

By Jenny Clark

CEO, Solvability

There are all kinds of support for companies getting started in Federal Contracting. During the startup stage, companies set up their businesses and get registered in SAM.gov and start networking with large primes. What is needed next is a road map to show them the stages of growth, and identify what steps they need to take to reach the next level. That is why we created the GovCon Small Business Growth Model.

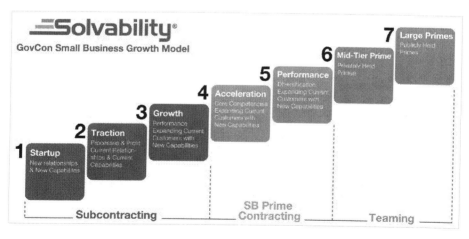

Within the GovCon Small Business Growth Model, we're showing small businesses in federal contracting what they need to do to move to the next level of growth, and give them options on how to accelerate and scale their businesses.

The GovCon Small Business Growth Model is a framework for understanding the requirements at each stage of growth. Small businesses may move back and forth between different stages. The Growth Model lets you see what it will take to move up to the next level, in terms of systems and processes, scalability, and the momentum gained with headcount and revenue growth.

However, achieving the next level creates a new set of challenges, because what got you to that level is never enough to take them to the next level. Additionally, most small businesses outgrow some of their staff as they reach the next stage. Some of the people that you started with will not have the capacity or interest to keep up with the company's growth.

It's important for companies that are "starting with the end in mind" to understand this growth model. Using this model helps to set a realistic strategy with a timeline to get to a revenue or headcount level characteristic of each stage, within a 5, 7, 10 or 20-year timeline. It also helps to see what your potential exit strategies could be, and what goals you need to achieve to make those exit strategies viable. So many entrepreneurs in GovCon say that they're lining up their company to be purchased by a large prime, but are they putting the steps in place to make that happen over a 10 or 20-year period?

The GovCon Small Business Growth Model applies generally to Department of Defense (DOD) contractors providing professional and IT services that are US-based, US-owned and privately held by the founders and their key leadership team.

Why do we need the GovCon Small Business Growth Model?

So much information is available to the Startup community. What if we could help more of the "Beyond Startup" companies accelerate their growth by better understanding the business practices of the federal market?

The growth model shows how to find and use industry expertise of the greater GovCon community in addition to training and advice from mentors and peers, while leveraging resources from federal contracting that are specific to small business requirements.

What Are the Resources Available to Small Businesses for Federal Contracting?

Small Businesses can use the following resources at no cost or minimal cost to get started in Federal Contracting:

- Small Business Administration (SBA)
- Procurement Technical Assistance Centers (www.aptac-us.org)
- Small Business Development Centers (SBDC) in each state
- Community Banks
- Economic Development Organizations
- SCORE Mentors (Service Corps of Retired Executives - SBA program)
- DCAA.mil Information for Contractors
- Industry Organizations such as:
    - National Defense Industrial Association (NDIA)
    - Armed Forces Communications Electronics Association (AFCEA)
    - Women in Defense (WID)
    - National Contract Management Association (NCMA)
    - Association of the US Army (AUSA); and
    - Many more.

Once beyond startup, the resources and guidance to expand are more difficult to find. What you accomplished during startup stage is not enough to get you to the next level.

At each level, you're faced with a new set of more complex challenges. Finding answers and choosing what will work best for your company can be frustrating. What if we could create a community of resources and connections specifically for your company - beyond the startup stage? That is what this episode all about!

What are the Boxes in the Small Business Growth Model?

Customers and Capabilities. Moving to the right means adding more capabilities. Moving up means adding more customers.

Traditional business growth says that adding new customers is an expensive proposition. Taking better care of that customer and solving more problems for that customer is the best way to grow. The most expensive way to grow is to add new customers and new capabilities at the same time. That would be like going from Stage 2, Traction, where you're working with Boeing on a network architecture project to Stage 5, Performance, where you're going after a prime contract with the National Security Agency (NSA) in artificial intelligence.

Starting with Stage 2 Traction, companies add more capabilities with the same customer, to get to Stage 3 Growth. At the Growth Stage, there is recurring revenue and longer-term contracts. You're able to invest in your infrastructure. You've successfully gone after IDIQs and have a GSA Schedule. You are now a prime contractor and can get work directly with the agency (though there is still competition and proposals required). You are spending more time setting up teaming relationships because that gives you a broader base and more access to other agencies.

From Stage 3, Growth, the company takes its expanded capabilities along with the IDIQs and starts working with more customers. At this point, you've brought in professional management and built out systems and processes so they are scalable. During this acceleration phase, you're leveraging contract vehicles and going after larger and more complex contracts.

Stage 4, Acceleration, is the point where you have to decide whether to *grow big* or *stay small*.

If you choose to stay within small business ceilings, you can operate as a Stage 5 Performance company. A Stage 5 Performance your company may go very deep within a single niche, but still stay within the size standards of small business; or operate a diversified portfolio of customers and services so that a downturn in any segment of customers and services doesn't impact you as much.

If you want to blow past the size standards, a company in either Acceleration or Performance realizes they need to quickly triple when they move to mid-tier, or they won't have the cash to compete for programs at the higher level. Exceeding the small business size standards by just a small amount can cripple company growth and cause you to fall back to small business standards. Many companies encounter this pitfall. One large contract can blast you out of small business size standards. You may not be ready compete as a Mid-Tier and that large contract is not enough to sustain your growth. Many will wait it out until they shrink back down, a disheartening and dangerous path.

Stage 6 is Mid-Tier, where you can no longer compete as a Small Business. In Mid-Tier, you must develop the business development discipline and cash liquidity to sustain large scale programs and pursuits.

Stage 7 is Large Prime. The only way they'll get to that level is to be acquired - which is not a bad outcome, although it's a very low probability. For a Large prime to acquire another federal contractor, the backlog of prime contracts has to be strong for several years, with contracts that the prime can operate on, not the ones set-aside for the various socio-economic statuses. Large primes operate from a pipeline. Their investments are focused on maximizing shareholder value. The follow directives set by their boards and executives for return on investment.

An example of how the GovCon growth model could work: INSIDE THE BOX with MITCH and SCOTT at Avalanche Research.

Let's talk about an imaginary company, Avalanche Research, and take our company through the Small Business Growth Model. Our company, Avalanche Research is just the two founders, Mitch, who is great at Business Development and his buddy Scott, who served with him in the military and agreed to join as the Operations Manager. Both Mitch and Scott spent three years at a major defense contractor and were tired of the meetings and constant BOGSAT (Bunch of Guys Sitting Around Talking). They knew that they could accomplish more on their own, continue their service to the mission, and create financial security and legacy in their community.

Mitch and Scott completed all the startup steps: setting up the corporation, getting tax IDs, buying QuickBooks, getting registered in SAM.gov (System for Award Management), working with their local PTAC (Procurement Technical Assistance Center found at aptac-us.org), setting up a website and getting business cards. They've reached out to old friends and associates, and started going to all kinds of networking meetings. They registered on portals for the large primes, and created their Capabilities Document. It took over 18 months, but their work paid off, and they're now working at a client site for a large prime. Mission accomplished - two "butts in seats" ready to turn into a real business. Mitch keeps calling people while Scott makes sure the bills are paid and their customers get invoiced.

Avalanche Research is ready to move to the Stage 2, Traction. Their prime contractor asks them if they can find "more guys like them" to work on the subcontract. Within a few months, they have enough work so that Mitch can come "off contract" and start working on the business full-time, while Scott continues to work nights and weekends on the company handbook, researching benefits, and writing proposals. At Traction, they are still serving the same customer with their core capabilities.

Mitch and Scott talk to their prime contractor regularly, finding out what additional work is out there that they can help with. Eventually, they find out about an existing contract where the subcontractor isn't working out, and pitch their own team. There are three years left on the contract and this is the exact step that will boost them to Stage 3 Growth. However, they aren't sure they're ready. Just like any other mission, they sign up and will figure it out as they go.

Before they can move up to Stage 3 Growth, they have to address infrastructure issues. What do they need to do for onboarding? How will they handle the more advanced billing and contract reporting and can they start working on a facility security clearance? There's so much going on and they don't want to be held back.

They also realize that the pipeline spreadsheet they are using is not enough. They aren't quite ready to hire a full-time business developer. They can get more billets on the subcontract but do they use an outsourced recruiter or find one part-time? That friendly banker that was so insistent about taking them to lunch has all their paperwork for a line of credit and isn't returning their calls.

Avalanche Research powers through. With the resilience of Mitch and Scott, they get their third subcontract. They've added a second capability with the same customer and are now in the Growth Stage. They want to start going after Prime Contracts and people are talking to them about getting on an IDIQ or going after a GSA contract, but they're not sure which way to go. They're looking at the effort and expense and want to make sure the agency they've been talking with will actually use that vehicle. It seems like there are mixed signals about GSA or NASA SEWP or OASIS.

It will be several years before Mitch and Scott get to Stage 4 Acceleration. They're growing steadily and cautiously. To get to the Acceleration stage, they'll have to go after more customers, which means lots of conferences, shaking hands, meetings, teaming agreements, and proposals. Oddly enough, Scott is all for it but Mitch is tired of all the travel he's doing and a bit frustrated.

Avalanche Research can grow in several ways. They can bounce back and forth between Stage 2 Traction and Stage 3 Growth, following the ups and downs of the federal market, learning their way along. They could also connect with a community of resources that focuses on federal contracting. Or they can follow best practices for the industry by investing in their infrastructure and becoming scalable. The GovCon Small Business Growth Model gives them a tool to see where they are, communicate their needs and accelerate their growth.

How do you define the GovCon Growth Model Stages in terms of employee headcount or Sales?

- Stage 2 Traction: typically, 10 to 50 employees, $1M to $5M in sales
- Stage 3 Growth: 50 to 100 employees, $5M and $10M in Sales
- Stage 4 Acceleration: over 100 employees, up to $50M in Sales
- Stage 5 Performance: over 100 employees, $50M+ in Sales

Beside Headcount and Sales, how else can we measure or compare small businesses in federal contracting?

There are two ways I've found to evaluate company maturity and the ability to generate growth. One is called a Systems Assessment, focused on the financial side. The second is a Benchmarking of the company's maturity and infrastructure. This identifies strengths and weaknesses that could help them grow faster or be holding them back.

In federal contracting, there are compliance rules specified in Federal Acquisition Regulation (FAR 31) and with Cost Accounting Standards (CAS). While most small businesses are exempt from the CAS, they still end up following the same basic rules, such as: identifying direct costs by contract; grouping indirect costs by pools; using employee timesheets to track contract, labor categories, hours and costs; and computing indirect rates such as fringe, overhead and general and administrative (G&A).

A Systems Assessment determines if the company can accurately track and report costs and reliably use historical data for proposal pricing. Without an accurate cost / pricing system and methods, a small business will struggle to be competitive. They'll either price too high and fail to win work or price too low and fail to generate the profit they need to grow.

Benchmarking

To help define where a small business falls in the GovCon Growth Model, using headcount and revenue is just the starting point. To evaluate infrastructure and maturity levels, the Growth Model includes a benchmarking tool. The benchmarking tool assesses 20 areas unique to federal contracting:

Benchmark 1 - DCAA Compliance: Do you know the basic rules of Defense Contract Audit Agency (DCAA) Compliance and does your accounting system meet these requirements? DCAA Compliance means you can pass a DCAA Pre-Award Survey (Form SF1408). Here's the quick fail test - if you can't calculate indirect rates based on your income statement detail, then you'll fail.

Benchmark 2 - DCAA Audit Readiness: Are you ready for a DCAA audit or have you already passed one? Can you print reports from your accounting system that show your labor hours and costs broken out by contract, overhead, G&A, and leave? How do you show that the overhead and G&A percentages you are using to bid are based on your actual costs and projected costs?

Benchmark 3 - Indirect Rate Management: How do you know that the indirect rates you use to bid will cover all your costs? You've been bidding a Wrap Rate[6] of 1.7 - but could your actual costs be higher? How often do you update your bid rates? Should you have more overhead pools or a materials/sub handling pool?

Benchmark 4 - Bid & Proposal Costs: Do you know how much you're spending on bids and proposals? Do you have a target budget for bids and proposals based on current and future sales? Are you using internal or external resources? How do you decide what to pursue and your probability of win (PWIN)? What about business development and proposals? Who writes the management volumes and the technical volumes? Do you have a defined process for preparing proposals using

---

[6] The Wrap Rate is the hourly billing rate that you'll charge a client for each hour of time. It's usually associated with Labor Categories such as Program Manager, Senior Engineer, Junior Analyst: job titles that match a specific proposal or contract, and are based on the average rates that you pay your employees.

some boilerplate information for pieces such as past performance, overview of accounting system, and indirect rate pools?

Benchmark 5 - Business Development: What is your process for finding opportunities and how do you manage your pipeline? Is your pipeline target-value 4 to 5 times your planned revenue? What tools are you using to identify opportunities? How do you cut opportunities from your pipeline?

Benchmark 6 - Marketing: Does your capabilities brochure show how you solve problems for customers? Is it easily customizable so it can be sent after your meeting with updated information specific to the customer's issues and priorities? Does your website reinforce and expand on what's in your capability statement?

Benchmark 7 - Pricing: How do you choose what kind of fee or profit to bid? How do you respond when your prime tells you what billing rate to use? Do you have salary targets for filling the positions based on the billing rate and can you find people at those rates? Do you make a conscious decision to accept a low rate in cases where you want to break into that customer or agency?

Benchmark 8 - Billings: How fast are you at getting billings done and do you have complex billings that you're having to do in spreadsheets? How is the delay in billing and reporting affecting your cash flow and your reputation with your primes? How does completing billing affect the timeline of your financial reporting and its accuracy?

Benchmark 9 - Accounting System Integration: How integrated is your accounting process and does it provide all the reporting you need? Everybody wants an integrated accounting system and every software vendor swears they can integrate with the other products you're using or considering. However, they never mention the cost or complexity of the bridges between systems. When we're buying systems to solve individual problems for each functional area - for human resources, for the program manager, for contracts, for accounting and executive reporting, we're not looking across the entire organization. It's easier for each organization to ask for $30K to solve their problem than it is to spend $150K across those 5 departments and tie it all together. But that is the only way to be scalable.

Benchmark 10 - Onboarding: Just think about how complex the recruiting and onboarding process is and how critical it is to your success in federal contracting. You have to reach out to the people whose resumes you submitted and find out if they're still available. You have to finalize salary and start dates. You have to get the program manager's approval, issue offer letters, get acceptance, and put them through your HR and payroll portal. Now you have to sign them up for benefits, get their badges and access, and set them up for their contract assignment with the right labor category and bill rate. Then you set-up their charge numbers on timesheets and turn that around in time to make payroll and billing deadlines.

Operational efficiency is a top challenge in federal contracting and this is just one example.

Benchmark 11 - Recruiting: One of the ways that small businesses can grow rapidly is by developing subcontracting relationship where the large prime contractor needs them to fill specific positions and labor categories. This is how a nimble small business can find their team and turn these openings into revenue. Can you recruit and sign these people quickly? Do you have a dedicated recruiter with contacts and tools? Are you having to spend money on placement fees and can you negotiate a lower commission rate or find alternative sources?

Are you strategic about what slots you'll go after, considering the locations and limitations of those slots? Is your prime contractor just giving you the slots they can't find, in expensive locations, where there are only one or two slots to fill, where you'll have to add state tax IDs and registrations and pay higher taxes and benefits?

Benchmark 12 - Outsourcing: Are you outsourcing your payroll and human resource processes or doing it yourself? Do you have the handbooks and legal requirements? How do potential employees find your company? Is your benefit package competitive? What about your accounting services? Are you prepared to train and manage experts in federal contracting?

Benchmark 13 - Contract Administration: How do you handle contract administration? What is your process for setting up new contracts and subcontracts? How do you share the paperwork with accounting, the program manager, billing? Do you have a contract kickoff meeting? What is the process for keeping track of the start and end date, the period of performance, contract value, and funding? What are the labor categories? When do the billing rates on those labor categories change?

Benchmark 14 - Program Management: What reporting does your program manager get and how frequently? Who reviews contract performance across the company? Initially, the CEO and the Chief Operations Officer (COO) were reviewing, but who maintains an active contract listing showing the headcount, the funding, and the backlog on each contract? Are we notifying the customer at 80% of funding? Are we watching for modifications to extend the contract and add to it?

Benchmark 15 - Cybersecurity: What are your corporate policies and who is responsible for cybersecurity? Are you prepared for the audits and reviews that are coming with the Cybersecurity Maturity Model Certification (CMMC)?

Benchmark 16 - Security Clearances: Do you have or will you need a facility security clearance as you continue to expand in DoD? What is your plan for getting the facility security clearance and how will you administer it?

Benchmark 17 - Contract Vehicles: Do you have the contract vehicles in place to reach your agency customers? Do you know what GSA contracts or IDIQs they will be using for future opportunities? Do you have teaming relationships with other companies who have those vehicles or will you need your own? Which Best-In-Class (BIC) contracts should you pursue?

Benchmark 18 - Financial Capacity: Do you have a line of credit or are you using factoring?[7] When bidding on larger contracts are you including a letter in your proposal showing how you will increase your financial capacity? Are you taking money out of the business when there are still large loans outstanding? Does your balance sheet show how you're managing cash and working capital? Do you show consistent net income? Do you have a budget through the next 18 months? Are you tracking the actual rates for fringe, overhead and G&A to your bid rates to make sure you're covering all your costs?

Benchmark 19 - Risk: Risk could mean financial risk, funding risk, or other liability risk. Some risk can be mitigated and some can be protected by insurance. Do you have a line of credit with a personal guarantee and loan covenants and can you meet those covenants? Can your line of credit be increased as you win more contracts? What is your financial risk as a

---

[7] Factoring is a financial transaction and type of debtor finance in which a business sells its accounts receivable (i.e., invoices) to a third party (called a factor) at a discount. A business will sometimes factor its receivable assets to meet its present and immediate cash needs. https://en.wikipedia.org/wiki/Factoring_(finance)

subcontractor if your prime contractor, another small business, does not pay you on time? Do you have adequate insurance to meet contractual requirements, from general liability and auto coverage to worker's compensation or Defense Base Act coverage (DBA) for overseas? Do you have Key Man insurance and Buy-Sell agreements in place? Do you need Directors and Owners Coverage or Professional Liability Insurance?

Benchmark 20 - Advanced Certifications: Are there advanced certifications that would differentiate you from competitors or that are needed for you to be a "player" in your agency? Do you have or need Capability Maturity Model Integration (CMMI) or International Organization for Standardization (ISO)? What level Cybersecurity Maturity Model Certification (CMMC) do you need to attain?

Summary

The Federal Market is backwards because *you don't sell to the Government.* You find a way to meet their requirements so that *they can contract with you.*

It's a long sales cycle, 18 to 24 months at a minimum. It's a relationship business. You need to connect with agencies and teammates and be seen actively in the marketplace over a long period of time.

Successful companies find a commitment to the mission and believe they can do it better. Ongoing risks in federal contracting are those you cannot control. You have to factor in potential funding delays and cancellations. You have to take into account government shutdowns and agency reorganizations and changes. However, you really can't build shutdowns into your pricing because of the downward pressure on cost and because other companies are not adding the increased cost of healthcare and other rising costs.

Persistence pays off. You need to focus on the fundamentals. Don't count on the home runs and big wins. Focus on the Money Ball Strategy - more hits means more runs. Keep going!

* * *

Jenny Clark is the CEO of Solvability. Solvability works with "Second Stage Federal Contractors", defined as small businesses serving defense and aerospace with 10 to 100 employees, $2Million to $10 Million in Sales. These businesses are committed to the mission of serving the warfighter. They are beyond the startup stage, committed to the long haul and ready to grow. They've built past performance with subcontracting, have developed teaming relationships and joint ventures, are listed on GSA, SeaPortE or other agency-wide agreements. They are investing in scalable systems and processes so they can get ISO certified and DCAA compliant. They go after small business opportunities as a prime contractor.

Solvability teaches you how to price more competitively and win more contracts so you can improve profits substantially. We help set up simple, integrated accounting systems so you can stop living in fear of DCAA compliance and be prepared for growth.

Solvability helps small businesses win federal contracts by focusing on competitive pricing and profitability. Find her at www.linkedin.com/in/solvabilityjwc/

Episode 8.
Hyper-Growth for Construction Companies

By Doug Reitmeyer

CEO, Government Construction Experts

Want to exponentially grow your construction business in the fastest time possible? Then this might be the most important episode in this book.

Here's why...

The biggest opportunities are often right in front of you, yet invisible. What if you had been an early investor in Microsoft, Facebook, Google, Starbucks, or Amazon? While hindsight is 20/20, foresight takes new knowledge and action.

And with the knowledge available in this episode, you can better predict the future with 100% accuracy.

"In the Federal Market, there will be more construction opportunities for any and every construction contractor and subcontractor to get and substantially increase their business profits, year after year, than anywhere else on the planet."

You can repeat those words every day and it will always be true.

So, what's stopping you? Most likely one thing. No one told You that You could actually learn HOW to build Your own personal *Federal Money Tree*.

Here's How It Works

I first committed to becoming a National federal contractor and building a *Federal Money Tree*. Then, the more that profits came in, much of it was reinvested in enhancing that money tree.

Over the past 25 years, more than a half-million dollars ($500,000+!) was invested in creating systems, tools, templates, developing scripts, software and advanced technologies to enable any successful construction contractor or subcontractor to double revenues and profits consistently, year after year, by simply getting and completing hundreds of highly profitable federal contracts.

For the first time, here are a few of the insider secrets; what it will take for You to build Your very own *Federal Money Tree* and achieve hyper-growth in Your business. In the process, you'll discover how to utilize Your *Federal Money Tree* and start making a lot more money in a lot less time and with a lot less stress than you ever thought possible.

Ready? Let's get started.

An Introduction

I am, at heart, a construction project manager; not a slick salesman, marketer, website, or funnel expert.

Yet, without any advertising, Facebook/social media marketing and without any salesmen or estimators, I've been awarded millions of dollars of federal contracts with no competition. Twice I've received "Contractor of the Year" awards from the US Army Corps of Engineers.

You can do this – start a new business or grow an existing one to $100 million per year and more with federal contracts. And You can do it fast.

How do I know this? Because I did. And quite honestly, you're probably smarter than me.

Did you get through high school in 4 years? It took me 5 years. I'm a college dropout and was drafted during the Vietnam War because my birthday was #54 of the 1969 Selective Service Lottery.

Yet, by all measures, I've enjoyed a very successful career, all because I figured out how to build a *'Federal Money Tree."*

It was a BIG DISCOVERY that others had built their very own *Federal Money Tree* and that collectively there are thousands of *Federal Money Trees* that pour billions of dollars into the bank accounts of contractors, subcontractors, and the American economy every week.

Understanding the Streams of Federal Money

Billions of dollars are sent from the US Treasury directly to the bank accounts of contractors that know how to tap the money streams of 400+ federal agencies that operate and maintain the U.S. Governments' over 900,000 buildings.

All of these near one-million structures require upkeep, repairs, and replacements of roofs, HVAC systems, floor coverings, masonry, electrical, painting, fire protection testing, upgrades and replacements, water and sewer maintenance, and all types of other construction services.

Because 97+% of Contractors and 99+% of Subcontractors have not made the effort of getting in on the action, they are excluded from these thousands of opportunities and all that money. It's a money-making game that they are being left out of.

FACT
*The largest construction businesses in the world actively seek
out and get federal contracts for one simple reason,
"That's where the BIG MONEY is!*

If you're not in this unique and highly profitable market, you're losing out, big time.

Building Your Federal Money Tree

The **roots** of the *Federal Money Tree* are the deep base of knowledge of how the federal money-stream flows that keeps the tree nourished and hydrated.

The **trunk** of the tree are all the business systems that are needed to support the structure of the tree.

The **leaves** are the millions of hundred-dollar bills that the Government prints out every day to trade for all of the construction service requirements of its over 400 agencies. These hundreds of thousands of $100 bills only fall into the bank accounts of those that have taken the time to build their own *Federal Money Tree*.

Road Map of Building Your Federal Money Tree

The Road Map starts with these 7 relatively simple steps.

1. Decide if the Effort is Worth the Risk.

Does it make sense for you and your business to go after highly profitable federal contracts? One of the most common reasons for getting into the federal market and why I decided to become a federal contractor is because it did for me.

In the private market there is often great difficulty in getting customers to pay in full for the materials and services that get delivered to them.

In the federal construction market, *a real person, known as* **a Contracting Officer, is being paid to pay you for your services** via the U.S. Treasury with funds automatically deposited to your business bank account, usually within 14 days of an approved progress payment. Not sure about this? Just Google the "Prompt Payment Act" and read it.

2. Get Registered:

Go to www.SAM.gov and take the time to get registered and qualified to get federal contract awards. Free help is available at any of the more than 300 PTAC offices around the country. Find the closest one using their website, www.APTAC-US.org. If you don't have the time, then pay a consultant to help you get registered.[8]

3. Get Qualified:

If you meet the requirements for any of the "set-aside" contracts such as woman-owned small business (WOSB), service disabled veteran owned small business (SDVOSB), Indian-owned, HUBZone, 8(a) for minorities / social disadvantaged, and/or others, be sure to get those qualifiers because many of the solicitations (*thousands of opportunities!*) are restricted to only businesses that have these certifications.

4. Get Connected:

Find and reach out to others that are already successful federal contractors. My group on LinkedIn, "*Federal Construction Professionals*" has over 5,500 members including both active and retired federal procurement officials, contractors and subcontractors, inspectors (also known as Contracting Officer Technical Representatives (COTRs), consultants, attorneys, and material suppliers. The resources available via the members of this group are endless.

5. Get Training:

The U.S. Army Corps of Engineers (USACE) and many other agencies offer free training, seminars, webinars and there are many federal market consultants that offer both free and paid training, much of it online.

Most construction opportunities advertised by the various federal agencies offer site visits prior to the bid date where you can meet with those that need work done. They are actively seeking qualified contractors and subcontractors that are registered in SAM.gov.

And for the most seriously interested, there is the *Mastering Federal Contracting Workshop* where a few times each year, I personally train experienced construction contractors and subcontractors on how to build their own *Federal Money Tree*. You'll find dozens of interviews with the

---

[8] Registering in the System for Award Management (SAM) is a free service provided by the Association of Procurement Technical Assistance Centers (APTAC), www.aptac-us.org.

Workshop graduates. Download the brochure and get the details at www.GCExperts.com/workshops.

6. Get Experience:

Participate by bidding on and submitting proposals to federal procurement officials. They are actively seeking contractors to get their agency's work done. Each time you don't 'win,' do a complete analysis of why you lost. If your proposal is rejected, request a "debriefing." A debriefing can be provided via a phone conversation or in writing. Either way, get the information of why you were not selected so you can get better at getting selected on the next one.

Remember, you either get it right and make some money, or you can get a lesson learned on how to get it right the next time.

7. Be In It For the Long Game

Winners win because they make the effort to constantly improve and learn from their failures. Never give up on doing federal contracts. If for no other reason because it's the only construction market that *never suffers a bad economy*.

During the meltdown of 2007 to 2010, Congress passed the "American Recovery and Reinvestment Act" (ARRA) which allocated an extra $787 Billion for all the federal agencies to buy whatever they needed just to pour fresh money into the US Economy. $147 Billion of that $787 Billion was specifically provided for all the federal agencies to spend on construction services. The result? Many construction contracts that were awarded under the ARRA funded allocations had profit margins exceeding 50% simply because there were not enough qualified contractors that knew how to tap this unique market.

If you're worried about another economic downfall, and you certainly should be, take the time now to get into the federal market, build your own *Federal Money Tree* and reap the rewards when all your "not-so-smart" competitors are crying the blues.

The Secret Sauce

The problem for most contractors and subcontractors is that they have developed skills in a niche. They have identified themselves as being competent in that niche and their ego compels them to relate only their skills in that niche to potential clients. Their websites and marketing tools scream, "I'm the best _____ (put the niche here) ___. Use me!"

This creates a two-fold marketing-to-conversion problem:

a) Nearly everyone else is shouting, "I'm the best, use me.", which leads potential clients into the despair of "paralysis by analysis." Competitors can't all be "the best," so clients have to struggle with figuring out which contractor truly brings the best value; and

b) this type of marketing is extremely limiting to only those particular, potential clients that actually have a specific problem that is perceived as needing a specific "niche experts' solution."

On the other hand, ask yourself, "How can I eliminate competition? Those that cause the above described conversion problems?"

The answer is to simply ask yourself this question:

"Where is the BIG MONEY?"

In a highly competitive construction market, where all the bidders are low-balling and cutting their margins, there's rarely any "big money."

So where is the BIG MONEY?

Answer: "The BIG MONEY is in getting a high value contract, defined as a contract that requires very little time, little or no resources yet provides a huge cash return."

Put another way:

a) There are people in the construction business trading their time for $20/hour to $200/hour because their mindset is, "I get paid for the actual construction work that I do and the on-site services that I deliver."

The $20 to $200/hour mindset is, "I'm the best, use me." This concept puts the whole conversation around the seller's need to get some work going so they can make that $20 to $200/hour.

b) There are also those that make $1,000 to $10,000/hour and more for their time working in the "construction business."

For the $1,000 to $10,000/hour and more individual, their mindset is, "Tell me about the problem you're trying to solve, the budget you have to get it done, and the time frame that it must be completed within." These are the people that are customer-focused and providing a solution to the client's immediate need(s).

The B-type contractors are focused on getting high value contracts that others, working for $20 to $200/hour, can perform the services for. A business that is focused on getting highly profitable contracts and know how to get others to get the work done in a way that meets or exceeds the customer's perceived expectations, in the federal market, can easily grow their business to a $100 million/year and more, as many have.

Where and How Does it Work?

To find what types of projects you may be most interested in going after, start by going through the newly transferred Federal business opportunities at SAM.gov.

The process goes something like this:

Facilities managers and engineers determine construction needs, such as a roof is starting to leak and it requires replacement. They make a request for the funds and send it up the chain of command all the way to the "Office of Management and Budget (OMB)" under the Executive Branch which has the responsibility to run the Government. That request for funding and its justification is then sent to Congress. If and when Congress approves the request, they send the funding to the agency's "Contracts Division" who then assigns a Contracting Officer to solicit or advertise to get someone to bid or submit a proposal for getting the project completed.

Once an award is made to a competent contractor, the government will call for a preconstruction conference meeting and subsequently issue a notice to proceed with the work to the contractor.

There will be an assigned government inspector, aka the Contracting Officer's Technical Representative (COTR), that will work with the project superintendent, review the submittals for contract compliance, observe construction progress, determine compliance with the plans and specifications, and approve the payment requests, etc.

Most federal construction contracts allow for monthly billings based on percentage of work completed. Once you do the work, they owe you the money and will pay you *within 14 days* for all progress payments in accordance with the Prompt Payment Act.

Want Hyper-Growth in Your Business?

To start making more money, send in bids *every day* in response to federal solicitations. Study the results of each bid to understand how to make the next one better.

When you get a contract award, get the project done as quickly as possible. Enjoy watching the money wired directly into your business bank account. And **just do it** over and over again. That's what I did. You can do this too!

Now, go back over the road map. Take the actions I've listed above. Start building Your very own *Federal Money Tree* and grow Your business exponentially!

* * *

Doug Reitmeyer: After personally completing more than a thousand federal construction contracts throughout the United States and several offshore locations, Doug Reitmeyer is now known as "The Federal Construction Expert." In 1998 Doug and his team of programmers started building the BidTrakker software system utilized daily by the most successful federal contractors.

Since 2010, he and his son, Sean Reitmeyer, have trained over 100 individuals and businesses on how to build their own *Federal Money Tree* in the 3-Day *Mastering Federal Contracting Workshop* events in Austin, Texas. Discover dozens of video testimonial interviews with the graduates, download the brochure, read the reviews and get the details at www.GCExperts.com/workshops.

Doug can also be reached via email:
DouglasReitmeyer@Gmail.com

97

You can get connected with Doug at
www.Linkedin.com/in/DougTheExpert.

Doug's connections on LinkedIn are invited to join the over 5,500 members at his LinkedIn group *Federal Construction Professionals*.

Episode 9.
Building Powerful Government Relationships

By Ashley Haass

CEO, The Daily Brief

"If you want to win something, win the hearts of the people"
-Anonymous

Relationships add value. Relationships also provide a platform for you to *give* value. You need other people but other people need you as well. In the world of government contracting, relationships and kindness will get you far.

As Ellevest CEO Sallie Krawcheck says "Networking is the #1 unwritten rule of success." Without relationship building, none of us would accomplish much. It's not only who you know *and* what you know, but how well you can mesh the two.

This was in fact the way I started my career. As a rookie in the world of Government Contracting (GovCon), using my relationship building skills was (and still is) by far the best and most fruitful asset in propelling my career. Curating and maintaining good relationships opened doors for me that I never could have opened on my own, or even imagined in many cases. In fact, the very reason I am writing an episode in this book is the result of curating and maintaining a strong professional relationship.

Relationships enable you to win contracts by teaming with others; allow you to utilize other's past performance and skill sets to qualify your organization; help create successful Joint Ventures (JV); and position yourself to *win*. Relationships with certain agencies can also open the door to a world of opportunities, such as what to be prepared for *before* an RFP release; what an agency's needs are; getting an inside look at what is coming down the pipeline; what's expiring; and possibly win sole-source work. The list goes on.

Today, it is relatively easy to find people within the GovCon community and reach out to them. So easy, there's no excuse not to. It almost feels like cheating. People are more accessible now than at any other time in history. Simply by utilizing the everyday technology at your fingertips, you can find almost any information you desire, on any company or any individual working in a particular position. With minimal searching, you can find exactly who you'd like to speak to, their email, their contact number, their colleagues, their credentials, their professional affiliations, how to reach them and possibly even their ancestral data. This also applies to research on incumbents, but that's another episode on capture strategy.

Track down the people you admire and who have achieved what you want to achieve. Find the people and companies who are winning the contracts you want to win. Ask them questions. Ask them to mentor you. Ask them to connect you, to introduce you, or to refer you. This could be an introduction to a professional affiliation, mastermind group meetings, conferences, contracting officers, agencies, or individuals and CEO's.

Is there an industry related podcast you enjoy? (All the authors in the book, myself included, have been guests on the leading national podcast *Game Changers for Government Contractors*). What is your go-to industry related reading material? Who are the active social media influencers whose professional content is valuable to you?

With a quick search of the host, the author, or the publisher, you can find them and reach out to them. Send them an email. Start replying to their Instagram stories and liking their LinkedIn articles or Twitter posts. Comment on their blog posts. Give their podcast a positive review. Send them a direct message, an InMail on LinkedIn, and ask them if they would be willing to schedule an intro call with you.

Making Connections

My top 3 recommended sources to utilize for making meaningful connections are 1. Industry Days (+ Conferences), 2. LinkedIn, and 3. Podcasts.

Once upon a time, there was a workshop I wanted to attend when I was just starting out. Like many at the beginning of their career, my funds were not abundantly flowing and the workshop was not free. However, I knew the value it would yield. I reached out to the host of the workshop, explained my situation, and asked if she'd be willing to sponsor me. She agreed, and I was able to attend. *You never know unless you ask.*

Meet people at conferences. Join your local organization chapter. Connect with your local PTAC. Become a member of the council. Are you a HUBZone certified small business? Join the *HUBZone Contractors National council.* Go to these events and talk to everyone there that you can.

Typically, when I am attending an event or industry day, I already have a target list of who I want to be sure to speak to and to exchange cards and capabilities with. This list is based on the research I've done prior to the event. Typically, there are other unexpected connections made as well.

Schedule a coffee with another small business that you feel could be a great fit to partner with down the road, who you have not yet sat down with in person. Ask to take them to lunch. People have to eat lunch anyway (except when an RFP is due because who eats or sleeps when that is happening?) Show up with a couple Cadbury eggs if you know that is their favorite desktop snack. Or better yet, introduce them to another contact who they could potentially team with as a good fit. Introduce them to another opportunity that was a no-bid decision for you, but you see how they could bring value and bid the opportunity on their own. Inform them of an upcoming industry day you're attending that's within their wheelhouse and send them the information. People typically don't forget that. And don't be afraid to ask what current opportunities they are aware of that would be a good fit for your business.

Now, clearly, we are not talking about bribery here. Operating with integrity in business will never come back to bite you. Also, people can usually sense real genuineness. When you are genuine, you make people feel they can trust you. In the words of Dr. Steven Covey "it is better to be trusted than to be liked." This sentiment rings true in the GovCon world.

You have to look at the market from an abundance mindset, not a competitive one. There's enough for everyone. When you are not coming from a competitive stance, your sense of genuineness will flow naturally. Share your tips on things which have helped you win; perhaps a proposal tip on how you use high resolution logos from agency websites. Send them a recap of a relevant webinar you recently attended that might be useful. Share industry news such as rules and regulation changes or what the section 809 Panel recently recommended to congress. *Add value*.

The key here is once you meet someone, follow up with an email after meeting *that* day. Even if you have to type an email from your phone, or it's late and you are in bed in your hotel, send them a follow up. Just as time kills all deals, time also weakens relationships, not to mention the individual you just met likely met a lot of people and exchanged many business cards. You need to ensure you are remembered (not forgotten). In addition, send them a LinkedIn request so they can put a face to a name. Begin piecing professional connections together. Make a point to stay in front of them and keep in touch after your initial contact. Write reminders on your calendar every 2- 3 weeks to check in with them.

When you remember the names of their children, what passion project they're working on, that they like to play chess, etc., these are all great building blocks. Most important, remembering these things makes them feel that you were listening, that you remembered, and that you care. All of this breeds trust. If you can win people's trust, you can eventually win their business.

Of course, there's nothing like meeting people in person, which I want to stress. This goes for your professional network, customers and clients, agencies, and the like. This is very important when you are not based out of the District of Columbia (D.C.) or surrounding area. It is *very* possible to succeed in Government contracting while being located anywhere in the U.S. However, you must make it a point to take regular trips to the District to stay in front of agencies, customers, attend events, and to network.

A lot of teams work remotely in today's ever evolving workplace culture. Naturally, this equals less human interaction. Although it is easy to find the right people through technology, you have to be intentional about getting out to meet people face to face. As tempting as it may be, do not hide behind your computer screen or phone. These are just a bridge to in-person communication to foster quality relationships.

If you truly cannot meet in person, video meetings are always second best.

In my experience, CEOs and smaller business owners don't have the time and energy to dedicate themselves to really curating and maintaining the relationships they need to be strategic and create solid partnerships. This is why a relationship builder within your organization is key. A dedicated business development person who can focus on these relationships can really be a powerful tool for growth and strategy.

I've seen it time and time again. A business owner starts down the trail to get to a specific contact on a specific opportunity. However, they stop their efforts at a certain point, before reaching the target, due to everyday fires and running their business.

A federal business developer is a key piece to growing and maintaining a long-term federal portfolio. If your business is not in a financial position to hire one full time, try finding someone to work on an hourly basis or for a set amount of time each month. There are freelancers and many GovCon consulting firms who can perform this work for your company on a contract basis with a little negotiation and resourcefulness.

I recently attended an Industry Day for a client and in typical fashion the CEO was too swamped with business to fly up and attend a Baltimore agency-based event. I attended in representation of the company and secured a one-on-one presentation with the agency. We virtually called-in the CEO and she was able to give the presentation live on the spot. I simply assisted by running the presentation in person.

There are always ways to get things accomplished if you look for a solution instead of a problem. Be willing to be resourceful, shrewd, relentless and innovative.

All of the typical entrepreneurial business owner traits work in our favor when applied to relationships. But, don't forget to be kind. Where there's a will, there's a way.

To put this into context, relationships are about 20% of the equation for the *government* side, from a contracting officer's perspective. As you have to adhere to proposal requirements regardless of relationship and no matter how much a contracting officer likes you, if you don't submit an RFP on time, in the right font, or fulfill their small business set aside requirements, they simply cannot give you the contract.

Teaming

The same does not apply to relationships with other businesses in order to create Teaming Agreements (TA)[9], receiving subcontract work and sole source contracts. These are the areas where relationships are most valuable. I would actually go beyond 80%, to say it's really about 95% relationships in regards to winning business with those aforementioned avenues.

Another form of business relationships in the GovCon world is the All Small Mentor Protégé Program. These are very valuable for small businesses who don't have many resources or past performance. This relationship gives you the guidance, name/brand, and the budget and resources of an experienced government contractor. A mentor is often a larger organization that has full teams dedicated to everything your company does on a day to day basis. The mentor has access to finances and costly certifications. A mentor has access to the type of large contracts you otherwise wouldn't be able to get close to.

There are many forms of business relationships that provide extreme value when approached the right way with the right partners. These include Joint Ventures (JV) and prime / subcontractor teaming agreements. There are rules, requirements, and technicalities to follow and thankfully, there are also many good literature and resources explaining these in depth. *Koprince Law* is a favorite resource of mine for navigating these types of government contracting business relationships.

Mentors

Although a large, highly competent, and experienced company can provide your business the mentorship it may need, you should still have personal mentors as well.

Don't just find a mentor, find several. The goal is to be able to call on many individuals for different strategy or industry questions and guidance.

---

[9] A Teaming Agreements (TA) is an agreement between two companies, given by a Prime contractor to each Subcontractor for the purpose of teaming together to jointly pursue a specific and unique government bid opportunity.

You don't want to rely on just one. Weighing different perspectives always proves valuable.

Also, find a sponsor. A sponsor in the professional world is someone who will advocate for you when you're not present. Don't be shy. Sometimes people in the industry can seem stoic. Some folks may feel unapproachable or intimidating but guess what? People are just people. They shouldn't make you nervous. At the end of the day, they are human beings like you who eat, sleep, and have families. They all had to start somewhere. You have nothing to lose by reaching out and everything to gain. Most people in this industry are actually more than willing to respond, connect with you, and give you their advice and time over a quick phone call.

Be sure to thank people. You'd be surprised how a simple email or handwritten note with a few sincere words of thanks will please someone if they gave you a referral or have mentored you.

View this as planting seeds all around. Just as you may wait for what feels like an eternity for a specific contract to award, these small investments in your professional relationships may not bear fruit in the short term, but you will eventually reap the harvest. You may even make some great friends along the way!

You won't be everyone's cup of tea. This doesn't mean you cannot do business together or make a successful agreement. Just as the rule of bidding goes, you can apply that to relationships also. Your average win rate will fall between 35-50% so you can expect to "win" 3-5 out of every 10 people you meet and network with.

Sometimes relationships can go sour. It's a part of being human. It's going to happen. We are still realists and expecting people to be sincere, because you are sincere, is like expecting a lion not to eat you because you wouldn't eat the lion.

As large as the GovCon community might be, it is also very small. Diplomacy in the world of relationships and business is a key asset, one that we should all strive to master.

Everyone has a different skill set and can bring something different to the table that you don't have. View expanding your network as a greater extension of your ability to win business, not as competition. Be genuine. Be sincere. Gain people's trust and bring value to them as well.

These may seem like basic principles, but there is beauty in simplicity. There is success in the application and follow-through of these simple steps.

* * *

Ashley Haass founded and manages, 'The Daily Brief,' a government consulting firm specializing in assisting businesses develop, expand and diversify their Federal acquisition strategies cost effectively. She personalizes each engagement and thoroughly analyzes a company's capabilities and strengths to align with their goals.

Ms. Haass assists businesses with the following services: development and refinement of new business pipelines; analysis and vetting of new opportunities; capture strategies; development of capability statements; teaming strategies; and proposal development. She has direct experience with the following agencies: National Institutes of Health (NIH), National Institute of Environmental Health Sciences (NIEHS), Centers for Disease Control and Prevention (CDC), Defense Intelligence Agency (DIA), U.S. Army Intelligence & Security Command (INSCOM), and U.S. Central Command (CENTCOM).

In constant pursuit of forging strategic relationships, she is always seeking ways to further develop and curate her knowledge and passion for government contracting. Connect with her via email at Ashley@thedailybrief.us. Find her at https://www.linkedin.com/in/ashley-haass/

Episode 10.
Finding Success as a WOSB in Government Contracting

By Linda Rawson

CEO, DynaGrace Enterprises

I am the owner of DynaGrace Enterprises (DGE). We are a family-owned business based in rural Morgan, Utah. Morgan is a small, religious, farming community. Moreover, somehow, I broke the gender barriers, and one of the ways was to get into government contracting.

I never intended to be an entrepreneur. I was a software developer in a cube, writing all kinds of software from bioinformatics, radar, geographic information systems, and many database utilities. I worked on and off at an Air Force base since I was 18 years old.

One day, a blast from my past whom I had worked with on an environmental information systems program came to me and said, *"Linda, would you like to be a sub on a contract for NASA? You will have to quit your W2 job and become a sub-contractor, with a corporate structure of some kind."*

I was taken aback. I was divorced. I had three children in high school. I just decided what is the worst thing that can happen? If things didn't work out my kids might have to sleep on somebody's couch for a while. It isn't a bad thing for kids to experience short term poverty. I thought about it for a weekend and jumped into business. However, It was an educated decision. I had software skills. I knew if my business failed that I could go back and work for someone. I still feel that way to this day. I jumped into owning my business and I've never looked back. We are still running almost 15 years later.

I get asked a lot about government contracting and I also wrote a book to help other people interested in government contracting, in particular, *The Minority and Women-Owned Small Business Guide to Government Contracts: Everything You Need to Know to Get Started (Available on Amazon)*

Success

Sometimes success happens when somebody you know, sees talent in you and says, why don't you try something else.

After I got into business, it was a different world. A woman in my industry had been awarded her Small Business Administration (SBA) 8(a) certification. 8(a) is a business assistance program for minority and disadvantaged businesses, and like me, she was a white woman in a technical field. She had achieved this endeavor by proving gender discrimination.

Comparatively, I was a female software engineer in Utah. That meant I made 10 thousand dollars less than my male counterparts. I'm a good writer. I'm up for a challenge. So, I decided to apply for the program.

I had to prove gender discrimination, but when I thought about it there were many subtle things. I had gone to conferences and had been asked to wear a low-cut shirt. I had been restricted from going on company travel because I was a woman and women shouldn't travel alone. I had to get signed affidavits about all these discriminations.

However, the SBA was mainly concerned with the salary discrepancies. The 8(a) program is based on socio-economic status.

Right before we got awarded 8(a), the SBA almost held up my 8(a) certification because the IRS had established us as a single-member LLC. The SBA said an LLC is defined as one or more people and we cannot approve your application unless you get this changed.

I had ten days, so I added my daughter, Jennifer Remund, as the other member, expedited the articles of incorporation, and our 100 percent Women-Owned Small Business (WOSB) expanded to two people. She had already been working for me doing the financial books, so this was a smooth transition.

Not knowing what the program was or what the program could do for me was a problem. Once awarded, I wasted the entire first year because I didn't understand the value of the program. Then, a blast from my past arrived on the scene, again.

Select Engineering Services (SES) approached me about utilizing my 8(a) in a mentor-protégé program. We joined forces, established a Joint Venture (JV), and proceeded to contact their existing customers about using this new procurement avenue.

I got lucky. SES was a terrific mentor. I wasn't just a checkmark to them. SES taught me how to respond to RFP's, prepare my accounting system, negotiate with contracting officers, market to the government, and analyze solicitations for go/no go strategy. One important lesson that I have always admired and respected about them was how to treat employees and compensate them appropriately.

They have been my mentor and business partner for many years. They taught me so much and provided expert advice and friendship over several decades. Without them, DynaGrace Enterprises (DGE) would not have grown. Anytime there was a question about something new, they had the answer. The introductions they made for me were invaluable.

Just like that, I was in business for a few years and I made a move from one employee, myself, to multiple employees. I took business in college, but I didn't have a clue what I was getting into. When things pop into your lap and you have success, you figure out how to continue that success and maintain those relationships to get more 8(a) sole-source awards.

With 8(a) certification, if a government customer likes you, they write your name on the contract and give it to you. It is still the best way to get government contracts. *This method is also the hardest way if you don't go through the steps to figure out your target market and maintain those relationships.*

Four different types of government customers

- **Procurers** (including contracting officers / specialists)
- **Influencers** (including program managers/high-level decision-makers)
- **End Users** (recipients of the services)

- Potential teaming partners who have existing government customers and need a contracting vehicle to service those government customers

The following table breaks down each type of customer and the benefit of marketing to that customer.

Name	Description	Benefits
Procurers	Contracting officers and specialists are an example of *Procurers*. The "gatekeepers" decide on the contracting vehicle to use to procure services from you. Because contracting, officers and specialists may not be familiar with WOSB or 8(a) set-asides, you need to educate them on the ease of the process.	The ultimate decision-maker on what contracting vehicle to use is the Procurer. If you can influence the Procurer, then your services will likely be procured.
Influencers	*Influencers* are program managers and high-level decision-makers. *Influencers* generate the requirement and are responsible for making sure the requirement gets procured. *Influencers* do not do the procurement but *can produce documentation to justify what contracting vehicle to use*.	Just knowing the Influencers is not enough. You must educate this group on the ease of using WOSB or 8(a) set-asides. If they do enough of the leg work before the procurement goes to the *Procurers*, then the process is streamlined. You educate and help this group to create the necessary documentation to ensure the *Procurers* use WOSB or 8(a) set-asides.

Name	Description	Benefits
End Users	*End Users* are the recipient of your services. They are familiar with the quality of your employees and management and want to get the job done on time and within budget.	Many times, the *End User* will only want your company. They can push the requirement up the chain to obtain your services any way possible. Because the *Procurer* can utilize the WOSB or 8(a) set-aside contracting vehicles this gives the *End User* one more way to obtain to your company's products or services.
Subcontractors	Another company may be providing excellent service to the government customer. The government customer wants to continue using that contractor but has no way to procure their services. You can form a subcontracting agreement with the *Subcontractor* and perform most of the work and help that company keep their relationship intact.	You can utilize the experience that the Subcontractor brings to increase your past performance portfolio.

Table 1 - Type of Customers

I once had a contracting officer decide that they wanted to use their local favorite small business instead of me. Even though I was popular with the End User and popular with the Influencer, I was not popular with the Procurer or contracting officer. My contract didn't go through.

There are many ways to find out agencies that don't meet their socioeconomic percentages. You can go to events and find those people. However, it would be best if you were good friends with all the levels of procurement, or your contract will likely not go through. If you have a great relationship with your End User, do they have enough pull with the contracting officer to get it through the procurement process? Recently, I had a delayed procurement action because I used an emoji in my email. Be professional all the way through.

111

Another way to reach the End User is to attend local events or even national events. There are matchmaking events and in five minutes I can find out their forecasts and what they are doing at their installation. In those five minutes you have a chance to give them your capabilities. Just make sure that you follow up. You should follow up immediately. Do that and then wait a month and send them another email. Keep them on your list and do this every three or four months. It takes a year to 18 months to get government work. You can't stop at two months.

Employees bring on a whole new level for your business. I'm not a selfish person and wanted to make sure that they were well taken care of. Moreover, they need to work hard and be professional. Most important, they need to show up. For the most part, on an 8(a) professional services contract, you almost always know the people that you hire.

As an 8(a), you are either taking over a project from another 8(a) that has graduated or it is a new task order. The project arrives and you learn how to hire people. You will learn how to screen prospective employees and how to trust your gut feelings… and don't forget to call their references. Figure out whether they're going to be a good fit. If they don't work out, fire them at the first sign of trouble. The last thing you want to do is negatively impact your company's reputation by placing a person at a government installation, someone that represents your company, and that person doesn't have the right personality or work ethic.

I have a screening process, but much of the decision hangs on gut feel. I have fired people and I will fire quickly because I don't want anything toxic in my company. You also have to explain to the government customer why you terminated an employee and why they were not a good fit. Let them know you listened to them and you are replacing that person with a much better fit.

Swapping on-site personnel is a sensitive situation. The best way to handle delicate situations is to be direct. Sit down with the customer, walk them through what is going to happen and why this is the best-case scenario. Chances are they have been frustrated with that employee as well and are relieved that you have enough guts to replace that person. Some companies have a reputation for leaving toxic people because of the difficulty in getting a replacement.

The statement, *"it's good enough for government work,"* doesn't fly with me. The truth is, it's not good enough. To get the second, third and continuing contract awards, you need to be better than the rest. Perform and deliver above the standard. Step up. Fix things. Help the government customer find relief.

I've experienced some surprises during my career. My biggest surprise was that I never intended to be an entrepreneur. I'm also surprised that gender discrimination is still a thing in today's world. I'm always surprised at the amount of discrimination, even when obtaining financing. I believe that funding for single women remains complicated and difficult to obtain.

The government contracting market still has an "old white guy" mentality. No offense to anyone reading this but that's the market we operate in. *You have to overlook discrimination to be successful.* Work around it and don't play the victim. Have the confidence to make it work despite the difficulties.

Speaking of financing, I didn't have any money to start my business. DynaGrace Enterprises is a service-based company and the SBA and banks don't give out loans unless you have assets. Your invoices are worth a lot of money. If you need to pay employees, you might invoice factor or use some other method to be able to borrow on that invoice and then pay it back when you get paid by your customer.

I have never participated in outsourced sales. The feedback I have heard from other firms has prevented me from hiring that outside salesperson. Here's the scenario: The sales guy, a retired colonel or general, is charismatic and he's got *all* the connections. After retirement he decides to work for Company A and receives an enormous amount of sales. Company A gives him a salary for a year and the next year all the contracts flow in. Now he has a track record.

The Sales Guy is done with Company A and tries to find the next company. Company B says, "Wow! You are just what we need," and hires him. But here's the problem - he's already gone through all his contacts with Company A. When he goes to present to his contacts again, he now has *several companies that he's representing.* How does he differentiate between all of them? These new companies are paying his salary and after a year, he fails to win work for them. I caution people to be careful when choosing outside sales. Do your due diligence for anybody that represents your company.

Michael LeJeune and his consulting staff recommend never outsourcing a couple of things. One of them is proposal writing and the other is an outside salesperson. He says that proposal writing can be outsourced if the person has a deep understanding of your company and when you're going to use the proposal writer repeatedly.

One of the things that I would tell a new 8(a) is to find a niche and focus on that niche. My standard response is, *"Oh, you need an 8(a)? I'm your 8(a). I can do it."* We did all sorts of things, construction, demolition, water quality studies, engineering services, and information technology. Too many avenues to explore. Whereas if you find a niche, you can focus on those government customers that need that niche, and then get to know them, reach out to them, and you have a much better opportunity to get that government contract award.

You will experience fear. There may be anxiety and fear every single day. Just ask yourself, *"what is the worst thing that can happen?"* That's how you get past fear.

My final advice is simple. Have confidence in your abilities and to analyze yourself. Know what you want and put your intention into everything that you do. You need to be passionate about what you are doing and communicate that passion to others. If you know what you want and you're excited about it, the money is going to follow.

*   *   *

Linda Rawson is a CEO, author, public speaker and serial entrepreneur. Linda is a technology entrepreneur and executive focused on providing innovative information technology, system integration, cybersecurity and writing services to government and commercial clients. Her background as a software engineer, combined with her corporate executive experience, merges the technical with the business world. She founded DynaGrace Enterprises (previously Sensory Technology Consultants in 2006). DynaGrace Enterprises (DGE) is a 100% Women-Owned Small Business and is an SBA 8(a) certified graduate with several million dollars in DoD government contracts.

Linda was raised in a small farming community, Morgan, Utah by her mother, who was a single mom raising five children. She never thought about being an entrepreneur even though there were childhood tendencies. From meager beginnings came the experience of how to work hard and how to achieve results. She has exceeded expectations and never let various challenges and obstacles associated with being a woman impede upon her path to success. Find her at https://www.linkedin.com/in/lindarawson/.

Episode 11.
How to Scale Any Business

By Michael LeJeune

Partner at RSM Federal, Federal Access PM, and Podcast Host
for Game Changers for Government Contractors

Companies always struggle with figuring out how to scale their businesses. During any calendar year, I'm invited to four or five corporate offsites. The owners of these companies bring their management teams together to discuss vision, strategy, and the direction of the company. Without fail, the primary theme is growth, the scalability of the business. I bridge my concepts with those of the CEO or president in order to drive home the strategic and cultural shifts that must take place. My point is that learning how to scale your business applies to all size businesses.

I get quite a few calls these days from business owners who are running companies with annual revenue in the thirty to fifty million range. The call is almost always the same. There is one burning question: *How do we scale?*

The first thing I always say is that they are clearly doing something right. You don't make fifty million a year by luck or chance. It takes hard work, a great business model, and doing a lot of the right things.

This goes to show that no matter what level you are at, business professionals always hit a plateau. There always comes a point when you don't know what to do next. Some reach that plateau at $150,000 and some at $50 million. It's normal. Just be willing to ask for help.

One more item before I dive into my top four strategies for scaling any business. Profit *must* come first. *Do **not**...under any circumstances...try to* *scale something that is not profitable*. The fastest way to go out of business is try scaling something that's broken. Growth is expensive. Trying to scale something broken is just plain foolish.

#1 – Your Business Model

It doesn't matter if you are product-based, service-based, or a blend of the two, you still need an overarching model for your business. That said, you need to understand what the core pieces of your business are; where you make your money; what your obstacles for growth are; and where your potential is for massive growth.

There are different business models depending on what you are selling. Here are some questions that you need to ask yourself to uncover the core pieces of your model.

- What is actually being sold? Time? Talent? Stuff?
- Who is fulfilling the orders?
- What kind of talent does this take? – high or low skill
- How hard will it be to recruit and train?
- Is this sold one to one (1:1) or 1 to many (1:M)?
- Does it work while you sleep or does it require billable time?
- Are we a manufacturer, distributor, or both?
- Who is our customer?
- What is important to our customer?
- Is it clear what we do?
- Is this model sustainable?
- Is it profitable?

Your model is built on (1) how you make your money, (2) who fulfills the orders/does the work, (3) your profit margin, and (4) how big your market is.

When you look at these areas of the business, always ask the question, "does this limit our ability to scale?" If so, how? Do we hit a plateau at $1M, $5M, $50M? What are the limitations? How can we overcome these limitations?

Think in simple terms. For example, McDonalds was once limited by a single drive-thru. As a result, many restaurants added a second drive-thru. The McDonalds in my town still has a single drive-thru. It holds about nine or ten cars. My daughter was telling me the other day that the restaurants in the city with a double drive-thru hold 35 cars! That's a massive increase in capacity. *Where can you add something simple like this to your business?*

If one of your challenges is profit margin, can you increase profits by narrowing your niche? Can you eliminate a vendor and develop your own products or services? Can you come up with a unique marketing strategy to significantly reduce upfront costs or significantly increase exposure to the market? What if you eliminated resellers and went direct to market?

In one of my earlier companies, we had two significant problems with our model. The first was that we only used resellers to sell to the government. Our resellers were lazy but had easy access to our ideal customer. We found ourselves in a situation where we were doing all of the selling and then passing the orders to large system integrators (SI). The SI would then double the price of our products to achieve massive margins.

When I looked at this, I found it completely ridiculous that I was paying six sales people to hand deals over to these large companies. So, I changed our model. I gave notice to resellers that we were going direct. This created extensive drama internally at our company and with our resellers. At the end of the day, we exponentially increased revenue. More important, we increased profit because we were able to charge significantly more than before while our pricing appeared to be drastically less than what the government previously paid to our resellers. Remember, the big guys were adding a massive markup. So even with our price increase, we were less expensive for the customer.

By going direct, we also increased our cash flow because we were receiving the order directly from the customer. This allowed us to invoice the work directly and bypass the need for money to flow through the reseller. By my calculations, we increased the speed of payments by 45 to 60 days.

The second challenge in our model was that we were built on a third-party platform owned by Microsoft. As luck would have it, Microsoft had recently purchased the platform from a former partner and Microsoft wanted to meet us because we were a significant piece of that business.

I told Microsoft that their cost was too high and that it would eventually drive us out of business. They didn't care much. So, I made them an offer. I asked if we could get a break on costs if we increased sales ten-fold over the next year. I'm pretty sure they thought I was out of my mind because they said yes. They ultimately said they would reduce their cost by over 75% if we committed to that volume. My other stipulation was that I wanted our discount to start right away. Again, they said yes. As a result, we increased our gross profit margin from 23% to nearly 75% when coupled with the direct sales approach.

We hit our numbers, increasing our sales ten-fold. One of the reasons we successfully increased our numbers was *our ability to reinvest the higher margins into improving our products and services.*

Always ask the question: What is holding us back from scaling? It's a simple question. You may not like the answer. It may not be an easy fix. Getting your model right is the first step to scaling. If you don't have the right model, you will continue to hit roadblocks. The model is easier to correct in the earlier stages of your business.

Put every option on the table. You don't have to implement every option, but you need to be open to all the possibilities. Do you think my company was receptive when I proposed cutting out our resellers and going direct? Of course not! Change is difficult to manage. In fact, for several months the only two people that were onboard with the change were the CEO and myself. No one wanted to anger the resellers. While I was sensitive to that, I was more concerned with the thirty-five families that we employed. If we didn't take drastic action, the company would not have survived.

#2 – Systems are the Foundation of Scalability

Every area of your business needs basic systems and processes. Without this, you are operating in chaos-mode. Without systems, you won't know what's broken or where problems are coming from because you aren't really managing the business. You're reacting to it. Chaos-mode is basically a free for all where your business is surviving in spite of itself.

The fundamentals of a great system are:

- It starts with a flow-chart / map for every step
- The flow-chart is your guide for creating the system
- It's documented in a way that's easy to use (McDonalds uses photos at workstations)
- It's easy to follow (makes sense)
- It covers 80% of the situations that can pop up

- Employees are trained how to deal with or escalate the remaining 20% of decisions that the system doesn't cover
- It *NEVER* puts process above people
- It includes a review/improvement process

I could write an entire book on systems, but instead, what I want to do is bullet point some key systems that are essential for each department in your business.

Sales

- Your sales process. From identifying prospects all the way through to bringing them on as a client.
- Scripts for each stage of the sales process. They don't have to be read verbatim, but sales people need a best practice guide.
- KPI tracking and reporting for each stage of the sales process.

Marketing

- Marketing collateral development and distribution
- Campaign (lead generation) creation, execution, and tracking
- Conference attendance, speaking, and booths

Operations

- Leadership roles and responsibilities
- Leadership development

Finance

- Cash flow management
- Financial reporting
- Payroll
- Accounts receivable

Employee

- Hiring
- Training
- Retention

Service / Delivery of your products

- Order processing

- Customer service scripts
- Customer service processes and procedures
- Escalation procedures

#3 – Marketing / Lead Generation

Marketing is so important to your business that it deserves its own section. You will often hear me say, "keep filling your pipeline." No matter what happens in your business, never stop filling the pipeline. Money won't solve all of your problems, but a lack of money will create problems on a regular basis. You solve this by having a pipeline that is overflowing with potential.

Most companies make three major mistakes with their marketing. The first major mistake is that their marketing is not trackable. A lead comes into their system and they have no idea where it came from or how they heard about the prospect. This one is easily fixed by adding tracking codes to your marketing and even then, always asking "how did you hear about us?"

If you have ever submitted a form on our website or signed up for one of RSM Federal's programs, you will see how we practice what we preach. A lot of the tracking happens behind the scenes via link tags and Google Analytics. But we still ask, "how did you hear about us?" We ask because we want to know how we connected.

For example, most of our leads don't come directly from the Game Changers podcast, **but**… the podcast is often the first place they learn about us. Many folks will start with the podcast, follow us on LinkedIn, pick up one of our books on Amazon, and then reach out to us. The strategies are working together to deliver leads. If we didn't ask the question, we wouldn't know that all the strategies are working together. You need this information to figure out where to invest your time and money.

Now for many readers, it's more about marketing for business to government (B2G). How do you know if the $3,500 you paid to exhibit at that conference was actually worth it? Do you have the metrics to prove that five opportunities in the pipeline are directly attributed to that conference? For every marketing dollar you spend, can you prove the value of that dollar? If not, you're likely wasting money.

The second big marketing mistake people make is counting on a single strategy. A good example of this is SAM.gov. As I write this episode, contractors are going through the FedBizOpps (FBO) to SAM.gov transition. It has not been pleasant. Forget about the new user interface for a moment. The first week of the transition was anything but flawless. In fact, during the first few days most people couldn't even login. For some companies, this was their only lead generation strategy. Quite a few companies did not know what to do.

When you think about your lead generation strategies, you want three to five pillars that you can count on. It's ok if one or two of those strategies produce the bulk of your leads, but it's not okay if those are your only strategies.

The best scenario is when your lead strategies *work together*. I've already hinted at this via the way we market our company. We have a podcast, multiple books on Amazon, over 15,000 connections on LinkedIn (btw, if we are not connected, please reach out to Joshua Frank and myself), a website that is SEO optimized, we speak at conferences, we have a partner channel that features us on their webinars, and we have a growing email list. All of these strategies work together to regularly introduce business professionals to our company.

What about your company? Examples include local, regional, and national conferences; industry days; federal agency and DoD events, other companies and potential teaming partners. All of these *work together*.

The third big marketing mistake that companies make is relying heavily on strategies that either aren't repeatable or have massive limitations. Many companies don't have an unlimited marketing budget. In fact, quite a few companies I talk with don't have a budget line-item for marketing.

What typically happens is that someone in management or on the sales team hears about a marketing opportunity and decides it's a great idea. So, the idea backer and the marketing team energetically come up with an idea that is going to drive more leads than they know what to do with. Then the campaign runs and you get little or no leads. Everyone now hates the idea of marketing because it's such a waste of time and resources and we go back to only using our bid-matching tools to search for opportunities.

When it comes to marketing, remember this...*If it's not repeatable, it's not dependable*. Let's say you attend a conference and it's a bust. You gain little to no value from the event. Are you sure it was the conference? It may have been how you approached the event! Keep an open mind.

Using strategies that are limiting is also a problem. If you can only use the strategy once a year, that's a fairly large limitation. If the strategy is going to wipe out your budget for the year, that's limiting. To one level or another, everything has limitations, but you need to watch out for the slippery slope of going "all in" on any one strategy that only gives you a single shot.

The best strategies have low acquisition costs per lead and are repeatable at will. This allows you to have a predictable marketing budget AND it allows you to buy more leads ON-DEMAND because you know exactly what they cost.

#4 – Your Team

One of the largest limitations to scalability are your employees. It doesn't matter what you sell, at some point, you need more people. You either need them doing the work, selling the work, or serving customers.

Building and managing a team isn't hard if you love people. It can be a nightmare if you are an introvert or a process person. However, being in business and scaling a business is dependent on the happiness of your team and their abilities. If you don't like managing people, find someone that does. A lot of companies hire a Chief Operating Officer (COO) to manage the team. There's nothing wrong with this. In fact, it could be the best hire your company ever makes.

Here are a few areas that you need to focus on in order to build a scalable team.

Hiring

- A process for finding and interviewing candidates
- Clearly defined roles and responsibilities
- Employee agreements (including compensation plans)

Employee on-boarding

- Welcome to the company procedures
- A 90-day roadmap for training and success
- Streamlined HR / paperwork procedures

Ongoing training

- Monthly / quarterly training schedule
- Industry training (if required)
- Incentives for completing certifications and training programs

KPI's

- By department
- By individual / position
- Reporting mechanisms
- Reward systems

Goals

- Company goals
- Individual goals
- Quarterly performance planning and review

Company Culture

- Vision statement
- Points of culture - the rules of the game
- Employee expectations / guidelines

* * *

Michael LeJeune is a Partner with RSM Federal and Program Manager for the Federal Access Knowledge-Base and Training Platform. He is an award-winning business coach, author, and host of the podcast Game Changers for Government Contractors. He has been consulting and mentoring companies in the government market for twenty years. Michael is also an Army Veteran. Find him at www.linkedin.com/in/michaeljlejeune/

Episode 12.
Understanding Joint Ventures

By Matthew Schoonover

Managing Partner, Koprince Law

If your business has been in the federal marketplace for any period of time, it will come as no surprise that winning a federal government contract is a very competitive endeavor. In fact, this competitive nature is enshrined in the United States Code: the presumption for acquisitions is that the federal government will obtain "full and open" competition to the extent practicable. See 10 U.S.C. § 2304(a); 41 U.S.C. § 3301(a). Competition has become more intense as the federal government has consolidated contract opportunities and shied away from lowest-price technically-acceptable awards towards best value tradeoffs.

Given the intense competition that often exists for federal contracts, how might a business—particularly a small business—best position itself for an award? One option is to consider forming a joint venture with another company to jointly bid on and, if awarded, perform a contract. In this episode, we'll discuss some considerations in forming a joint venture that complies with the Small Business Administration's (SBA) regulations.

A couple of quick caveats before we dig in. First, though this episode is written by an attorney, it is not intended to be (and should not be considered as) legal advice. Instead, this episode is for educational purposes only. Reading this episode does not create an attorney-client relationship with the author. Second, this episode discusses the pertinent regulations as they existed in September 2019; if you're reading this episode after that date, the regulations might have since changed. Again, don't rely on this episode for legal advice.

With that, let's dig into joint ventures under the SBA's regulations.

What is a Joint Venture?

According to the SBA, a joint venture is an association of individuals and/or concerns with interests in any degree or proportion consorting to engage in and carry out no more than three specific or limited-purpose business ventures for joint profit over a two-year period, for which they combine their efforts, property, money, skill, or knowledge, but not on a continuing or permanent basis for conducting business generally.

13 C.F.R. § 121.103(h). The regulation continues to say that a joint venture "[m]ust be in writing and must do business under its own name; must be identified as a joint venture in the System for Award Management (SAM);" and must be a separate, unpopulated legal entity. Id.

That's a definition that only a lawyer can love. In a nutshell, it means that a joint venture exists when two or more companies (venturers) form a new legal entity (the joint venture) that will itself bid on work. To perform this work, the joint venture will rely on the venturers' resources, equipment, and property, as well as their past performance. The joint venture may not, however, be *populated*—that is, it cannot employ any of the personnel that will perform the work under the contract; instead, the venturer members will ultimately employ those personnel and perform the tasks required under the contract. Both venturers, moreover, will remain responsible for ensuring that any contracts awarded to the joint venture are performed.

As the regulations state, the joint venture entity must itself be registered in the System for Award Management (*SAM.gov*). To first do so, the company will need to be organized in a state of the venturers' choosing; have its own federal tax identification number; DUNS number;[10] and Commercial and Government Entity Code (CAGE). The joint venture must also complete the appropriate representations and certifications on its behalf as part of the SAM registration process. Because each of these steps can take some time to complete - and because an entity must be registered

---

[10] GSA has announced its intention to replace the DUNS number with a Unique Entity Identifier beginning in December 2020. Learn more at: https://www.gsa.gov

in SAM before it submits a bid for a federal government contract - it's worth starting this registration process as early as possible.

How does a joint venture arrangement differ from that of a traditional prime contractor/subcontractor team? Under a prime/subcontractor team, only the prime contractor is responsible for contract performance. To facilitate that performance, it contracts out a portion of that work to one or more subcontractors, who are usually paid on a pre-determined basis. Some of the key differences between a joint venture and a prime/subcontractor team follow:

	Prime/Subcontract Team	Joint Venture
What is the contractual relationship?	Only the prime contractor has a contractual relationship with the government. The subcontractor's contractual relationship is with the prime contractor.	All venturers have a contractual relationship with the government (through their status as venturers).
How is contractual eligibility determined?	The prime contractor must be an eligible offeror under the contract's size and socio-economic requirements.	The joint venture must be eligible. Both venturers must be small businesses under the contract's size standard (unless the joint venture is between an approved mentor and protégé); socio-economic requirements must be met as well.
Is a new entity formed?	No—the prime contractor will bid on and perform the contract.	Yes—the venturers form a separate, unpopulated legal entity to bid on and perform the contract.
Who performs the work?	The prime contractor is responsible for ensuring that the work is performed. It can enter subcontracts,	Each venturer is individually responsible for ensuring that the contract is performed

	but must comply with any applicable limitation on subcontracting.	(as *de facto* prime contractors). It can subcontract to third parties, but must comply with any applicable limitation on subcontracting <u>and</u> the performance of work requirement.
How is profit shared?	The prime contractor receives payment from the government and then pays its subcontractors for their services.	The joint venture is paid by the government, and the venturers split their profits commensurate with the work they each perform.

What are the Benefits to Forming a Joint Venture?

Creating a joint venture is more involved than simply bidding through a prime/subcontractor team. So why might a company decide to enter into a joint venture relationship, instead of simply bidding as a prime/subcontractor team?

Joint ventures carry several unique advantages over a prime / subcontractor team. These include:

1. **Past performance and experience.** One of the primary benefits to forming a joint venture is that a contracting officer is required, when evaluating past performance, to not only consider the past performance and experience of the joint venture entity itself, but also that of the individual venturers. E.g., 13 C.F.R. § 125.8(e). This rule is a significant benefit compared to the treatment of a subcontractor's past performance or experience. Under the FAR, a contracting officer *should*, but isn't required to take into account a subcontractor's past performance. See FAR 15.305(a)(2)(iii). In other words, an inexperienced service-disabled veteran-owned small business (SDVOSB) might benefit from forming a joint venture with a well-established 8(a) Program participant under an SDVOSB set-aside, instead of a prime/subcontractor team.[11]

2. **Management assistance.** Along these same lines, the joint venture might benefit from the venturers' combined management of the contract. True, the venturer upon whose eligibility the joint venture's eligibility is based must serve as the joint venture's managing venturer. E.g., 13 C.F.R. § 125.8(b)(2)(ii). But there's no prohibition under the regulations from the managing venturer relying on the assistance and support of its partner venturer in managing the contract. Assuming the performance of work requirement is met, one venturer should be able to augment its management capabilities by relying on its partner.

3. **The potential for a larger work share.** For contracts that are set-aside for small businesses, the limitation on subcontracting restricts the amount of work that the prime contractor can subcontract to non-similarly situated entities. See 13 C.F.R. § 125.6. This percentage varies depending on the type of contract at issue: under a services contract, for example, the prime contractor cannot subcontract more than 50% of the work (measured by the dollars paid by the government under its prime contract). Under a joint venture agreement, however, the non-managing member can perform up to 60% of the work that the joint venture itself performs. E.g., 13 C.F.R. § 125.8(c). In some situations, a company might be eligible to perform more work under a joint venture than it would be through a traditional prime/subcontractor team.

4. **Avoiding ostensible subcontractor affiliation.** Remember: a joint venture is a combination of two or more companies—and their respective efforts, property, money, skill, and knowledge—to jointly bid on and perform work. In the context of a prime/subcontractor team, however, this combination of assets and resources to pursue and perform a contract might lead to the SBA finding the prime contractor affiliated with its subcontractor. And, where this affiliation is found, the combined size of the prime subcontractor with its ostensible subcontractor could lead to it being ineligible for the award. See, e.g., Size Appeal of Equity Mortgage Solutions, LLC, SBA No. SIZ-5867 (Nov. 16, 2017) (finding a prime contractor affiliated with its subcontractors because the prime relied too much on the subcontractors for the personnel, experience, and resources needed to win and perform the contract).

---

[11] The joint venture would, of course, have to meet the applicable eligibility requirements.

To facilitate the joint venture's combination of the assets, equipment, or personnel needed to perform, the SBA's regulations grant a *properly-formed* joint venture certain immunities from a finding of affiliation. 13 C.F.R. § 121.103(h). It would be a perverse result, after all, if the SBA's regulations encouraged venturers to combine their resources in this manner through a joint venture, but then penalize them for doing so through a finding of affiliation. Thus, if the prime were to need to heavily rely on its subcontractors for these items, it might consider instead forming a joint venture to help guard against affiliation.

5.   **Ensured performance.** Unlike a prime/subcontractor team (where only the prime contractor is obligated to ensure the successful performance of the contract), all venturers are obligated to ensure that a contract awarded to the joint venture is successfully performed, even if one venturer withdraws from performance or the joint venture. To the government, this assurance can be a great benefit, particularly where the work is difficult or one of the parties has a less-certain performance history.

Consider too the benefits from ensured performance from the contractor's perspective. Because the venturers own a portion of the joint venture—and because each venturer is obligated to ensure performance—it is difficult (if not impossible) for one venturer to terminate the other from that performance. This can itself be an advantage compared to a prime/subcontractor relationship, where a prime contractor might enjoy broader discretion to terminate subcontractors.

The benefits to forming a joint venture can be significant. But to avail themselves of those benefits, the venturers must form a *compliant* joint venture. Let's turn our attention to what goes into forming a joint venture.

Joint Venture Eligibility

Forming a joint venture isn't as simple as creating a new limited liability company. But at the same time, it's also not mind-bogglingly complex. It just takes some foresight and, yes, some paperwork.

The first consideration to keep in mind is whether the joint venture itself qualifies as a small business (if it intends to bid on work that is set-aside for small businesses). The general rule is that both venturers must both independently qualify as small businesses under the solicitation. 13 C.F.R. § 121.103(h)(3)(i). An important exception exists: a joint venture between an

SBA-approved mentor and protégé[12] will qualify as an eligible business for any procurement for which the protégé is itself eligible, so long as the joint venture has a compliant joint venture agreement. 13 C.F.R. § 121.103(h)(3)(i), (ii).

This exception is a boon for small business protégés. Not only do these companies get the business development assistance promised under the mentor/protégé agreement, but they get an additional benefit of being able to joint venture with a large business to perform work reserved for small businesses. Because an agency might look favorably upon a joint venture that boasts the participation of a large business (and that business's attendant resources and experiences), this exception helps give a competitive advantage to mentor/protégé joint ventures.

Beyond qualifying from a size standpoint, the joint venture must also meet any applicable socio-economic requirements. For example, a joint venture that wishes to bid on and perform a solicitation that is set-aside for HUBZone concerns must qualify as a HUBZone joint venture.

The specific socio-economic requirements that must be met will vary somewhat depending on the socio-economic program at issue.[13] But in

---

[12] The SBA currently has two mentor/protégé programs: one under the 8(a) Program, and the other open to all small businesses (including 8(a) businesses). On November 8, 2019, however, the SBA proposed to consolidate the two mentor/protégé programs under the All-Small mentor/protégé program. Consolidation of Mentor Protégé Programs and Other Government Contracting Amendments, 84 Fed. Reg. 60846, 60846–47 (Nov. 8, 2019). This consolidation has not yet been finalized as of this writing.

Under either program, the protégé receives identified business development assistance from its mentor, including the possibility of entering into joint ventures. And though other agencies run different mentor/protégé programs, only a mentor and protégé under an SBA-approved agreement are eligible for this joint venture size exception.

For additional information about the SBA's mentor/protégé programs, refer to 13 C.F.R. § 124.520 (8(a) mentor/protégé program) or 13 C.F.R. § 125.9 (All-Small mentor/protégé program). See also Matthew Schoonover, 5 Things You Should Know: All Small Mentor-Protégé Program, SmallGovCon.com (Sept. 20, 2017), available at http://smallgovcon.com/five-things/asmpp/.

[13] These requirements are found at 13 C.F.R. § 124.513(c) (8(a) joint ventures), 13 C.F.R. § 125.8 (small business joint ventures), 13 C.F.R. § 125.18(b) (SDVOSB joint ventures), 13 C.F.R. § 126.616(c) (HUBZone joint ventures), and 13 C.F.R. § 127.506(c) (WOSB joint ventures).

general, a compliant joint venture must have a joint venture agreement that includes the following provisions:

1.   **Purpose.** Because a joint venture is a limited purpose entity, the joint venture agreement must specifically designate its purpose—usually, to bid on and perform work under a specific solicitation. If the joint venture later identifies another solicitation upon which it intends to bid, it should amend the joint venture agreement to reflect that new solicitation.

2.   **Managing member and project manager.** The joint venture agreement must designate the venturer with the applicable socio-economic category as the managing venturer, and name an employee of the managing venturer as the joint venture's project manager with responsibility over contract performance.[14] For example, if an SDVOSB and a woman-owned small business form a joint venture to bid on work reserved for SDVOSBs, the SDVOSB venturer must be named the managing venturer. Those venturers could then form a second joint venture to bid on WOSB work, so long as that second joint venture named the WOSB venturer as managing venturer.

3.   **Ownership.** The joint venture agreement must specify that the managing venturer owns at least 51% of the joint venture entity.

4.   **Profits.** The joint venture's profits must be split between the venturers commensurate with the work each performs.

5.   **Special Bank Account.** The joint venture must set up a special bank account in the name of the joint venture, into which all payments due the joint venture will be paid. All expenses from the joint venture must also be paid from this account; and withdrawals must require the signature of all venturers (or their designees).

6.   **Itemization of all major equipment, facilities, and resources.** The joint venture agreement must itemize the major equipment, facilities, and resources that each venturer will provide the joint venture to meet its purpose (and provide an itemized value of each item). For indefinite

---

[14] A joint venture between two small businesses that will bid on work reserved for small businesses does not need to have an agreement with any specific provisions. 13 C.F.R. § 125.8(b)(1). But it should still have a written joint venture agreement.

contracts, the joint venture should include a narrative of how the venturers will identify and provide these items once a definitive scope of work is made known.

7.   **Specification of the parties' responsibilities.** The joint venture agreement must also specify the venturers' responsibilities regarding contract negotiations, source of labor, and contract performance. For indefinite contracts, the parties can explain how they will decide and provide these items once a definitive scope of work is available. Regardless, however, the joint venture agreement must also explain how the parties will meet the performance of work requirement.

8.   **Record keeping and financial reporting.** The joint venture agreement must also include SBA-required provisions about where the parties will keep their records and when the joint venture will provide various financial reports to the SBA.

Beyond these requirements, there are other provisions that venturers might wish to be included in their joint venture agreement - provisions relating to the confidentiality of information, solicitation of employees, and indemnification for any losses, among others.[15] But the provisions discussed above are, in general, those that the SBA requires to be present in a joint venture agreement.

Though these provisions might seem simple, the difficulty often lies in the details. For a joint venture to be considered compliant, it must meet these requirements exactly. If a joint venture agreement falls short in some respect, the SBA may find the joint venture to be ineligible for the specific contract at issue.

If compliance is such a big deal, does that mean that a joint venture agreement must be pre-approved before the joint venture can be eligible for the award? No, with two limited exceptions. First, the SBA must pre-approve joint venture agreements under the 8(a) Business Development Program.[16] Second, the Department of Veterans Affairs' Center for

---

[15] Some of these provisions might be included in a separate operating agreement for the joint venture. Just be sure that these provisions—or any others—don't conflict with the SBA's required provisions.

Verification and Evaluation must approve a joint venture that wishes to bid on work set-aside by the VA for SDVOSBs or veteran-owned small-businesses. For all other joint ventures, pre-approval will not be given; instead, the SBA will review the agreement to ensure compliance with the regulations in response to any size or status protest.

In addition to meeting the applicable size and socio-economic requirements, a joint venture must also meet a few performance-based requirements. The first requirement to keep in mind is the "3-in-2 rule," which essentially prohibits the joint venture from performing more than three contracts over a two-year period (measured from the date of the first award).[17] This is an affiliation rule, meaning that violations may lead the venturers to be considered generally affiliated with each other. But although compliance with the 3-in-2 rule can be tricky, the SBA offers a way to avoid violations: simply form a new joint venture. See 13 C.F.R. § 121.103(h).

The second requirement to keep in mind is the performance of work requirement. This requirement mandates that the managing venturer performs at least 40% of the work that the joint venture itself performs. E.g., 13 C.F.R. § 125.8(c). But keep in mind that the limitation on subcontracting is likely to apply too. So, for work that is set-aside for small businesses (or any other socio-economic category), the joint venture, as prime contractor, must first make sure it complies with the applicable limitation on subcontracting. Then, for the work that the joint venture performs (or, stated differently, that the joint venture doesn't subcontract to third parties), the managing venturer must perform 40% of that work. The managing venturer's work, moreover, must be more than administrative, so that it gains substantive experience; moreover, all work performed by the non-managing venturer and its affiliates, at any subcontracting tier, will count against that compliance. All told, this provision exists to make sure that a

---

[16] Any amendments to an approved joint venture agreement, as well as any addendum to allow the joint venture to bid on another 8(a) job, must also be pre-approved.

[17] On November 8, 2019, the SBA proposed to modify the 3-in-2 rule, to essentially remove the 3-contract limitation. Under the proposed rule, joint venture members would instead run the risk of affiliation if the joint venture was long-standing—that is, still bidding on contracts more than two years after it received its first award. See Consolidation of Mentor Protégé Programs and Other Government Contracting Amendments, 84 Fed. Reg. at 60847–48. As of this writing, the SBA has not yet adopted this change.

joint venture itself doesn't become a mere pass-through to an otherwise ineligible business.

Finally, the joint venture will have to meet various ongoing reporting requirements. These requirements obligate the venturers to confirm that they have - and are performing pursuant to - a compliant joint venture agreement, and that they meet the applicable performance requirements. To help them prepare these reports, the venturers should each keep detailed records about the work they perform, the work subcontracted, and the amounts received under each contract.

Conclusion

Joint ventures are an important tool for small businesses with the goal of winning federal government contracts. Done properly, a small business can augment its experiences, capabilities, and technical approach to stand out from its competition.

The discussion in this episode only scratches the surface of this important topic. To better understand joint ventures and for assistance in forming a compliant joint venture, consider reaching out to experienced counsel.

* * *

Matthew is the managing partner of Koprince Law LLC, a boutique law firm that counsels clients about the unique legal issues they experience working with the federal government. In addition to advising clients about regulatory and socio-economic compliance issues, Matthew prepares effective and compliant teaming agreements, subcontracts, mentor/protégé agreements, joint venture agreements, and other key documents. A significant portion of Matthew's practice, moreover, involves representing contractors in bid protests, size and socio-economic category protests and appeals, and in claims and appeals matters under the Contract Disputes Act.

Matt has presented on government contracting legal issues to a variety of audiences across the country. He has also been quoted in articles appearing in Bloomberg.com, Law360.com, Westlaw Journal, and Contract Management magazine.

You can read Matt's government contracting posts on SmallGovCon.com, including his 5 Things You Should Know series, or following him on Twitter @mtschoonover. Matt's email address is mschoonover@koprince.com. Find him at
https://www.linkedin.com/in/matthew-schoonover-89098933/

Episode 13.
What it Takes to Win
SBIR & STTR Contracts

By Matt Miller

Owner, Electro Magnetic Applications, Inc.

The Small Business Innovation Research (SBIR) and the Small Business Technology Transfer (STTR) programs have been extremely beneficial to the companies that I have worked for (as an employee and as an owner) over the past 18 years. In this episode, I will provide a brief history of these programs and then talk about the approach I have taken for writing winning proposals and commercializing the technology funded through SBIR and STTR contracts.

In the 1970's, there was concern that the United States was losing competitiveness in an era of increasing globalization. Around this time, Roland Tibbetts was appointed as the Senior Program Officer at the National Science Foundation (NSF). Mr. Tibbetts had worked for both large and small companies and understood the importance of small technology companies. He helped establish the SBIR program at the NSF and eventually it was adopted by many government agencies including Department of Defense (DoD), Department of Energy (DoE), Department of Homeland Security (DHS), National Aeronautics and Space Administration (NASA), Environmental Protection Agency (EPA), Department of Education (ED) and the United States Department of Agriculture (USDA).

The STTR program began in 1992 and differs from the SBIR program in that it requires participation by a nonprofit research institution (RI). The role of the STTR program is to bridge the gap between performance of basic science and commercialization of the resulting innovations.

To understand the impact of the SBIR and STTR programs, let's take a look at the numbers. According to the www.sbir.gov website, approximately \$3.1B in funding was obligated by the U.S. government to 3,142 firms for a total of 5,630 contracts in 2018 alone. The DoD issues the largest number of SBIR/STTR contracts followed by the Department of Health and Human Services. DOE, NASA and NSF issue roughly the same number of contracts and then there is a fairly sharp drop in the funding and number of contracts issued by the remaining government organizations participating in the SBIR and STTR programs.

Of the 5,630 contracts issued in 2018, the vast majority of contracts awarded were from the SBIR program (4,838 for SBIR and 792 for STTR). The breakdown between Phase I and Phase II awards (more to come later on the multi-phase approach) was 3,703 Phase I awards and 1,927 Phase II awards. It is also interesting to look at the distribution of awards by state. As one might expect, California had the largest number of contract awards with 1,102. Massachusetts came in second with 599 contracts and then several states including Virginia, Maryland, Colorado, Texas, New York, Pennsylvania and Ohio received between 200 to 300 contracts per state. Poor North Dakota and American Somoa only received one contract each.

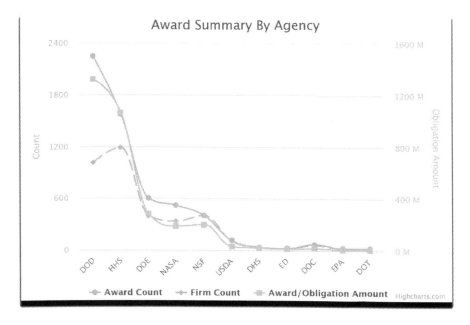

While we are talking numbers, let's look at some fun facts. Over half of SBIR awards are to firms with fewer than 25 people. Over a third of SBIR awards are to firms of fewer than 10 people. One fifth of SBIR awardees are minority or women-owned businesses. These are all truly small businesses. These are people that have taken great risk to start their own company and more often than not, they dearly need the SBIR contracts to help fund their ideas. I know this from first-hand experience.

I started my first company in 2005. I was a one-person company working out of a home office surrounded by corn fields in central Illinois. I spent my days performing consulting work for various companies and my nights and weekends writing proposals including SBIR and STTR proposals. Without the first SBIR contract that the Air Force awarded to my small business, I never would have had the chance to grow the business and eventually sell it to the leading company in our industry a decade later.

On average, 25% of awardees are first-time winners. So, it's not just the same companies getting contracts over and over again. About 15% of SBIR and STTR proposals are awarded a Phase I contract and about 50% of Phase I awardees continue on to the Phase II contract. So, it's not easy to get the Phase I contract but if you are successful, you have about a 50% chance of winning the Phase II contract where the real opportunity exists.

The SBIR and STTR programs use a multi-phase approach. Phase I can be thought of as seed funding to test out the ideas proposed by the small business. The details of the contracts vary from one funding agency to the next. However, there tends to be some common structure to the SBIR and STTR contracts.

Phase I contracts typically consist of a Base and an Option contract. The length of the Base contract varies from 6 months to 13 months depending upon the agency. This is the time for the small business to demonstrate to the customer that the ideas described in the proposal are as good as advertised.

The Phase I Base contract is very important because there are typically at least two Phase I awardees. So, it is very much a competition between your company and another company. With every company that I have worked at, we took the approach of throwing everything we could at the Phase I, even if that meant losing money on the Phase I, because so much was riding on the potential Phase II award.

Typically, a Phase I Option contract is only awarded if the company has been selected for the Phase II contract. The Phase I Option is intended to continue the work started during the Phase I Base and bridge the funding gap until the Phase II is turned on. Again, not all agencies have Phase I Options. Some go straight from the Phase I Base to Phase II. If you are notified by the awarding agency that your firm has been selected for a Phase II contract, pop the bubbly and celebrate.

OK, enough fun, let's get back to work. Now, you need to make sure that your accounting system is compliant with the requirements of whatever agency is issuing the award. For DoD contracts, the Defense Contract Audit Agency (DCAA) will perform a pre-award audit to ensure that your accounting system meets its requirements. In particular, they will want to see that you are tracking Allowable and Unallowable expenses and Direct Labor in a consistent and well-documented manner.

Initially, this can be very overwhelming as there are many nuances to DCAA and FAR requirements. If you have a strong accountant or finance person on your team, they can probably work with DCAA to implement a compliant accounting system. And to be clear, it's not about having the right piece of software. My companies have used very expensive software programs that were made specifically for DCAA rules and we have used affordable and widely used tools such as QuickBooks.

If most of your revenue is coming from government contracts with DCAA accounting requirements, it's probably a good idea to invest in a software tool designed for those types of contracts. If government work is a small portion of what your company does, I recommend sticking with whatever you were using before the government contract award. However, make sure that DCAA is satisfied with your accounting system. You do not want to fail an audit.

If all of this accounting talk is making your head spin, consider hiring a firm that specializes in helping small businesses set up a compliant accounting system. There are such firms located throughout the country. They generally are not cheap but you want to get your accounting system set up correctly with that first Phase II contract. I have only worked with DoD and NASA on SBIR and STTR contracts. So, I cannot speak to the details of the accounting requirements for other government agencies.

So, why do they care so much about all of these accounting rules? When you submit a proposal in response to a solicitation, you include a cost proposal. Part of that cost proposal includes your indirect rates. It is common for small businesses to use one all-encompassing indirect rate that includes all allowable indirect expenses. However, companies can have multiple indirect rates for different categories such as Fringe, G&A, and others. These indirect rates factor in the cost of rent, benefits, computer equipment and many, many other allowable expenses. So, when you submit a proposal to the government, you are saying that your company's indirect rate(s) is a certain percentage of the employees' direct labor rate. If the government accepts the rate, then you apply that rate plus profit to your employee's hourly rate for every hour worked on the contract.

To keep everyone honest, the government has what I call a "true up" process at the end of the year. The small business has to submit an Incurred Cost Report (ICE report) to DCAA showing in great detail what the actual expenses were for the year. If your rate was higher than what you billed the government, they owe you money and if your rate was lower than what you billed the government, you owe them money. You really want to be as close to your billed indirect rate as possible. For example, there may not be any money left on your contract and if you under billed the government, there is no additional money to be paid out.

Let's go back to the solicitation period. Some government agencies, like the DoD, issue solicitations for SBIR topics multiple times a year and other agencies, like NASA, only issue solicitations one time per year. Each agency issues schedules for when solicitations will be released and most have a mailing list that you can subscribe to for notifications when the solicitations are released.

Solicitations are typically issued two months before the proposals are due. However, as I will say many times in this episode...be sure to read the instructions. It is not uncommon for rules, requirements, time periods, etc. to change. It is your responsibility to understand the requirements.

With most agencies, but not all, you can contact the technical point of contact (TPOC) during the "open" period. The open period is typically a few weeks to a month when interested parties can submit questions to the TPOC either directly or through a web-based system where anyone can see your question and the answer posted in response to it.

Given the opportunity, I will always speak directly with the TPOC. I do this for several reasons. First, sometimes the TPOC is not the person that wrote the solicitation. It can take several months and sometimes, over a year for a solicitation to make its way through the agency's review process. A lot can change in that time period including the TPOC leaving the agency or being promoted to a different role. Maybe the new TPOC has a slightly different objective in mind with the topic or maybe the technical requirements have changed from when the original solicitation was issued. If you don't talk to the TPOC, you will not know this really important information and potentially write a proposal that does not address the TPOC's true interests.

Another reason to speak with the TPOC is to get to know them and to tell them about your company. They may be interested in other technical areas of expertise or services that your company offers.

Now that you have spoken to the TPOC and read the instructions at least twice (seriously...don't lose a proposal because you used the wrong font size, page margin settings, didn't follow the page limit requirement, or some other silly mistake that could have been avoided by reading the instructions), it's time to start writing.

One of the biggest mistakes that companies make when writing SBIR and STTR proposals is that they spend 80% of the proposal talking about all of the great things they have done in the past and 20% of the proposal talking about what they are going to do. In my opinion, the breakdown should be roughly inverted. The reviewers need to know that your company and staff are competent, well-educated and have been successful on other projects. However, what the reviewers really want to see are your very clear and detailed plans for solving the problem.

If you write in generalities with many assumptions or ambiguity in your approach, you might as well not waste your time writing the proposal. Your chances of winning are almost zero. Instead, lay out a clear vision for your solution to the problem and then back it up with a detailed technical proposal.

Writing a winning proposal is not something that you do in a day or two. At one of my previous companies, we won roughly 85% of our SBIR/STTR proposals. We had such a high win rate because we worked really hard on writing clear and well thought out proposals including writing prototype software to demonstrate the validity of the ideas as part of the proposal process.

I estimate that 40 hours was the least amount of time that we ever spent on writing a wining proposal. It was not uncommon for proposals to require 80 hours or more including peer reviews throughout the process. As I mentioned before, a lot is riding on these proposals. We did not want to seek outside funding from venture capital firms or other sources. So, we needed to win the SBIR/STTR contracts to fund our technology development.

This dovetails into another topic regarding common mistakes with SBIR/STTR proposals. Many companies submit proposals for topics that are outside of their areas of expertise. Sometimes, companies pursue topics because they work in an adjacent technical area and think they can make the leap to a new area without really understanding what they are getting into.

If you ever review a proposal and it just sounds like a bunch of "fluff", this is probably a topic that the company should not be pursuing. Fluffy proposals have little chance of being selected. Rather, I recommend that companies go after topics that are within their technical wheelhouse or very close to it. This isn't to say that you shouldn't ever veer away from the traditional strengths of your company. However, if you want to expand into other areas, you need to hire someone with the technical chops to help your company break into a new area or spend significant time conducting research to gain the necessary knowledge. Otherwise, you are probably wasting time writing the proposal. I say this as someone who was forced by management early in my career to write SBIR and other proposals that just did not align with our company's expertise. Our win rate for those proposals was probably close to 5%.

The shotgun approach of writing proposals is not a good one. In addition to being a demoralizing exercise for the people writing the proposals, it is a waste of time and money. *Instead of using a shotgun approach, I much prefer to use a rifle approach where I develop relationships with customers and learn about their needs.* I explore ideas with the customers that may someday turn into a solicitation. There is no guarantee that such ideas will eventually show up as a solicitation but if they do, your chances of securing at least a Phase I award are significantly better.

I hope that the information in this episode has been helpful to anyone wanting to learn more about winning SBIR and STTR contracts. They are both truly great programs for small businesses and can result in intellectual property for your company that you can subsequently commercialize.

Matt Miller is a Principal Scientist at Electro Magnetic Applications (EMA) where he leads a group providing analysis services for cosite interference, installed antenna performance and radar signature prediction. Mr. Miller has 20 years of experience in electromagnetics, business development, marketing and sales. Mr. Miller worked for The Boeing Company from 1998-2001 as an Electromagnetic Effects (EME) engineer supporting various defense and space programs providing analysis in the areas of antenna-to-antenna coupling, electro-static discharge (ESD), lightning effects, receiver intermodulation product generation and shielding effectiveness. From 2001-2005, Mr. Miller worked for SAIC-DEMACO in Champaign, IL as a Research Scientist performing code development and analysis for various types of electromagnetic phenomena. In 2005, Mr. Miller co-founded Delcross Technologies, LLC where he served as the President. Delcross developed commercial simulation tools for cosite interference, installed antenna performance and radar signature prediction. Find him at https://www.linkedin.com/in/mattdelcross/

Episode 14.
Winning Sole Source Contracts

By David Neal

Managing Partner, David Neal Consulting

I wanted to start this episode off by saying thank you to RSM Federal and in particular Mike LeJeune and Joshua Frank. There are others to thank as well but let me get started.

My name is David Neal and I come to you as a warrior who has been in the heat of battle for over a decade. My knuckles have been bloodied, my knees have been skinned up and I have been through the trenches. So what am I talking about? *I have spent the last decade or so selling to the Federal Government via 8(a) firms.*

The journey has not been an easy one. This journey is not for the faint of heart. If you have the intestinal fortitude to take on this challenge it will be the greatest roller coaster ride of your life.

The United States Government is the largest consumer in the world and if you are reading this book then your thought is, "Well, I want a piece of that pie!" With that said, there are people who take on this challenge and at the first sign of resistance - they bail. Like I mentioned before, this is not for the faint of heart. Just because you have sold your product or service to the commercial world, does not mean that the US government will all of a sudden start buying from you.

I'll add another wrinkle to the mix. This episode and my focus is on small business. Now, imagine trying to compete with a company that has a larger budget for trash removal than you will make in a year! Are you ready and excited to take on the challenge now?

The great thing about selling to the United States Government as a small business is that you get your own category to sell in. You also get small business officials that are there to help you. You get access to the same Federal contract and information websites as large companies. As a small business you also have the spending goals for each agency. But wait a minute, let's start from the beginning…

What's your North American Industrial Classification System (NAICS) code? Do you need a GSA schedule? What is the difference between a Sources Sought and a Request for Proposal (RFP)? Do you need to be registered in the System for Award Management (SAM)? Do you need a security clearance? So many questions!

In order to do this right, let's assume you are a small business. That will be determined by your number of employees or your revenue five-year average. Let's also assume that you are registered in SAM and that you know what your NAICS codes are.

What I have learned and developed is an 18-step program, that involves hard work and determination. My first sources sought that I answered, I won. A sources sought gives you a chance to tell your firm's story. It gives you a chance to answer the questions: Who out there can do this and do it well? It also gives you a chance to brag. Yes, that's right, go ahead and brag about what you have done.

Selling to the Federal Government is about proving that you can do what they are asking for and that you have done it successfully. For my company, it took knowing our NAICS code, knowing our capabilities, knowing our teaming partner and knowing where to look to find the opportunity. That first sources sought turned into two million dollars in contracts.

In addition to working hard, you need to work smart and properly take advantage of your small business status. Consider looking for a large business for your teaming partner. Large businesses that have a product that fills a small business category, requires strong fiscally responsible small firms to resell their product.

Large businesses also need small business partners to help them meet the government's small business goals. That being said, here are ten of the eighteen steps that I want to share with you to help accelerate your entry into the government market.

Step 1) Once you identify several NAICS that are relevant to your company, you will need to verify each one. It's very important that we get this right - up front. We currently use the Federal Procurement Data System (FPDS.gov) to help in this process. When I wrote this episode, FPDS was being migrated into SAM.gov.

Step 2) Once we identify the NAICS codes that most accurately fit, then we narrow them down to the most relevant. Again, we use FPDS (SAM.gov) in this process. The goal here should be to formally identify no more than 5. You can always have more NAICS codes, but in the business development phase this will help us to focus.

Step 3) Now that we have done steps 1 and 2, we can again use the FPDS/SAM data and target the agencies that buy products and services under those specific NAICS codes. We use this data to prioritize which agencies we will be spending time trying to cultivate relationships with. We will also use this data and our existing relationships to introduce our capabilities.

Step 4) Now we can search for and pursue opportunities. The primary government sources for opportunities are SAM.gov (FedBizOpps), Fed Biz Connect, and Fed Bid. These are the standard websites used today to find Federal opportunities. We will also and more importantly focus on procurement forecasts. Once we've identified our agency targets, we look for their annual forecasts. This allows us to validate each agency's procurement strategy for the next fiscal year. This step is crucial to getting out in front of opportunities before they are released to industry.

Step 5) Build a FUNNEL and a sales forecast for the next twelve months. This will give us an internal report that we can use to calculate what the potential will be for the next year. We can also use these targets to choose which small business conferences to attend and how to build past performance references.

Step 6) Engage the small business offices. Now that we have a funnel and sales forecast, we can lean upon several people to help us in the process. Each agency has a small business office. Interestingly, I will tell you that these folks could be nothing but a road block if you don't know what you are doing. That is why steps 1-4 are so important. By the time we get to these folks we know *WHO* we need to talk to. We won't need them to help us find, identify, or even qualify an opportunity. We should have that information in hand. From my experience, this is what separates a good small business firm from the rest.

Step 7) Our goal is to confirm who the contracting officer is that will be releasing the RFP or RFQ. If we can get a call or introduction with them, that would be great. However, our objective is to identify the Program Manager.

Step 8) Talk to the program manager. The key to a successful winning strategy is knowing the what and the why. What is the customer looking for and why are they writing the RFP or RFQ in this manner? The Program managers have been influenced by someone or by research that they have done on their own. Most likely, they will tell you what they have in mind. *THIS* is critical to finding and obtaining any opportunity. It is vital that we stock pile a list of all program managers and contracting officers.

Step 9) Build relationships. Introductions are nice, and they are the good start, but the goal is to build relationships with the *right people*.

Step 10) Capability debriefings (CD) - I can't stress enough how important it will be once we have a CD lined up that this is where we will need to shine. We will need to show proof that we have the capacity, the capability and the overall know how to accomplish the task at hand. Past performance is everything. For the government to make a decision they will need to have 100% confidence in your company.

*   *   *

David Neal is the owner, operator, and managing partner of David Neal Consulting. Husband to Joy for over 26 years. Father of three beautiful daughters and one son-in-law. Adventurer at heart which has led him to be a scuba diver, bike rider, runner and cruise enthusiast. After working for three 8(a) firms, David turned work into a passion at 45 when he started working as a consultant. His goal is to help small, minority, woman and veteran-owned companies sell their products and services to the federal government. You can find him at https://www.linkedin.com/in/david-neal-13b4bb2/

Episode 15.
Leveraging Your 8(a) Certification

By Bellandra Foster, Ph.D.,P.E.

President, BBFoster Consulting

When to Apply for an 8(a) Certification

The 8(a) certification application process will take time to complete if you are completing the application without the use of a third-party consultant. The 8(a) regulations require that a business must be in existence for 2 years prior to submitting an application to the SBA for consideration to become 8(a) certified. If your business has not been in existence for 2 years, there is a provision to request early consideration for entrance into the 8(a) business development program. To be considered under this provision, the manager(s) of the business must have significant business management experience to be considered under this special stipulation.

You also want to thoroughly review the financial requirements to be considered for 8(a) certification. Be sure to apply for 8(a) certification while the owner(s) still meet the personal net worth, business size, and maximum revenue requirements.

I completed the 8(a) application for my company. It took approximately 3 months to complete the written sections in addition to completing the required forms, compiling the various documents that included taxes forms, proof of ethnicity, articles of incorporation, by-laws, and other documents. The current process to apply for 8(a) certification consists of entering information electronically into the SBA 8(a) certification website and uploading the required documents for review.

2 Key Aspects in Deciding
To Apply for 8(a) Certification

1) Do you have the time to compile and complete the information requested?

2) Do you meet the personal and company financial benchmarks?

Application Self-Completion Vs. Hiring a Third-Party

When determining whether to complete the 8(a) application yourself, as opposed to hiring a third-party, it boils down to time and money. I received offers to complete my certification documents in the range of $5,000 to $10,000.

I decided to review the requirements for submittal and determined that if I took my time, I could complete the application on my own. I also determined that even if I did hire a third-party, there would still be a time requirement for me to supply the required information to the third-party completing my company application.

I looked at the time to compile all the information, some level of heavy lifting that the third-party wouldn't have been able to do anyway, and completion of all the questions. After looking at the level of effort, realized that I may as well take the time to complete the submittal myself.

It took about 3 months to thoroughly review the requirements, compile all of the information and respond to all of the questions within the application. The process was not painful, but did require time, patience and perseverance. During my application review process and prior to my information submittal, I met with my local PTAC (SBA procurement technical assistance center) representative. I determined that it was important to provide the SBA with the exact information they requested within the application.

Not everyone has the time or desire to complete the application on their own. So, before deciding whether or not to hire a third-party consider the following questions:

Do you have the funds to pay a third-party provider? Most companies require the entire fee to be paid in advance. Be sure to consider that you will still need to provide information about your company to the company you hire to complete your application. If you do decide to hire a third-party to complete your application, request references from the company you plan to hire and contact companies they have done "successful" work for in the past; and -

Do you have the time required to compile the information required for the submittal?

Benefits of Obtaining SBA 8(a) Certification

There are several benefits to becoming SBA 8(a) certified. The SBA 8(a) business development program allows small disadvantaged businesses to bid on federal projects set-aside for 8(a) certified companies to bid on. This is especially important since the federal contracting market is extremely vast and there are hundreds of companies competing for opportunities. It is extremely helpful when there's a smaller pool of contractors engaged on any given opportunity.

There are also training sessions provided by the SBA that 8(a) businesses can participate in to achieve a higher level of success. Some of these course titles include:

- How to do Business with the Federal Government and Win Contracts as an 8(a) Certified Firm
- Bids and Proposals
- FAR and Other Regulations
- Market Research in Federal Procurement
- Capabilities Statements and Briefings
- How to do Business with the Federal Government – Refresher
- Marketing & E-Tools: Identifying Opportunities
- Teaming: JVs, MPAs & You
- Managing Growth
- Network, Capturing & Leveraging
- Preparing Your Company to Succeed After 8(a) Graduation
- How to Market to the Federal Government as a "Small Business Concern"
- Prime Contracting
- Teaming and Mentor-Protégé Program

Keys to Successful Self-Submittal of an 8(a) Application

First, it is critical that you first review the requirements and make sure your company meets *all of them*. This includes business size, income, and personal net worth. When searching for information pertaining to the 8(a) certification program, the federal SBA website is https://certify.sba.gov/8a-docs. This website includes a document detailing "guidance to submitting and 8(a) application" which is very useful.

Most people typically overlook the need to very carefully follow directions. In the case of the 8(a) application, it is *imperative* that you follow the application directions closely and submit your information, as requested by the SBA, in an organized manner.

From a timing perspective, you want to submit your application 6-months prior to the time you desire your 8(a) approval.

Past project and managerial performance are very important. Your application should map out past performance in an orderly and logical manner. Your company and staff past performance timeline should include all relative past projects and their associated project descriptions, dates, and references.

When I completed my submittal, I spent significant time detailing my past project managerial experience. My former company no longer existed and I was starting over as a small business owner. As a result, my application relied heavily on my past managerial and engineering technical experience. I detailed the types of projects I had undertaken as an engineer and/or manager. At least 90% of the projects I had worked on over the prior 10 years were federally funded projects. However, my contract was not directly with the federal government. Most of the contracts were either with local governments or private subcontracts.

List all of your relevant projects. Do not be shy on listing your experience. Remember, even if the opportunity or position was completed early in your career, it still counts as experience. Don't deny yourself the ability to shine when it comes to listing your management and hands-on experience.

Attempt to start the application *on your own* once you decide to submit for consideration into the program. Start by dedicating 30 minutes a day by reviewing the application information and what is required for submittal.

You may soon realize that you can submit the application without using a third-party!

Once your submittal information is uploaded, within a few months, an SBA representative may contact you. If you are contacted, respond to the SBA specialist requesting information in a timely manner...within 24 hours, if possible. Submit the requested information and communicate with the SBA representative, as needed. I learned that most companies do not communicate with the SBA 8(a) representative during their application process. Communication can be a key aspect in your application process to making sure you are supplying the right information to the SBA in a timely manner. This helps facilitate a faster decision on your application.

Approach your 8(a) application like you are writing a proposal. The only difference is your expected outcome, approval into the SBA 8(a) business development program!

My Company is 8(a) Certified...Now What?

(Finding the right teaming partners)

Many companies that become 8(a) certified think the money will start rolling in once their application and entry into the 8(a) program is approved. In reality, once my company obtained approval into the 8(a) program, the real work began.

It was important for me to locate the best federal client for my company to provide the services we supply. It was also important to locate good teaming partners with integrity, who perform ethically, want to do a good job, on time, and provide a good service to the client. Compensation will come once your company obtains a strong reputation and top-notch client performance evaluation.

The main goal to grow your company should be to locate the right client, best project, and best teaming partners. Accordingly, locate the best staff to grow your company. I have been successful in locating several great staff members using Indeed.com.

Always keep in mind that the 8(a) business development program mandates that your client portfolio should include *both federal and non-federal clients* (local governments, municipalities, state government, private industry).

To boost your opportunities to obtain clients, you want to attend industry events. You want to request appointments to speak with the procurement and small business agency managers.

Prior to locating teaming partners, determine what makes your firm an attractive company to partner or team with. Find companies that do the work within your company's primary and secondary NAICS codes.

Your goal is to find the right client and best teaming partners. One of the biggest challenges is finding the right teaming partners. The key to locating the best teaming partners is to start searching for the right solicitations and exercise capture management. Locate the opportunities early. Form a capabilities matrix with all of the deliverables. Make sure the team can fulfill *all of the requirements* of the solicitation.

Obtaining approval into the 8(a) business development program is just the beginning!

Long Term Benefits of the 8(a) Program

It is important to know the stages of development in the 8(a) program. Years 1-4 are considered the development stage; years 5-9 are the transitional stage. Once a firm completes its first program year in the transitional stage, it is required to meet certain non-8(a) business activity revenue targets. These targets are based on the most recently completed fiscal year numbers submitted during your annual review. Failure to meet these targets will result in a sole-source restriction: a restriction whereby the district office cannot accept sole-source offers on your firm's behalf. The non-8(a) percentages required during the transitional stage are as follows:

Participant's year in the transitional stage	Non-8(a) business activity targets (required minimum non-8(a) revenue as a percentage of total revenue)
1	15%
2	25%
3	35%
4	45%
5	55%

The most prevalent long-term benefit of the 8(a) program was having the privilege of starting my new company, being part of a program that helped me find new ways to open doors. This helped me enter into opportunities with federal agency clients. I learned that the federal market was wide open and full of opportunities!

Programs and Assistance Available to Enhance 8(a) Experience

Once accepted into the 8(a) business development program, your company will have access to training courses to assist in your 8(a) solicitation pursuits. I outlined some of these classes earlier in the episode. The federal procurement data system (FPDS) (currently being migrated into SAM.gov) will assist you in locating companies that have been successful at winning contracts under various NAICS codes and opportunity types. The website USASpending.gov will help you to look up contract awards by company name and/or keyword search.

SAM.gov has replaced FedBizOpps (FBO.gov). SAM will allow you to filter data, locate sources sought opportunities, and find information on upcoming procurement events at the various agencies.

Your local PTAC advisor can also be instrumental in assisting you in locating procurement events being held at low or no cost. It is also advisable to meet with agency small business representatives once you narrow down the types of opportunities you would like to pursue.

Meetings and events often take place at military bases and agency locations. You'll find a multitude of SBA events, agency and DoD events, and other workshops and training sessions. Don't stretch yourself too thin…make the right connections that will best benefit your company and your clients. Be selective about attending events to locate teaming partners and potential joint venture opportunities.

Many 8(a)'s go out of business after their 9-year period because they don't focus on the right revenue mix AND don't know how to properly differentiate from their competition without using their status. So make sure you not only focus 8(a) acquisitions, but also focus on non Federal government as well.

Dr. Bellandra B. Foster, P.E. is the president of BBFoster Consulting, PC. The North Carolina based corporation specializes in civil engineering, program management, facilities management, utility coordination, and coaching. Dr. Foster is a licensed professional engineer in the states of Georgia, Illinois, Michigan, North Carolina, Ohio and South Carolina with over 30 years of experience in civil, construction, and transportation engineering.

She is an experienced program manager with vast experience providing project engineering, contract administration, and utility coordination. She has managed engineering, construction inspection, and client technical support operations for private, state, local, and federal projects. Bellandra Foster is a former Director of Highways and Streets for the City of Atlanta Department of Public Works and former Director for State DOT Utilities and Permits Engineer for the southeastern Michigan Region.

Learn more at www.bbfosterconsulting.com, www.bellandrafoster.com.
You can email her at bbf@bbfosterconsulting.com.
Find her at https://www.linkedin.com/in/bbfoster/

Episode 16.
I Didn't Know You Did That... Too...

By Tim Burt

Owner, Tim Burt Media

Your phone buzzes. It's a text from the team leader trying to grab that massive contract. "We didn't get it." Those four words just ruined your month. Maybe your year.

You stare at your phone in disbelief so intensely, your gaze could burn a hole through the screen. In your mind, your competition just got – no...STOLE – a massive government deal that should have gone to *your* company.

A handful of antacids - coupled with an aggressive swig of your beverage of choice - don't begin to fill that canyon-sized hole in your gut. The refrain of "How in the hell did we lose this?" echoes in your head.

Sound familiar? You're probably saying to yourself right now "Oh, that was the _____ contract." "Sounds like the time we got screwed out of the ___ deal."

What Happened?

In your mind, you did nothing wrong. Your best people were on the job. The proposal was rock-solid. The pitch was stellar. But there is one key area in which your business might be leaving money on the table, and you don't even know it.

I'll tell you what you (and a lot of businesses) are doing wrong in just a moment...and how to fix it.

You may never get the full explanation of why you lost out on a contract. You think the person who had the final say is going to give you a straight answer? Probably not. They have to sanitize their answers. These things happen. It's business, baby.

Obviously, I don't know you and you don't know me. But without knowing you or your business, I can virtually guarantee you why the other guys get the contracts.

Let's Look at the Root Cause

The one area where practically all businesses struggle? Marketing.

It doesn't matter if it is internal or external. In this episode, I'm going to highlight some commonly misunderstood areas and bring clarity to them so you can gain an advantage over your competition.

If you want to learn some ways to create a message that can sell your business 24/7, keep reading.

Getting a government contract is (or should be) no different than selling to the public. There are, however, a few key differences which you may (or may not) be aware of.

Yes, every selling situation and client is different. While you might be able to yuck it up with Steve in one office, Dave at another department may have zero sense of humor. But there is one thing that Steve, Dave, and Suzy Cream Cheese (my loving name given to any member of the public) all have in common. They'll only buy from you or your company if your overall marketing message is clear. Some people call this your "brand."

Just to be clear, "brand" and "branding" are two words that I, as a seasoned professional marketer, absolutely hate. After I explain what they are and how they should be used, you will hate them too.

I despise them because they are nothing more than buzzwords. When asked to define "brand" or "branding," most people can't – especially marketing "experts."

In a few moments, you'll learn the true definition of branding. And you'll never be fooled by clueless advertising agencies ever again. Yet, experienced – but mostly inexperienced – business owners hear these words and instantly apply them to their business, regardless of size.

After speaking with thousands of small business owners around the planet, here's one thing that is true world-wide: most small business owners don't have a brand. They think they do, but they don't. To paraphrase Marc Cuban, they have a hobby with business cards.

But because your company is big enough to go after government contracts (or will be soon), you most certainly do have a brand.

We'll talk about what yours is in a moment. But first...

What Branding Isn't

I believe it is important to define the term "brand" and all that it encompasses. Let's bust some myths you've been told by others that simply aren't true.

Despite what you may have heard, "Branding" is NOT:

- A logo
- A color
- A font
- A sound

When you see the iconic "swoosh" on a pair of athletic shoes or other apparel, you instantly recognize it as Nike. The image of Colonel Sanders means KFC. The "Golden Arches?" Of course, McDonalds.

All of those images and sounds (the Taco Bell "ding," Coca-Cola's red and white font, Apple's "apple," etc.) are very important devices. However, they are NOT the "brand."

What you're about to read isn't taught to those with marketing degrees. Those symbols and pneumonic devices do one thing: they lead TO the brand itself in the mind of the audience. They are NOT the "brand."

You don't buy because of the device that led you to the brand. You buy from a brand because of what they can do for you. Your customers are absolutely no different than you. And let me bust a myth that you've been told which is complete garbage…

The Biggest Branding Lie You've Heard

While watching one of the many cable business networks such as CNBC, or Fox Business, etc., have you ever heard a story about a business claiming that they're "rebranding?" You've probably read these types of stories in your trade publications, too.

Let me interpret that line of marketing "guru" crap for you: it means they're either changing their name, and/or their logo.

As you're about to discover, simply changing your company's name and/or logo is NOT "rebranding." In most cases, it's simply giving the Titanic a new coat of paint.

Here's What Branding is (and Why it's so Important)

What is the definition of "brand" or "branding?"

My good friends Blaine & Honey Parker (who do "branding" for a living) summed it up beautifully in their book "Billion Dollar Branding." As a side note, the Parkers also hate those words.

Their definition: Branding is the one way you want your core customer to *feel* about your business. You might want to re-read that about a dozen times to burn it in your brain.

Now that you have that memorized, let's dissect that definition into bite-sized chunks:

1) **The ONE WAY…**

Not five, not three, ONE. While you may have 50,000 items in your catalogue, we're going to want the public to focus on one thing.

2) **You want YOUR CORE CUSTOMER…**

You may have heard a lot of self-described marketing "gurus" talk about building your "tribe," "raving fans," etc.

Before we can speak to your core audience (the ones who will actually buy things from you), it is imperative to identify and define who these people really are.

Why is that so important?

Because once you determine who they are, what they like, what they don't like, and what they're willing to do to get your product or service, you can then take the critical next step: figuring out the best way to talk to them.

You can then speak to them in a way that is evocative and drives them to a single action. This is where your core marketing message comes in. More on that in a bit.

3) **To FEEL about your business.**

As an example, let's talk about one of the titans of branding: Apple.

(In the interest of full disclosure, I used to be an Apple fanboy. That was until I returned from my first speaking tour of South Africa in 2013. My iPhone 4S was moments away from becoming bricked, which would have meant all the photos and videos I took would have been lost. At that moment, I jumped to Android and haven't looked back.)

Say and believe what you want about Steve Jobs. His tenure was marked with controversy and he clearly wasn't the nicest person to work for. But you cannot ignore what was accomplished under his leadership.

When you see the Apple logo, what do you *feel*? Slick products. Well designed. Expensive. Trendy. Global. Intuitive. Built solidly.

In fact, you don't even have to see the Apple logo to know someone is using an Apple product. The white earbuds give it away, too.

In your mind, does Apple have an advantage over Samsung, LG, etc.? If so, *why*? Only you can answer that question. Yet, however you answer that question, *that* is the Apple "brand" - in *your* mind.

Take it from Amazon

As Jeff Bezos said, "Your brand is what people say it is when you leave the room." If that's true, then I'll ask you: what is *your* brand? What do people say about you when you leave the room? Are you sure?

161

If you're wondering, yes, you CAN change your brand. But be warned, it is tricky. It takes a lot of research and can be costly. But if you get it right, the payoff can be beyond your wildest dreams.

Oh…you want a real-world example? Okay…

Possibly the most prolific example of a company changing their brand is Bezos' empire, Amazon. Do you recall what Amazon first became known for in the late 1990's? They were the world's largest online bookseller.

Today, Amazon is where you can buy approximately 606 million items from around the world (at the time of this writing).

And did you notice that Jeff Bezos didn't change the name or logo of his company? He was the first to dominate the online retail shopping niche. In fact, can you recall when you first heard that Amazon went from just selling books to other "stuff?"

My recollection of that shift was when they started to offer the handheld Kindle devices. Then he stepped on the gas, and hasn't let up. It was a masterful marketing transition which deserves to be studied for decades.

The Million-Dollar Question: What is Your brand?

Here's a pro tip for you. Ask your customers what they think your business is known for. Because to them, that is your brand. Does it match up with your company's mission statement?

If it does, then you've cleared one of the biggest hurdles in marketing. Then, marketing for your business is just a matter of getting your message (your "brand") in front of as many people as possible, as quickly as possible.

But what if you ran a survey of your core customer base and received surprising answers? If the consensus of your customers isn't what you believe your brand is, then you have a massive problem that must be solved quickly. At a minimum, you're leaving money on the table. At worst, your company is going full steam ahead while following the wrong map.

A conventional "rebrand" (new name and logo) is not what you should do. If you conduct the survey of your customers as I suggest, then perhaps a new name and logo would be in order. Again, a decision not to be taken lightly.

How to Sell Yourself 24/7

In my marketing seminars, I will flash the KFC logo on the screen. I then ask everyone to tell me what their slogan is. When I do this around the world, without fail, the audience will all shout out "Finger-Lickin' Good!0"

Then I put the Nike logo on the screen. I ask again what that slogan is. Without fail, worldwide, audiences proclaim, "Just Do It!"

Now we get to another tough-love question: what's your company's slogan? Do you have one? If you do, is it strong enough to sell for you 24/7?

What Makes a Good Slogan, and How to Strengthen Yours

In the same marketing seminars, I also touch on key strategies to create a slogan for you that's going to SELL.

Here are two of those key strategies:

1) **State Your Case, Make Your Promise, and Plant Your Flag.**

Your company's slogan must be bold. The public will rarely buy things from people or businesses they deem as inferior.

Here are some examples:

- Duracell: The Copper-Top battery
- Burger King: Home of the Flame-Broiled Whopper
- Las Vegas: What Happens Here, Stays Here
- Men's Wearhouse: You're Going to Like the Way You Look, I Guarantee It

Food for thought: what does your business do that makes you completely different from your competition? Whatever that one thing is, it is the thing you should be highlighting.

2) **The second key I'll share with you is: Solve Their Problem, and Show the Outcome in Advance.**

- Geico: 15 Minutes Could Save You 15 Percent or More On Car Insurance
- The classic FedEx: When It Absolutely, Positively Has to Be There Overnight.

163

- Indeed.com: We Help People Find Jobs.

Food for thought: can your business' slogan tell the story of what you do in 10 words or less?

When you create a slogan that can sell for you just by saying it (repeatedly, excessively, ad nauseum), that is how you permeate the consciousness of the public. And it's exactly the same route that KFC, Nike, etc. took to get where they are today.

One important reminder: once you have your slogan set, you will be tempted to change it within a relatively short time. When you do this, you are essentially setting your marketing efforts back to square one. Just like the logo and name change, this is not something to alter on a whim just because you're bored with it.

Here's real-world proof: DeBeers has used the same slogan for their company for 70 years. Yes. Seventy. "A Diamond Is Forever" continues to be used in every single piece of DeBeers marketing to this day.

Remember...

Doing all of these exercises take time. Self-examination and reflection is not a time for knee-jerk reactions. If your sales are stalled, or you can't land that government contract, it's probably because you're not giving people a reason to buy from you.

Just changing your logo and name – while continuing to do what you've always done – will not compel people to buy from you.

Creating a solid, effective marketing message (a.k.a. slogan), coupled with solid customer research can put your business in the forefront of the decision makers – whomever, and wherever they may be.

Tim Burt is responsible for more than 30,000 commercials worldwide, which have generated $500 million in sales. He is a highly sought-after marketing, branding, and messaging coach, producer, and public speaker. Tim still produces approximately 300 commercials each year.

He is also an international award-winning author. Tim's books include "High Performing Ads," "Inside A Buyer's Mind," and "A Kick in The Ads."

Tim has created or produced ads for such Fortune 500 companies as Toyota, Graybar, Burger King, South African Airways, and others. He also works with countless small businesses around the world. In 2017, Tim left his 25-year career in radio (CBS Radio) to focus on his ad agency.

Tim's websites:
http://www.TimBurtMedia.com
http://www.MarketAnything.co
http://www.SpeakerTim.com

Episode 17.
Social Selling in GovCon

By Mark Amtower

Managing Partner, Amtower & Company

The government contracting community is a relationship driven market. Building and managing those relationships is a multi-faceted task, not to mention time consuming.

The key to this is who you know, who knows you, why and how they know you, what they think of you, what they think of your company, and more. In order to be a player in government contracting (GovCon), you need to be known in whatever niche you serve.

When social networks started to impact the B2B community, invariably they started to infiltrate the GovCon world. Over the past decade LinkedIn has become an integral part of GovCon, to the point that there are now **2.4 million identifiable Feds on LinkedIn**, who can be located by agency and department as well as operating division and job title.

Contact information and agency lists you used to spend thousands of dollars on are now at your fingertips, just a quick search away.

This is the cornerstone for social selling in GovCon. Social selling is a multi-dimensional, multi-touch method of getting on the radar and staying there in a non-intrusive manner; becoming top-of-mind without being annoying.

It is **not** traditional selling. Traditional selling methods are frowned upon by most on social networks.

So, before we begin, here are a few LinkedIn facts:

- There are 645 million LinkedIn members worldwide
- 2.4 million Feds on LinkedIn
    - 15%+ with IT job titles
    - 40%+ program/project management
    - Searchable by agency and operating division
- All major contractors on LinkedIn
- Approximately 3 million groups on LinkedIn, with 200+ dealing with government contracting.

How can social selling be useful for <u>you</u>?

- You can find those you need to influence
- Build your own network around what you do
- Staying in touch with that network
- ABM- account/agency - based marketing
- Lead generation
- Thought leadership and building an SME platform
- Content marketing
- Branding and positioning your company
- And more

So, where do you start?

The simple act of being on LinkedIn is marketing, so *your LinkedIn profile has to resonate with the audience you seek to influence.*

A poor profile offers no reason to connect, no reason to engage, and will get you no traction.

Step 1 of your social selling journey is to make your profile more of a destination, a place where your prospects can get some information germane to their needs.

So, you need to decide *what* you want to accomplish: what are your goals?

- If you are a sales executive could you position yourself as a subject matter expert (SME) around whatever it is you sell?
    - Agency focused expert (USDA, DISA, DHS, etc.)
    - Technology focused expert (data access, cloud)
    - An expert on business processes
    - Combination of the above

- Do you need more relationships in specific agencies and with other contractors, especially those you want to partner with?
- Do you want to build a large network?
- Do you want to become a market resource, sharing information about a particular technology, process or agency?
- Or do you have other goals for LinkedIn?

Your goals will determine *how* you write your profile, who you connect with, the groups you join, the content you share, and they will be the core of your social selling strategy. This may strike you as mundane, but stay with me – this is important.

Your Profile - the key elements include:

- Photo
- Background photo
- Headline (120)
- About (formerly the summary, 2,000 characters)
- Experience (job title 100, description 1,000)
- Write in Microsoft Word, then cut & paste (LinkedIn does not have spell check)
- Endorsements & recommendations
- Education
- Use of graphics & content throughout

The opening screen shot needs to establish your credibility quickly: your background area, your head shot and your headline will determine whether or not someone will continue reading. Profiles with headshots are read 11x more than those without. The default headline is your job title, and most feds are not interested in connecting with yet another "Sales Associate."

Your "About" section

- 1st person narrative - if you have a relevant story, tell it and let people get to know you. Do NOT simply cut and paste your resume.
- Tell people what you do and who you do it for (the agencies or contracts you support).
- Write in short paragraphs (no more than four lines with a hard return to make white space between the paragraphs).

- Include a specialty area using industry jargon. This is where you will simply make a list of the skills you possess that are germane to your job.
- This is a good place to include the major contracts your company has.
- If you want people to contact you, show them how - include a phone, email address or both.

GovCon M&A guru, Kevin DeSanto has one of the best "About" sections I have seen: first person, focused on what he does, very short paragraphs with plenty of white space, making it very easy to read.

"Experience" (your jobs)

- What your company does
- Who they do it for (which agencies)
- Your role in the company
- Contracts where you are prime or sub
- Your preferred **contact method**
- Short paragraphs, 1st person, white space
- Endorsements
  - *Give to get*
  - *List them in the priority you want the visitor to see (default is the category with the most is first)*
  - *Invent them if you don't see them*
- Recommendations
  - *Give to get*
  - *You can ask for them*

If you want people to reach out, include contact information in your profile (summary or experience, or both). Do not make it difficult to contact you because no one is going through a multi-step process.

Social Selling

So now we finally get to the social selling process. As I stated at the beginning of this episode, social selling is a multi-dimensional, multi-touch method of getting on the radar and staying there in non-intrusive manner, becoming top-of-mind without being annoying. This means no cutesy crap. You're not sharing cat videos or meaningless platitudes - just stuff that can make a difference for you.

We all know that email is not always a viable tool. Emails may not be read for a variety of reasons; from spam filters to an admin responsible for weeding out the "unknowns" or just email overload.

We also know that getting through by phone to key decision makers and influencers is not easy.

This is why social selling is growing in popularity and will continue to do so for the foreseeable future.

So, what does social selling look like? On his blog, www.marketingthink.com, marketing guru Gerry Moran lists 30 ways to engage via social selling:

30 LinkedIn Sales Triggers to Help You Achieve Social Selling Success

1. Your LinkedIn profile is viewed
2. You receive an invitation to 'LinkIn'
3. Contact accepts your invitation to 'LinkIn'
4. Contact changes a job
5. Contact gets a promotion
6. Contact has a birthday
7. Contact has a work anniversary
8. Contact is mentioned in the news
9. Contact updates something in their profile - photo, summary, etc.
10. Your LinkedIn blog post is liked
11. Your LinkedIn blog post is shared
12. LinkedIn blog post is commented on
13. Daily update is liked
14. Daily update is shared
15. Daily update is commented on
16. Group post is liked
17. Group post is shared
18. Group post is commented on
19. Group member makes a comment in a group
20. You are endorsed for a skill
21. You are recommended by a contact
22. You have opportunity to ask for recommendation from a contact
23. You are invited to join a LinkedIn group
24. A shared group member reaches out to you
25. You receive an InMail
26. *A contact's contact likes a LinkedIn update post*
27. *A contact's contact comments on a LinkedIn update post*

28. *A contact's contact shares a LinkedIn update post*
29. *Your contact writes a LinkedIn blog post*
30. *LinkedIn's People You May Know feature presents a contact which is connected to someone in your network*

(https://marketingthink.com/30-linkedin-social-selling-sales-triggers/)

Each of these items presents an opportunity to reach out to current connections as well as to develop a relationship with those we wish to connect to.

While you probably won't take the time to do all of these, I strongly recommend using four or five that can pay quick dividends. For example, I use **items 4 and 5** regularly. When I see a promotion or job change, I will look at the individual profile, then the company profile. I want to say more than congratulations, so if I know other people at their company (especially executives), I might say, "Hey Bill - congrats on the new role. When you see Mr. X, tell them Amtower says hello." Or I might say, "Hey Bill, that looks like a good place for you. We should catch up soon. Let me know when you have time for a short call." I do the same things for birthdays.

We all deal with **item 2**, but in different ways. I vet every single connection request I receive. If they are not in the business of government contracting, I generally see no reason to connect. If they look interesting, I may send a note like this: "Thanks for reaching out but I am only connecting with those involved in US federal contracting. I don't see anything about that on your profile. Was there a specific reason you wanted to connect?" I do this because LinkedIn is *my business network*, and GovCon is my business. If I don't hear back within three days, I reject the request.

However, about 10% of the time I will get a message back that says: "We are looking into getting involved in government contracting…" or "I am involved in Federal contracting but haven't updated my profile." Even though this only happens 10% of the time, it is worthwhile for me because these people may be potential clients.

I share other content on LinkedIn, which will show up on your home page if we are connected. When I find an article germane to my network, this is my default for sharing. Often these will garner views, likes and comments. I try to respond to each person who comments to show that I am watching and that I care that they took the time to read what I shared.

This also applies to the items I write on my own blog (which is shared on my profile), my articles in other publications (also shared on my profile) and the articles I choose to write directly on to LinkedIn. I connect with my readers by responding, even if they disagree with me.

When I receive endorsements of recommendations, I always say thank you and many times I reciprocate with an endorsement, **if** I know the person well enough. I don't endorse them simply because they endorsed me. I really want to know what they do and that they are good at it.

Before "Endorsements" became a part of LinkedIn, you could (and still can) "recommend" people. This is a written recommendation and LinkedIn does want you to say how you know the person and what the business relationship was between you. I have given out nearly 400 written recommendations during my 16 (yes, 16) years on LinkedIn. And when I find someone in my network who deserves one, I still take the time to write it. These are all people who have impacted me in one way or another in my 36 years in GovCon and I like to show them that I appreciate whatever they did.

If you want to get on the radar of a thought leader or market influencer, look them up and "follow" them. This means anything they do on LinkedIn will show up on your home page. Read their posts and comments when you can, even if it just to say "Thanks for sharing this." If the post is really worthwhile, share it with your network. This kind of activity will put you on their radar.

If you are already connected to these influencers, when they are mentioned by others or are in the news, they will show up on your "Notification" page. This is another opportunity to comment. And when you do, use the hashtag before their name as you write so that LinkedIn tags it for you.

I am not going to comment on all thirty of Gerry's triggers, but it may have occurred to you that I am using his list and not my own. While I do most of the things on this list, it never occurred to me to itemize all of the social selling triggers. So, I use Gerry's, and am happy to give credit where credit is due. I appreciate that other LinkedIn experts are out there providing cool things like this list.

Study Gerry's list and start engaging via the social selling process. If you have questions, drop me a line, or connect with me on LinkedIn then ask.

The bottom line is, the better you get at this process the better off you and your company will be. You will have a stronger network as a result.

*   *   *

Mark Amtower is an award-winning GovCon consultant, Amazon best-selling author, columnist (Washington Technology), radio host (*Amtower Off Center* on Federal News Radio), adjunct professor of marketing in the graduate school of George Washington University, and perpetual student of the government market. He advises small, mid-tier and large government contractors on all aspects of marketing and he coaches companies on Social Selling.

Find him on LinkedIn www.linkedin.com/in/markamtower, email him at mark@federaldirect.net or reserve time on his calendar at https://calendly.com/markamtower

Episode 18.
Building Healthy Cultures

By Mike McDermott

President, InquisIT

I was reading through my daily articles in Medium the other day and saw a paragraph that rang louder than many ironically buried in an article about the greatest pitch deck seeking capital and what drives the wisest investors.

> "Product differentiation, by itself, has become indefensible because today's competitors can copy your better, faster, cheaper features virtually instantly. Now, the only thing they can't replicate is the *trust that customers feel for you and your team.* Ultimately, that's born not of a self-centered mission statement like "We want to be best-in-class X" or "to disrupt Y," but of a culture whose beating heart is a strategic story that casts your customer as the world-changing hero." - Alan Rasken

One may argue the impact of a mission statement, organizational differentiation, and the merits of relationship building in today's electronic world, but what we cannot argue is the sheer power of organizational culture.

No matter what business book, magazine, YouTuber, Ted Talk, or whatever informational resource you choose, you cannot escape in-depth discussions on culture and the importance of great leadership over management. However, in the actual execution of running a business, it is often overlooked, unmanaged, and more importantly, not a continued focus.

As leaders, we want to believe that we can define something and it stands forever. We can draw a proverbial line in the sand and others will abide, charging forward in the accomplishment of our vision. If only anything worked that well!

Culture is highly dynamic even in the smallest of organizations where we feel we have the most control. In large organizations, it gets away fast and scurries to the darkest places where some companies spend years trying to get it back when reinventing is sometimes the better answer. It is something we don't think about when it's going well, and then when it's not, it takes years to get back on track. In today's highly competitive markets, both for bookings and talent, (two of the hardest things to attain at quality), culture is one of the most important drivers.

So, how do we wrangle this concept when it comes down to something we "feel" and relates to things like decisions we make even at the speed of the subconscious? I oftentimes make people laugh when I speak to this concept…as a 250-plus pound bodybuilder covered in tattoos I am the unlikeliest of candidates to be writing and speaking about the softer side of business. But with a foundation in sports and the Marine Corps coupled with more mistakes and misfortunes in 20 years of my career than groups take on in a lifetime, you learn.

At one point in my career I fell the ultimate victim to not managing culture -- fired from a company I helped raise from very little and then having been rejected by what the culture morphed into. Having managed three businesses since getting this harsh lesson, culture has been an extreme focus. With this, I have created a fairly straight-forward method to Culture Management. Define, Communicate, Hold Accountable, and Repeat.

Define

Defining a culture, while it sounds easy, takes time and thoughtfulness. In the case of an owner/operator or long-term operator situation, the culture is often times very closely coupled to the personalities of the founders/long-term operators. It can be so tight that it runs well and the process of defining a culture seems a waste. However, when the time is taken to really define the culture even at the smallest of sizes, you not only create the foundation for something very strong at scale but can avoid costs of hiring mistakes and the like along the way.

In many instances, both in my experience and with clients, we see culture being defined as a result of a change in the business. Most often, it is as a result of senior leadership change or a downturn in the organization that culture starts to get a lot of attention. In those cases, it can be much more difficult as the definition of the culture must take into account the positive aspects of the foundation that is there. Otherwise, the risk of alienating the organization is high.

In either case, it is best to really think through a series of questions. Some examples of this encompass:

- What do we value?
- What are the characteristics of a successful organization?
- What do we believe in about how a business should be run?
- What are the stories of the organization today?
- What do we want the stories of the organization to be tomorrow?
- What are the behaviors that create the stories we want to be told?
- How do we define what employees tend to be concerned about (e.g. work-life balance, a good working environment in which people feel that they make a positive difference and are recognized for it, success, teamwork)
- How will we facilitate adaptation?
- It would be amazing if our company valued_____.
- If I were CEO and could create a business with only three rules, they would be_____.

In the execution of the definition of a culture, there are three ways to get it down on paper - (1) the primary leader creates a baseline and facilitates input, (2) a facilitator is used for all to contribute, or (3) the primary leader facilitates the group (typically answering questions beforehand).

The "best" way to do this really comes down to the organization, personalities, and size of the "executive team." I put executive team in quotes as I have seen in multiple organizations where this is comprised of 10 or more percent of the employee population. This is in no way a true top team.

The most important piece of the process, no matter how you get there, is building ownership among senior leaders. The head of an organization simply cannot come in one day and upon arrival announce the "new culture." This is a long process in which "buy in" as well as ownership and commitment are required from inception for success.

Once the culture is defined in a clear and concise manner, communicating the culture becomes the focus.

Communications

Communicating the culture is an overt exercise, and even more importantly, a behavioral one. Typically, organizations create posters, pamphlets, emails, social media campaigns, town hall meetings, etc. Think about these efforts as merely introductory and frankly necessary. They are the low-hanging fruit of communication and send only the simplest of messages.

Additionally, these meetings and communications need to be genuine. We live in a society where corporate executives tend to be demonized, marketing experts want to spend time on backgrounds, dress, keywords, etc., and we are addressing a "snapchat audience." You are trying to do something real - so be real in the process.

Communication, like the implementation of the culture, is an *iterative process*. Too often organizations put in an initial large communication plan, not prioritizing groups and thinking this is a flip-of-the-switch exercise. Culture change takes years in most organizations and you cannot rush the process.

As a leader, especially when the pressure is at its highest, it is our job to slow things down and ensure that a thoughtful and methodical approach is executed efficiently. Culture management is no different. As it pertains to groups and a roll out, this means actions such getting your HR team on board, spending a significantly increased amount of time with managers, and thinking about the already in-place communications and structures that can be leveraged.

Your HR Team and Managers are paramount. Managers are often overlooked as their own distinct group in this context; however, often times, they have the most interactions with customers and employees.

Bad Managers May Indicate Week Culture
*Data shows us that people stay or leave organizations because
of managers, and bad managers last the longest in
organizations with weaker cultures.*

Really getting managers involved and creating closeness with senior leadership teams will drive the health of the culture you are creating.

Lastly, those managers and senior leaders in your organization need to know their actions speak louder than any element of an overt communications plan, and they can invalidate elements of your culture in minutes. I tell clients, "Your culture is only as good as the worst behavior of the CEO," which easily stretches to senior leaders and managers. Their behavior is the strongest part of your communication plan. They, like you, live on a stage where decisions, actions, and words are judged carrying more weight than we often ever want to acknowledge. Our collective behavior, words out of frustration, a badly worded email, etc., can invalidate the culture quickly.

Accountability

Accountability often carries the connotation of negative reinforcement. The negative side is an unfortunate part of the process. But, it can be largely tempered and the organization will be made safer through an iterative emphatic approach that will guide employees through a lot of change.

We as leaders, especially new ones, need to give room and be as positive as possible while still enforcing accountability. First, realize people will NOT adopt and then follow your new culture immediately. Get over it! Culture change takes grit, empathy, patience, and a lot of judgment calls along the way. You are managing change, which is something that people generally resist. You are doing it on an organizational scale and at the same time typically pushing for a financial result. Overstating this financial result can bring about the quick demise of positive cultural change.

One of the most effective ways to create this change is vigilance for opportunities to reinforce and the willingness to have the open and sometimes uncomfortable conversations. There are hundreds of decisions and regular day-to-day transactions in any business that require judgment. Be on the lookout for the ones that go right and wrong relative to the foundations of the culture and talk about them. Laud those in the business whose decisions and actions embody the culture and openly discuss alternatives in how mistakes could be handled.

Acknowledge the organization is changing and mistakes will happen, thus creating a safe environment for mistakes and admission *versus* cover-up. Creating or improving a culture is a learning process and you are working with all kinds of students. Give them the opportunity to learn.

Work with your organizations, typically HR, to integrate the new tenets of the culture into your hiring and interviewing processes as well as employee communication and awards programs. Train hiring managers and talk to them about how to evaluate cultural fit through interview questions, as well as through analysis of behavior and small "tests" with candidates.

Use a "culture guard;" someone in the hiring process who you feel is protective of the culture and will ensure candidate fit. Many times, these people are not even part of the candidate's potential hierarchy - they are simply great at evaluating cultural fit.

Look at the awards program your organization runs and think about what can be done to positively reinforce culture and provide very public recognition. There are many ways to make this change positive and transparent within your organization; give some thought, engage employees at all levels, and if something doesn't work, scrap it and continue to the next one.

While these programs are effective, they are not 100%. You will always have resistance, employees who no longer fit, behavior that cannot be tolerated, etc. This is where you have to remember, especially when new, you're on the stage. Everyone is looking at how any negative enforcement will be handled, especially terminations.

Keep in mind, "it's not the one, it's the ninety-nine". Meaning it is not the individual you are punishing or terminating (though respect is always paramount), it is all of the others who know they may be in that position who are watching and then will decide how they act and how they perceive you going forward. Fairness and enough transparency that you are ensuring an accurate depiction of events sounds easy, but it is a maze, and I advise all to slow down to ensure you solve it correctly.

Repeat

We often talk about culture as a fixed asset of a company. Something that we set up and it prevails. If only it were that easy! The culture of an organization is constantly changing and incredibly fragile. Culture is impacted by every hire and exit from the company, events throughout day to day operations, and these days even national news and social media which has created a need for many companies to establish a stance on social issues. Leaders are challenged everyday with decisions that have culture implications.

Cultures are not stagnant; they are moving and that means they are moving in either a positive or negative direction; the only two options. As leaders, it is on us to influence and push the culture in a positive direction. This happens in two primary ways.

First, through the decisions we make including those we hire and promote in the organization. Promotion versus a new hire alone can send clear messages either consistent or inconsistent with culture (for example we all know companies that tout promotion from within and then hire senior staff with no explanation, destroying their integrity).

Second, it is through constant analysis and asking questions. Are there tools you can use to improve the culture? Are there areas in which you can further integrate culture? How will you scale culture with your business growth? It is important to look around the business, talk to employees at all levels, analyze programs for impact, and ask probing questions to continue to create the positive push.

Creating, changing, and managing a culture is critical work that often takes a back burner. An organization's culture is not defined and managed to a static mood; it is fluid and influenced by every new employee, decision, communication, and transaction. A culture is passed down and introduced to new employees through stories. As Rasken says, "A strategic story."

As you live each day in the organization, remember you are creating the stories others will tell and those who hear them will build their perception of you, your organization, and most importantly your culture.

Mike McDermott is President of InquisIT and Managing Member of Leadership Ignited. He coaches leaders, organizations, and is responsible for advancing InquisIT by defining corporate strategy and being the driving force behind marketing and contract operations. Prior to his current roles, Mr. McDermott was CEO of ATA LLC, a data analytics, program, and intelligence support firm. Mike spent over a decade at Phacil advancing from an onsite Cybersecurity and Information Assurance Analyst to President of the company logging over $500 Million in total sales along the way. He is a veteran of the United States Marine Corps, Amateur Bodybuilder, avid motorcycle rider, and proud father of four daughters.
Find him at https://www.linkedin.com/in/mike-mcdermott-b365a11/

Episode 19.
Governments Don't Buy Things People Do!

By Judy Bradt

CEO, Summit Insight

Game-changers include myth-busters, and I think that's why I was invited to share a few words with you here.

Come with me into the heart of darkness of federal sales. Our quest today is to vanquish two big myths. I promise I'll bring you back safely. But I can't promise you'll see things the same way again.

I've been an expert in federal business development for over 31 years. But for 25 of those 31 years, I had a dirty little secret.

I've helped more than 6,000 people win **hundreds** of **millions** of dollars in Federal work, on everything from strategy to cash-in-the-bank to recompetes.

I've given hundreds of presentations and over 300 webinars. I've published two books on the subject that have helped thousands of business owners just like you.

I could have told you almost anything about *how* the federal government buys. Anything and everything about winning federal business, except the one thing you most wanted to know:

The magical thing about how people really win contracts.

I'd landed a couple of small federal contracts for my company, sure, but it was all relationship-stuff, I told myself. It wasn't like I didn't want to tell you. *I honestly didn't know.*

...which didn't really matter 'til it really, really did.

See, I started my career as a business strategist, working for IBM Canada in Toronto. It took me six months to realize that I was working for what, at the time, was the planet's biggest sales organization. And that to be successful there I was going to have to SELL THINGS.

I was so horrified at the prospect of selling that I literally left the country, went to Washington D.C., and started a new career. By 2014, I'd been an expert in government contracting for 25 years, and a small business owner for ten of those. Then came the day I landed the big one: a sustaining contract with guaranteed revenue for a whole year. I was going to give seven companies targeting, training, and build their federal sales plans.

Heavy deliverables: two months. Coaching them while they sold: ten months. Sweet. There's no such thing as easy money in any business, but this sure looked a lot like that. Right up to the moment when I delivered the sales plan, and the client said, "Great! When are you making the introductions?"

Making the what? Whoops...

See, there was this *little* difference of opinion about the statement of work. I went through shock, then anger, then denial, bargaining; all the classic stages of grief. And I ended up at acceptance.

The thing I'd been running away from for 25 years had suddenly body-slammed my business.

I was on the hook for **thousands** of calls and **dozens** of federal buyer leads, every week for forty weeks. My problem was not just that I didn't want to do it - I had *three* problems.

First, I had just been turned into a full time sales person with quota and no experience. I felt overwhelmed and humiliated. *I have a graduate degree. I'm a strategist. I don't sell things.* The project I was so proud to win had brought me to my knees.

Second, I was terrified of being outed as a fraud, the contract expert who couldn't.

Third, this project was my company's major project for the whole year. I had no other irons in the fire. Failure, as they say, was not an option.

I had never failed a client before, and wasn't about to start now. There was only one thing to do. I took a deep breath, pulled up my big girl socks, and picked up the phone. This was my job: to cold call, find the right person, and get to know them well enough to introduce them to my clients. Who made everything from glass containers and power generation equipment to waterless shampoo to root-canal repair equipment.

Yep. I was dialing for dollars for endodontics. I can now report that nobody ever died from a phone call. I can also now tell you it's possible to *feel* like you're going to die from a phone call.

Despite being a seasoned speaker, a professional trainer, a national expert, when it came to these calls, I was...awkward. I didn't know what to say. I tripped over my words.

Once I strung together a sentence, I'm embarrassed to say it was some version of "I'm lost. Would you please help me?" all the while I was thinking *"Please don't yell at me."*

But then this happened:

99% of the Federal employees who took my calls didn't notice! I was nervous. They were kind. I was confused. They didn't mind! *They* wanted to help *me*! I made thousands of calls and spent hundreds of hours. Weeks and months went by. Then came the light bulb moment.

Do you know what Dr. Ned the endodontist for the Indian Health Service in Penobscot Maine was doing on his day off? He was sewing curtains. And his nephew was applying for medical school at Georgetown. Boy, was he proud! And, sure, he'd be glad to talk to the rep from the company that made the root canal repair system.

And I hung up the phone and sat there. And it dawned on me: *THIS was the heart of the job.* I had all the time in the world to hear **their** stories. Once they knew that I cared about them and what they were doing, something nearly magical happened: They told me what they needed. Even when I felt awkward, my research let me ask thoughtful questions that opened doors.

That lit up my sales plan with thousands of small wins! I'd built a sales plan around my client's best prospects. So, every conversation, every new call booking gave me a fresh dopamine hit. I was literally hooked...not on sales, but on human connection.

Army Warrant Officer Sarah at Fort Bragg was heading out to make a presentation at Fort Huachuca. Air Force Colonel Dr. Linda just got promoted to run the Postgraduate Dental College!

Ned and Sarah and Linda all had problems. And my client had solutions for them! Once I took my time to get to know them. I could connect people who could help each other. That felt great. Pretty soon, I looked forward to my dialing-for-dollars days.

What I thought was the heart of darkness was filled with hearts of gold.

Big Myth Number One
There's no such thing as selling to "The Government."

There's only selling to *people.* When you win a contract, there's going to be two signatures on that document. One will be yours. The other will belong to a real federal human who put everything on the line when they awarded that work to you.

The key to open up a federal sale was to start by finding and making friends with people who need you. Thousands of federal contractors struggle because they never connect with the buyers and partners who truly need your expertise.

Master the art of building relationships with federal buyers and you can leave those struggles behind.

That's the first message. The other is that with over $400 billion of federal contract spending, we are awash in contract opportunities. And there's never been a better time to find them. Lucky, eh?

See, back in the day, it wasn't so easy to find out what the federal government was buying. Vendors were hooked on CBD...but not the kind that's in the news these days. For years, the place you had to go to find federal contract opportunities was the CBD -- Commerce Business Daily. Published by the Department of Commerce in six-point type, on tissue paper, it came out daily. Hardcopy in the mail. In 1988, federal IT spend was about to hit the dizzying height of $12 billion. Total federal contract awards were busting through the $250 billion mark.

A private company could get federal contract award data, but if you wanted that in electronic form - to do any kind of analysis, you had to buy it from a commercial provider.

Then everything started to change. By 2002, the federal government had ceased publishing the CBD and replaced it with FedBizOpps – the predecessor to Contract Opportunities on SAM.gov. And federal contract data exploded onto the scene.

Government contractors today have dozens of options to find out about federal business opportunities. Joshua Frank and I are among many consultants who routinely teach companies about all the different sources that companies can tap into to find out what the federal government is buying.

Everything is so accessible, so transparent, that you'd think it would be SO much easier to win federal contracts these days than before it was all online, right? Yea...not so much.

Look around on our journey. The room is emptier than it used to be. 43,000 small businesses have LEFT the federal market since 2009. Why?

Well, for starters, the average federal contractor spends anywhere from $30,000 to over $233,000 in 12 months on the road to the win. It can take that long for the first win and not everybody wins that quickly.

If you're in the federal arena right now, as a business owner, congratulations. You're a survivor. But are you thriving?

You have every reason to be. You're a savvy business owner. You've got the expertise. You've probably got experience of some kind, and may even have millions of dollars' worth of past performance.

It's all too common to be a government contractor working harder than ever, but the new wins aren't coming in. If that feels familiar, you're not alone.

If you're running hard and going broke, you may be in the thrall of *opportunity illusion*. I'm going to shatter that for you right now.

80% of companies in the federal arena are overwhelmed by all the opportunities. They spend countless days sifting through all that contract data, all those opportunities, asking "What can we bid?" and pumping out proposals all year long... and losing... and losing... and losing. And wondering why.

Big Myth Number Two
Winners don't have better data than you do.

They have better relationships. They don't look at the data and ask, "What can we bid?" They're looking at "Who's my buyer?"

Just imagine for a moment...

What would open up for you if you could get in front of the right federal buyer months before the competition? How much more would you win? $1 million? $4 million? $12 million?

Successful federal contractors do **THESE FOUR THINGS**:

- First, buff up their sales game.
- Second, focus on a few target agencies.
- Third, build a structured sales plan around just those agencies; and
- Fourth, use that plan to get in front of buyers who need what you do.

Want to open doors more easily? Start by giving.

Whether you're meeting buyers or vendors, chatting up someone new, cultivating a connection, or getting back in touch with longtime colleagues, keep this question front and center in your thoughts:

"How can I help you?"

Generosity is a magic ingredient, in both your perspective and your approach to others.

Did you know? Even top vendors can't (and don't) win them all. A couple years ago, a report on government sales showed win rates for incumbents surveyed to be only 54%, and win rates on new projects (where there is no incumbent) to be only 26%.

Fact: you're going to lose some. So, consider helping others on the journey. It's an easy, powerful, way to stand out and be top of mind.

Want more leads - connections as well as opportunities? Start by bringing leads to others. *To others? Why would I give away pieces of my pie?*

Opportunity isn't pie, as in "only so much to go around." It's *dough*. When you add warmth, it expands. It rises and grows more to feed everyone. There is plenty of business to go around. You have relationships and contacts. If you're serious about the federal market, you're constantly and deliberately building relationships. Don't hoard those connections. Share them.

When you meet another business owner, start by being curious about what they do. After you learn a bit about them, *even if they might be a rival*, ask, "Who are your ideal clients? Who might you like to meet at this event? *Who should I be sending your way?*"

Listen to the answer, and jot a note on their business card. Take a moment to think about who *you* know who could help *them*. Also add that note to their record in your contact database. Rare is the company who is *only* a rival. Experienced federal contractors often compete with fellow vendors on one project, and team with them on the next!

Now, when you meet someone new in government, what introductions or industry reports or innovative ideas could you bring your government contacts to make their day easier?

Remember that all these people you're meeting are also human beings, with lives and pets and mortgages and hobbies. Maybe what the contracting officer most needs, she tells you one day in August with fiscal year-end bearing down on her relentlessly, is a decent dog walker - because of all the overtime she's working. Gosh, and you just happen to know one.

When I ask experienced business owners, "Where did you hear about the government business opportunities you've actually won?" ninety-percent of the replies are something like:

- "A friend told me."
- "Referral from one of my current clients."
- "My accountant had another client who needed me on their contract."
- "I followed up with somebody I met at a community event."

- "I got to know this woman through an association, and she told me about the opportunity and introduced me."

Just as relationships are how vendors hear about buyers... relationships are also one of the most important ways buyers hear about vendors!

Sales isn't slimy.

Sales – including federal sales -- is the glorious and precious art of human connection. Selling is about building trust and that's a very, very, human thing we have all been doing since the day we were born. Despite all the marketing automation in the world, people still do business with people they know, like, and trust.

Who's *your* federal buyer? What is their life like? What do they love about their job? What do they wish was different?

Find out. Your business depends on it.

* * *

Judy Bradt, CEO of Summit Insight, brings over thirty years' expertise in Federal business development and strategy to people who want to grow their federal business. She's an award-winning speaker and consultant, and author of the book Government Contracts Made Easier.

Judy believes that winning federal contractors don't simply have better contract data, more money, or stronger past performance. Winners use all those things to build better relationships, a lot sooner, than everybody else. Her clients include many of the country's top federal contractors, especially those in professional services and technology, who use her tools and techniques to reach the federal buyers they were meant to serve.

Summit Insight delivers an intensified approach to Federal business development that's the right choice for people who are committed to growing their Federal business. To find out more, visit www.GrowFedBiz.com!

Call 703-627-1074 or email Judy at Judy.Bradt@SummitInsight.com. Find her at https://www.linkedin.com/in/judybradt/

Episode 20.
Crowdsourcing RFP's

By Rob Rosenberger

CEO, Blackdragon

Introduction

Vince Lombardi coined the popular phrase, "Winning isn't everything. It's the only thing." As it applies to companies depending on winning competitively awarded contracts to generate revenue, this statement hits home. Business development is critical for survival but a more important metric deciding the fate of federal contractor firms is 'Contracts Won.' This is especially true for those who believe the adage, "If you're not growing, you're dying."

Business as usual is dead. Federal contracts are won differently than they were before although the enormous industry itself is well-known for its glacial-pace with respect to responding to major forms of change. Without winning, the lack of revenues earned can weaken a company.

I run a company called Blackdragon. It's quite unique in federal contracting. We entered onto the scene in 2015 and quickly rose to become globally recognized as a fresh, disruptive game changer throughout the industry. Within just a few years, we've revolutionized the way federal contracts are identified, qualified, pursued and ultimately won.

As the largest and fastest growing bid and proposal (B&P) company in the federal market, Blackdragon is the only full-spectrum outsource solution that wins entire contracts on behalf of bidder clients. Its disruptive platform

191

serves as a matchmaking marketplace combining powerful aspects of the rising Gig Economy that completely rethinks the value chain.

Blackdragon is also the first to have productized the full spectrum of identifying, qualifying, pursuing and winning the right contracts. The integrated suite of on-demand products (listed below) is designed to help bidder clients win targeted contracts in the shortest time with lowest investment risks and minimal disruption to daily operations. It is a powerful collection of complementary attributes for winning, sharing a common objective and the ability to easily exchange data with each other.

Similar to how productized tax preparation services use real-time access to a living, global network of talent, Blackdragon has productized all aspects of everything it takes to help companies win targeted contracts that are right for them. This is a conversion from the outdated model of hiring humans in increments of time such as, salaried employees performing work 40 hours/week or individual consultants hired hourly for temporary assignments to the improved alternative of providing outcomes performed by experts, or teams of experts.

The Gig Economy is Transforming Industries

The Gig Economy is famous for disrupting traditional business sectors. Business innovation and disruption are rapidly changing the scope, pace, and scale of technology work worldwide. The lack of overhead and inventory help share-based businesses run lean. The increased efficiencies allow these brands to pass-through value to their customers and supply chain partners. Traditional industries are being affected by the sharing economy—and many traditional brands will struggle if they do not adapt to the changing landscape.

The sharing economy is defined by the value in taking underutilized assets and making them accessible online to a community, leading to a reduced need for ownership of those assets. In the federal sector where companies must first win the competitive bidding process with the Government to stay in business, historically bidder firms have attempted to build empires by accumulating assets. Not the least of which are the human capital assets that embody the knowledge, talent and experience of winning these contracts.

Professional services via the Gig Economy are evolving to blend hand-in-hand collaboration between experts with business functions to concrete unprecedented value. As a result of the growing demand for rapid and efficient delivery of low-friction experiences and capabilities—on par with best-in-class consumer-grade online experiences—many technology teams are shifting from traditional project- and process-focused operating models to those that are more product- and outcome-centric, which prioritize cross-functional collaboration, acceleration of time-to-customer value and other user/customer needs, and business outcomes.

An essential factor in every federal business opportunity is having a trusted relationship with the right government decision-makers before the Request for Proposal (RFP) is released. Consciously or otherwise, they influence who wins and why. However, this is becoming harder to accomplish in scale for many reasons. Too few business development (BD) personnel can adequately nurture very many diverse relationships with so many government influencers who are kaleidoscopically rearranging their roles within agencies. Also, high turnover rates of BD personnel with established individual relationships often significantly affect a company's standing in the federal stakeholder's mind.

The key differentiator is instituted in the disruptive *power of the platform*—a new business model that uses technology to connect people, organizations, and resources in an interactive ecosystem in which amazing amounts of value can be created and exchanged quickly and inexpensively. Today's platforms empowered by digital technology and social connectivity are crushing barriers of time and space that connect producers and consumers more precisely, rapidly, and easily than ever before.

Federal industry experts of all types, backgrounds and skill levels are increasingly registering themselves as freelancers in the Gig Economy. This worldwide ecosystem of knowledge, talent, experiences, and relationships—a living network of networks—uses platforms to form Dream Teams of experts, on-demand, for any federal opportunity within a moment's notice. Companies can outsource complete contract wins to self-forming, self-managing teams of experts who will work for a moderate fixed fee plus reasonable incentive.

How this Model Differs from Traditional Models

1. **Client Agnostic.** Primary objective is to win targeted contracts for any bidder client, not to pursue any contract opportunity for select clients. Contrary to conventional consulting arrangements, Blackdragon starts with the optimum business opportunity and then seeks out a partnership with

the highest caliber prospect bidders deemed best fitted for winning a given opportunity instead of the other way around.

2. **Puts Strengths to Work.** Greater opportunity for experts to do more of what they like to do. The Deal Team model is the foundation for a 'Dream Team' whereby every member is carefully selected for a project for capitalizing on their respective strengths in unison with others, but does not expect any of its members to cover professional domains where they're weaker or less comfortable.

3. **Deal Teams Self-Form and Manage at Their Own Discretion.** Deal Teams initiate and manage their internal selection process for fellow expert members based on their own timing and dynamic preferences for best fit. Members are not picked autocratically by an external source or queue system. Deal Team members manage themselves, hold themselves accountable for achieving outcomes instead of processes and ultimately, they determine one another's compensation based on perceived contribution of value.

4. **Collaborate with Peers, Don't Compete with Them.** Consultants do not compete with one another to score the limited client funds available for distribution.

5. **Risk/Reward Sharing with Clients.** Deal Teams are not compensated on an hourly basis like conventional 1099 support. They work fixed price for the duration of each project. Deal Teams place most of their fixed fee as contingent upon contract award and must win the contract on behalf of the client to collect their full fee.

6. **Unparalleled Compensation Opportunities.** Contingent portions of fee for a project are technically calculated as a percentage of the total contract value (TCV) being pursued. Bigger wins result in bigger payoffs.

7. **Decision Making Autonomy.** Deal Teams are empowered to share final decision-making autonomy with their clients as it pertains to maximizing PWIN for each project.

8. **Shifts Market Power to The Value Producer.** The platform serves as the first special skills marketplace facilitating efficient, optimized matchmaking of experts into complete teams tailored in design around specific bid opportunities.

9. **Disrupts Old Balance of Power.** Freelancers proactively unite in the platform to self-form into 'Dream Teams' of experts for a targeted opportunity before they have a final client identified. This enables Dragons to seek out the client they prefer to win for vice shop for any firm that will pay their hourly fee as individuals.

10. **More Money.** Eighty-five percent of all revenue dollars earned, whether they be billable by the hour, fixed fees for projects or win bonuses, flow to the people that perform the work.

11. **Flexible Lifestyle.** With temporary assignments, all fulfilled remotely via personal schedules of the consultants, earning potential remains solidly within the hands of each consultant.

Crowdsourcing RFPs is a unique capability that I strongly recommend companies consider as they enter and mature in the federal market. If you have questions on improving your win-rate, don't hesitate to contact me.

*   *   *

Rob Rosenberger is the visionary CEO/CO-Founder of Blackdragon, a continuously growing and highly innovative global consulting firm that is increasingly recognized across the Federal industry as a major disrupter, radically changing the way contracts with the Government are identified, pursued and ultimately won. The first and only of its kind, the company breaks longstanding paradigms by revolutionizing one of the largest, most mature industries renowned for its resistance to change. In under three years from its initial launch, Blackdragon quickly rose to become the foremost unified group of for-profit Bid and Proposal (B&P) experts in the U.S. Find him at https://www.linkedin.com/in/robertrosenberger/

Episode 21.
Price to Win

By Michael McNulty

President, McNulty and Associates

"If you know the enemy and know yourself, you need not fear the result of a hundred battles. If you know yourself but not the enemy, for every victory gained you will also suffer a defeat. If you know neither the enemy nor yourself, you will succumb in every battle." — Sun Tzu, *The Art of War*

While the famous statement above is about warfare, it can be applied to any true competition. If we don't know our opponent and we don't know ourselves, we are destined to lose. And no one is going to be very sympathetic if we don't try to know our competition, at least as well as we know ourselves. Attempting to know our competition as well as ourselves, when bidding on Government Contracts, is the basic concept behind Competitive Assessment and Price to Win (PTW) analysis.

It is perfectly natural to want to know what your competition will do on any given pursuit. Who will bid? Are they weak or strong? Are they hungry? How hungry? How is the incumbent performing? The two big questions we are trying to answer with Price to Win Analysis are: What will our competitions' bid price be? And, how will they score on the non-price parts of the Section M evaluation criteria? If we can accurately predict how our competition will score and what price they will submit, we can leverage that information to greatly increase our chances of winning.

This episode is focused on the modern practice of Price to Win Analysis. To explore this topic, I've laid out the episode into the following sections: Customer, Competition, and Price.

Figure 1 is designed to get us oriented and thinking about Customer, Competition, and Price from a PTW perspective. Along the bottom, is a notional Government procurement timeline; capture activities are along the top of the Figure; and Price to Win activities and artifacts are shown in the middle.

Looking along the government procurement timeline, we see there is a historical RFP, spending or budget data on the current program and potentially on the upcoming program; an RFI release (always submit a response to the RFI if interested in the program); several Draft RFP milestones, including Draft PWS, Draft Section L&M of the RFP, Draft Cost Formats and Q&A's; then comes the Final RFP, Q&A's and Amendments (if any), before final Proposal Submittal.

There is not very much that bidders can do about the government timeline. All interested bidders will have to work to this timeline and decide to either submit their bids, or not. The middle of Figure 1 shows the various PTW artifacts, which we will cover, including a Top-Down Price to Win Analysis, Competitor WRAP rate analysis, Competitive Assessments, Solutioning that might be required, then the Bottom Up Price to Win Analysis with Gaming. Before we get to the actual Price to Win pieces, let's have a look at the Customer.

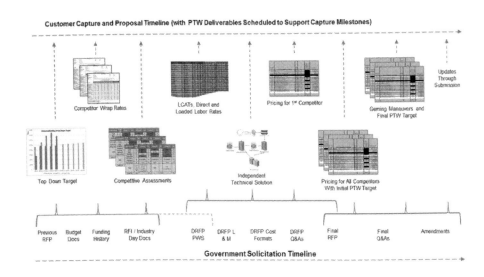

Figure 1

198

Customer, Customer, Customer

The best place to start, when trying to win a government contract, is with the Customer. After all, the Customer has the requirement(s) which will produce the RFP. Understanding the problem that the Customer is trying to solve by awarding the contract is key. Are they simply competing because the time has come to re-compete a services contract? Do they have new requirements based on advances in technology they'd like to exploit, like moving to the cloud? Do they have new requirements, based on changes in technology or changing strategy of U.S. enemies requiring new radar or stealth technologies?

Are they running a Low Price Technically Acceptable (LPTA) competition for a commodity or are they seeking to get the most for their budgeted dollars in a best value competition? All of these questions, and more, are key. You must fully understand what the Customer is trying to accomplish when bidding. After all, they set the budget, choose the type of competition, set the Section L and M criteria, write the requirements and ultimately choose the winner.

A recurring theme in this episode will be to *START EARLY*. You can never start too early, but you can start too late. Looking at Figure 1, if a bidder starts writing a proposal after the RFP comes out and they haven't done the necessary front-end capture work, they probably should not bid.

Customer visits, requirements shaping, teaming, solutioning, pre-proposal and proposal writing, along with early Price to Win activities have already been completed by the competition. When the RFP comes out, it has been shaped by the competition. Do you really want to try to write a winning proposal against an RFP that was shaped by your competition, without having done any of the up-front work that you know you should have done?

Bidder's chances of winning without doing these up-front activities are extremely low. Instead, start early and use this up-front time to truly understand Customer requirements, ideally shaping them to your capabilities, and analyzing Customer buying behavior to help inform your bid.

It is very important to understand how the Customer in question actually buys. Do they typically go out with LPTA procurements or Best

Value RFPs? Do they put on Best Value competitions and consistently pick the lowest bidder, making it a de facto LPTA procurement?

The best way to find out how the Customer really buys is to review protests on previous bids with the same Customer. Years ago, bid protests were extremely rare. Companies did not want to anger the Government, fearing down-stream retribution. Those days are over. Protests are extremely common today and the information is publicly available. Read the protests for the Customer in question. They often reveal how the Customer buys, settling the question about whether or not they typically pick the lowest bidder, even in Best Value Competitions.

The other important buying behavior you want to know can often be derived from a bid protest. Just how much of a premium is the Customer willing to pay for better non-price scores? The protest review may show that the Customer will pay more, sometimes quite a bit more, for what they perceive as better technical, past performance, management, or even risk scores. You want to know this information as it directly relates to the Price to Win Analysis and pricing strategy.

Competition and Competitive Analysis

Know your competition as well as you know yourself. Indeed, detailed competitive assessments are foundational to Price to Win Analysis. The goal of proper competitive analysis is to come to conclusions about what your competition will and won't do, when bidding on the procurement in question, and how they will likely score on the non-price items required in Section L and evaluated in Section M (i.e., management, technical, past performance, transition, risk, etc.).

This type of competitive assessment should be centered around the technical requirements in the RFP and the capabilities and motivations of the competitors. A competitive assessment should result in an unbiased mock scoring of your competitors against the Section M criteria.

The Technical Requirements of the RFP are the foundation of the Competitive Analysis (CA). The technical requirements, found in the PWS and associated documents, tell the CA analyst what to look for with the competitors. If the requirements are for cloud migration - leveraging commercial cloud technologies, operations and maintenance (O&M) of the resulting Cloud environment and associated call center and help desk support, then the competitors need to have these capabilities to be credible.

200

The CA analyst should build an analysis that sets the technical requirements as the baseline, then compares the capabilities of each competitor against those technical requirements, just as the government ultimately will. This is often done in table form, where the requirements are on one side and the capabilities are on the other, to show how each competitor meets the requirements. Likewise, the CA analyst uses the technical requirements to search for suitable past performance citations, the same ones the competitor will likely cite in their proposal.

This is also normally shown in a table format showing the key information about each applicable past performance program, including the name of the program, the government agency, a high level scope of work, the award date, the size of the program ($M of dollars), the length of the program or period of performance (PoP), etc. If the CA analyst can't find enough past performance citations which meet or exceed the technical requirements, then that bidder is likely going to have to team in order to meet requirements or will potentially score poorly on the past performance evaluation; or they may simply no-bid.

Price

The price you are going to bid on the program should be shaped by a few important factors: What the customer budget is and the *Should-Cost (i.e.,* what the customer thinks they should pay for the program), what the competition will bid and how they will score on the non-price items in Section M, and last but not least, your cost basis and profit goals.

We'll now delve into Should-Cost and the first look at what the competitions' likely bid price will be through a process called Top Down Price to Win Analysis or, more simply, the Top Down. Then we will take a look at Bottom Up Price to Win analysis or, the Bottom Up Analysis (BUA).

Top Down Price to Win Analysis – Setting the Likely Top-Line of the Program

Top Down Price to Win Analysis is a process by which the analyst researches historical spending on the current program along with budget data on the upcoming program, to determine the should-cost of the program. The should-cost is the amount the government thinks the program reasonably *Should-Cost* the government (i.e., the fair and reasonable price for the government to pay for the program). Once the should-cost is determined, the analyst, knowing that each competitor can likely determine the should-cost as they did will develop a pricing strategy to bid below the should-cost and win. No one is going to bid above the should-cost. How much below the should-cost will a competitor bid? Like so many things, it depends.

Bottom Up Price to Win Analysis (BUA)– Building the Competitors' Cost Basis Forecasting their Bid Price

Bottom Up Price to Win Analysis (BUA) is where the PTW analyst builds a working price model of the competition. Ideally it is a very accurate forecast of the bid prices that will be submitted by each competitor. It is also ideal that BUA will be used to fully populate the government's pricing sheets, just as the competitors would do, when developing their cost proposals. This allows comparison of the competitions' forecasted prices to your own internal pricing. An accurate BUA is a game changer. Imagine, with an accurate BUA, you have a very good estimate of your competitions' pricing, even before you develop your own pricing for the RFP.

BUA estimates all of the pricing the competition will do. It includes pricing all of the labor, all materials, travel, other direct costs (ODCs), everything that needs to be priced in the cost volume. Let's take a look at piece of the estimate – pricing labor.

The price of labor is made up of the Direct Labor (*i.e.*, the wages paid to employees), Indirect Expense (i.e., Overhead, G&A and Fringe Benefits) and Fee. Most companies buy subscriptions to human resources (HR) databases to get accurate empirical data on wages for all kinds of job categories all over the country. The most popular HR tools in use today are Salary.com and ERI. The Bureau of Labor Statistics (BLS) also produces quarterly reports of wages by job code. BLS data is free.

In our industry, when overhead, G&A and fringe benefits are combined, we call that a WRAP rate. WRAP rates are very difficult to determine so most companies buy WRAP rate estimates from reputable firms that do this analysis and sell the estimates.

The fee that is applied to labor is driven largely by the profit goals of the competitor in question and the type of bid. Let's say the competition is a best value competition and the competitor's last SEC filing of their 10-K, shows they have a current operating margin of 7%. It's likely they will try to at least maintain that 7% operating margin. But if the competition were to be LPTA, they will likely have to dive to around 4% to be competitive.

Pulling it all Together and Gaming

We have covered Competitive Assessment, Top Down Analysis and Bottom Up Analysis. Once these are done, the analyst can see the whole picture. They can see how the various competitors will likely score in the non-price items. They can see what the likely should-cost is and how the customer is thinking about the procurement. They can see the BUA and where each competitor is likely to come in. This is where the analyst applies Gaming. Gaming involves making adjustments to the BUA, altering it to be as close as possible to what each competitor will actually bid.

To explore the idea of gaming let's look at a case where there is an existing services contract which is up for re-compete. An incumbent and two other bidders are being modeled by the PTW analyst. The procurement is Best Value with the headcount dictated by the Government. The competitive assessment indicates that the incumbent seems to be doing a good job and has many other programs, like this one, they can cite in their past performance and technical volumes. If they write a good proposal and submit an aggressive bid, they will be hard to beat.

They *want* to be hard to beat, so it is likely they will write a good proposal and submit an aggressive price. It is reasonable to assume the Government does not want to go to the trouble of re-badging contractors to a new company or possibly losing a few good contractors along the way, if there is no real cost savings.

The other two bidders understand all of this and will *game their bids*, dropping their prices in an attempt to get below the incumbent, making it attractive enough for the Government to choose them. The PTW analyst will adjust the competitor models, making downward adjustments where they can, to drop the price. Remember, they can't drop the headcount, so they will likely drop the direct labor rates, maybe even bid a lower WRAP rate (that can be done within reason) and last but not least, drop their fee. All of these maneuvers are gaming moves to try to get the price down.

Now the analyst has an even better picture of the whole situation and what they are up against on this bid. From here a Price to Win recommendation can be made, taking all of the analysis into account, and recommending what price their company should bid to win.

The PTW recommendation is a target number in dollars. As you can see, there is quite a bit of complex, detailed analysis behind getting to that number. PTW targets aren't supposed to be the lowest possible number that can be bid. The PTW target is supposed to be the number you need to bid, to win, and not leave money on the table. It must also allow for successful program execution.

To leverage the PTW analysis the bidder compares it to the numbers obtained from internal pricing or maybe targets set by senior leaders. How close are the numbers? Where are they off, and why? They don't need to match. That isn't the point. The point is to leverage the PTW analysis so that decision makers can then drive their pricing direction internally, normally to get below the PTW target.

Winning bidders start early, obtain an accurate PTW analysis, target and leverage that information to improve their win probability.

* * *

Michael McNulty is the founder and Lead Analyst for McNulty & Associates, Inc. He is a highly experienced Business Development expert in the US Federal Government market.

Mr. McNulty holds both Bachelors and Graduate degrees in Engineering and over 25 years of experience as a Business Development executive, Capture Manager, Program Manager, Proposal Manager and Engineer specializing in Modeling & Simulation. He has been instrumental in providing Price to Win, Pricing Analysis, and Competitive Assessments on many successful competitive procurements across all Services and the US Federal Government.

Mr. McNulty's experience includes program values ranging from under $10M to over $3B, spanning all areas of acquisition from R&D to Systems Design & Development to Production, Deployment and Sustainment. Functional areas include Design & Engineering of Major Systems, Large IT Systems, C4ISR Systems, Training Systems, Flight Simulators, and Large-Scale Logistics and Support efforts. Find him at https://www.linkedin.com/in/michael-mcnulty-078a1429/

Episode 22.
Streamlining the Proposal Process

By Carrie Ann Williams

Principal, Andana Consulting

Often seen as a necessary evil to win more work with Government agencies, proposals can really be an energizing, engaging, and collaborative process. You may think of them as a means to an end, but maybe that is because you don't have a pursuit strategy, or maybe you are bidding everything you think you 'can' do and not being thoughtful about your internal resources or how the opportunity lines up with your business plan.

If you are responding to any solicitation because it checks a box or two, read on to learn more about how to develop proposals that are impactful to your bottom line and to your team's morale.

With all of the work it takes for a firm to identify an opportunity and finally receive the solicitation, letting the development of the response become an afterthought causes problems. In the Government contracting space, a response to a Request for Proposal (RFP) or a Request for Qualification (RFQ) is part of the process to get new contracts and build your business.

So how do we get beyond boilerplate responses done at the eleventh hour?

Analysis of Solicitation

First, a firm must conduct an honest analysis of the solicitation – its statement of work, evaluation criteria, and other requirements. Answering the question "Can we do this work?" is not enough. Many firms *can* do the work, but are they really *qualified* to do the work? Based on the documents provided by the agency, a firm can determine if they truly align with the requirements. Being close is not enough – designing a parking lot is not the same as designing a highway.

Read the documents and understand exactly what the government is looking for in your qualifications. Often the evaluation criteria show the details they want; a type of project, the size of the project, the costs of the project. These details help you narrow down your ability to qualify that you can competitively perform the work they want.

In addition to analyzing the solicitation documents, what other intelligence do you have on the opportunity? Do you have existing relationships with the agency or end user? Is your firm positioned as an expert to the agency you are bidding? Have you met with potential teaming partners who can add additional value to your offering? Does the agency know your firm and your capabilities?

Don't make the mistake of bidding because you 'can' do the work. Make sure you are qualified to do the work outlined in the solicitation and that you are positioned to win.

Strategic Go / No-Go

Once you've analyzed the solicitation and understand that you meet or exceed the qualifications required, the next step is to conduct a strategic go/no-go process. A go/no-go process will help your firm bid the pursuits that make the most sense - whether they are must-win's that you've been positioning and planning for or those that are your bread and butter contracts. They could be might-win's that will be a stretch for your firm but fit into one of your strategic pursuit categories.

Bidding isn't a numbers game, especially when qualifications are part of the equation. It is about a strategy. If your firm bids 10 proposals in one month and wins none, consider using a go/no-go process to narrow that down to three proposals in one month that can have dedicated resources and strategy, which may result in a higher quality proposal and more wins.

To tie the opportunity to your strategy, implement a go/no-go process early in the game. That process could look like a quick meeting with a company leader, or the capture manager and proposal manager reviewing the solicitation together. It could look like a form integrated into your CRM that is used by several people to get to a decision. It could be a narrative explaining the decision to pursue or not pursue. It could be a persuasive slide deck showing statistics and decision points.

Some of the considerations in the process are alignment with the company goals. Considerations include:

- Internal resources (can we facilitate writing the response?)
- Timeline (how much time do we have and what are our competing projects?)
- Relationship with the customer
- Who is the competition?
- Do we have the expertise in house?

Whatever the process looks like for your firm - it does not have to be complex. However, it must be a process that works for you and that is completed for each pursuit. Firms that have strategic processes also have a timeline to implement the process and review the decision. Often, the process is initiated within *24 hours of receipt of the solicitation* and the *decision must be made within 48 hours*. Successful processes also include multiple evaluators - not just the sales/BD/Capture managers, but also other members of the firm from leadership to technical staff to proposal staff.

Creating a process allows the team to see how the decision aligns with the company goals and business strategies. Was it a 'go' because it is a growth area for the firm? Because it is a target client? Whatever the reason, when the decision lines up with company goals, the proposal team recognizes that it will have a big impact on the company if they do well and write a winning response.

Just as important in having a reason to pursue, is a reason to walk away. A strategic go/no-go process offers firms the courage to say no to opportunities. This is hard to do, especially when the contract has a five-year term and it will be years before you can bid again; or when the project would be so great to perform but you just don't quite meet all of the criteria; or when your resources are already maxed out working on other priority pursuits.

Having the courage to say no, to walk away, will allow you to focus on the *pursuits that matter* and that you are *better positioned to win*. It will allow you to put resources into building a strategy for the next opportunity with that customer (gather some intelligence – set up a meeting, attend an industry day) rather than present a package that misses the mark.

Being able to execute the work is not a good enough strategy to actually winning a proposal.

Build a Motivated Team

Often, a proposal is the last thing internal teams want to be part of. They have other deadlines and client priorities already filling their days. But internal teams are the key to creating a successful bid. Internal teams include leadership, ownership, BD/Capture, technical staff, marketing and proposal managers. Each group brings their individual expertise to the proposal – the BD/Captures team knows the customer and end user pain points. The technical staff knows the solution your firm will offer to solve those problems. The proposal managers know how to orchestrate all the data and narratives to bring the package together, on time.

The proposal team can feel great about being on the project when they know that what they are working on is in-line with the company's goals and plans. They must know this alignment so they have a desire to win and are dedicated to the pursuit.

When ownership or leadership is excited about the opportunity, this can really motivate teams to see beyond the late nights and rounds of edits to know they are having an impact. It is hard to feel good about a process without solid strategy and encouragement. So, once the 'go' decision is made and the team is pulled together, understanding how this proposal helps the company reach its goals is integral to building a motivated team.

Momentum-Building Kick-Off Meetings

The proposal process can last weeks, sometimes months. Depending on the complexity, you may be dealing with a lot of moving parts - not only on your internal team, but with consultant team members and the agency's solicitation you are bidding (reviewing amendments can be a full-time job!).

Keeping momentum throughout the process starts with an impactful kick-off meeting. This meeting is the jumping-off point for the whole proposal. It *sets the tone* for the team and the *battle rhythm* for the process.

Here, you bring together the writers, the capture managers, the graphic designers, the subject matter experts, volume leads, company leadership, and other contributors. A killer kick-off meeting will define the roles and responsibilities for the team. When team members understand their role in the process and how their input affects the rest of content development, they have more *accountability*. The proposal leader should provide the team with the background of the opportunity, the strategy that has been developed, and the impact the pursuit will have if it is won. The kick-off is the time to build energy and excitement around the work that will result from the contract when it is won!

The kick-off meeting also manages the nuts and bolts of the proposal. The proposal manager should come prepared with the proposal directive, compliance matrix, and schedule. In the meeting, the team agrees to various assignments for data collection, writing assignments, and agrees to the proposal schedule for draft development, review meetings, and commenting times.

Note. Use review meetings as an opportunity to renew momentum and re-engage the team on producing the response. Celebrate the milestones along the way!

Whether at the kick-off meeting or in a separate session, bring the team together to review and develop the proposal strategy and win themes. Depending on the complexity of the response, win-theme development can take a lot of iterations to get to those that are most impactful to the customer.

When writers are provided with an outline for their sections, *include guidance from the solicitation instructions and evaluation criteria* (sections L and M usually). When you include your win themes, also include the proof-points necessary to demonstrate your successful solution.

In your meeting you should discuss the following topics as a team:

- What do we know about the client?
- What does the client know about us? Our competitors?
- What are the evaluation criteria? How will we meet/exceed them?
- What are the program goals? How will we meet them?
- Do we work with the customer today?

- What do they like? Dislike?
- Why should they hire us?
- What are our win themes?
- What features/capabilities do you bring?
- What are the benefits/impact of those capabilities?
- Proof of past successes?
- How you will eliminate keeping them up at night?
- What you want the client to remember when they finish reading your proposal?

Proposals are not just a necessary evil. They can also be meaningful marketing activities. They might not be fancy like a conference or a website but think of proposals as a highly tailored qualification package. It is a marketing sprint - you have 30 days to put together your best qualifications and create content that highlights your capabilities.

In the end, you have a package that showcases the best of your firm and your team. You get the opportunity to look at all of your accomplishments that have gone into the proposal and think of what you *will* accomplish after you win. It's a shift in mindset.

A Shift in Mindset
Proposals are not draining, they are energizing!

Sidebar: Pursue Intelligence

Tracking an opportunity before it becomes a solicitation can make the proposal more meaningful. You want to gather intelligence about the contract and learn information that is not publicly available in the announcement. This can be accomplished through primary intelligence gathering that includes face to face meetings with the customer, the end user, teaming partners, and attending industry days. You should also conduct secondary intelligence gathering by reviewing forecasts, finding past procurement documents, and researching on USASpending.gov and SAM.gov (previously FBO/FPDS). The data you collect during this capture process will set your team up for success in developing a winning proposal response.

As principal of the award-winning firm Andana Consulting, Carrie Ann Williams, CPSM, works with organizations to guide proposal development and create amazing marketing content.

She has worked with organizations to track, pursue, position, and propose on government solicitations - and private organizations. When not leading proposal strategy, she guides firms to develop lead marketing campaigns with clear goals and implementation plans.

Carrie Ann is known for leading interactive, insightful and actionable training workshops and presentations providing insight into marketing and business strategies for professional services firms. Her sessions have taken her across the country to train companies and organizations including local and national events for SAME, PSMJ, SMPS, AIA, and NVSBE.

A Certified Professional Services Marketer, Carrie Ann has an undergraduate degree in English Literature and a Master of Business Administration degree. Carrie Ann is also "Inbound Certified" and "Content Marketing Certified" from HubSpot. Find her at https://www.linkedin.com/in/carrieannwilliamscpsm/

Episode 23.
Getting Massive Value Out of an SF330

By Carrie Ann Williams

Principal, Andana Consulting

In 1972 the Brooks Act made it a United States Federal Law that requires the U.S. Federal Government to select architecture and engineering firms (A/E) based on their competency, qualifications and experience rather than by price. Commonly called Qualifications-Based Selection (QBS), it follows a process for selecting the most highly qualified firm, *then* negotiating the fee based on the project scope, schedule, and budget.

The creative services of a team providing A/E design services cannot be fairly priced as a "hard bid" without first knowing the full scope of the project, and more importantly, the owner's wants and needs. Prior to 1972 low cost bids for professional design services resulted in poor service, poor quality, and a lack of creativity. Enter the Brooks Act, requiring that owners of public projects follow a Request for Qualifications (RFQ) process over a Request for Proposal (RFP) process that includes rates and fees.

The RFQ process allows design teams to put forward their qualifications in response to a synopsis provided by Federal agencies. The goal is to be determined the "most highly qualified" firm out of the packages submitted. Prior to 2004, A/E firms used two standard forms to demonstrate their qualifications - the SF254 and SF255. The SF330 is a revamped, streamlined version of the SF254 and SF255 forms.

For A/E firms, the SF330 is *the form* to submit enticing qualifications to Federal agencies, and often to state and local agencies. Often, when a synopsis is posted, contracting officers tag it as a "presolicitation" rather than a "solicitation."

In the Federal realm, a "solicitation" involves a price proposal and an SF330 does not. This is something to watch for when monitoring opportunities from the Federal government. Do not ignore an opportunity because it is represented as a "presolicitation." That very well could be the announcement for submitting your SF330 form.

The SF330 can be used for stand-alone design services contracts, such as a barracks design, or for indefinite delivery indefinite quantity (IDIQ) contracts for environmental restoration. When firms spend quality time developing their SF330 packages, they can really highlight the best of their team's qualifications; what makes them different and why the agency should choose their team.

Reviewing the Synopsis / Instructions / Specialized Criteria

Review the synopsis for the scope of work that will be executed under the contract and all of the details required in the SF330. The outline of the SF330 is built around the selection criteria - key personnel are planned, top projects determined, team members identified. Be thorough when reviewing, watch for sneaky requirements, such as adding a DUNS / SAMMI number in unusual locations; adding the percent of work each firm will perform to Section H; or adding percent self-performed to project sheets.

Make note of content constraints such as length of resumes, number of projects, length of Part I, or length / format of Section H, and font requirements. More RFQs are also asking for past performance questionnaires (PPQs) and contractor performance assessment reporting system (CPARS) ratings, or copies of licenses and registrations, or joint venture (JV) agreements. Make a note if these details are required and build that into the preparation process.

Outlining each section of the response, either in a matrix or directive, is key to making sure that the instructions are followed, and all criteria addressed. Oftentimes, firms start with a matrix of personnel and projects to sort and determine which are the strongest - against the selection criteria and which choices will build a solid Section G.

Even though pricing is not involved in a QBS, the synopsis might still have some items that need clarification. Each RFQ has a point of contact and often a deadline for questions. Take advantage of this opportunity to get clear on exactly what to submit and ask for more defined instructions on unclear sections.

An Overview of the SF330 Form

The SF330 form focuses on relationships between personnel submitted; the projects they worked on; relationships of the team proposing on the contract; their history of working together; and the individuals who will be working on the project.

The SF330 is designed to streamline the process for the industry, in order to put together the qualifications and for the government to review the qualifications. From the architecture and engineering (A/E) side, the SF330 response is highly involved and detailed. When effort is put into making the form as strong as it can be, the result is a compliant, easy to review response that the government can evaluate to determine qualification.

Part I of the SF330 form includes nine sections. Part II of the form is a one-page synopsis of your firm.

Section A–C – Contract Information, Point of Contact, Proposed Team. Sections A and B are very straightforward. Section A is information from the synopsis. Section B is the firm's point of contact for the response. This person will receive any questions and information about interviews or award.

Section C is the list of the Project Team. This section has a row for each firm and each office that will be participating on the contract. Section C crosswalks to the Part IIs – the SF330 must include a Part II for each row shown in Section C. That means each branch office must have a Part II. This section also cross walks to Section E – Resumes and Section F – Projects.

If a resume for a team member firm in the Sacramento, CA office is shown, then that office must be shown in Section C and a Part II must be included. If that same firm provided a resume for a person from their Chicago, IL office, that office must also be shown in Section C and must have a Part II.

Section D – Organization Chart. The organization chart is usually one page, often 8.5" x 11" and can be up to 11" x 17" (this is usually defined in the instructions, if not, check the Q&A). The organization chart should clearly show the disciplines required in the synopsis and show the personnel that have resumes in Section E. From time to time, additional names or roles may make sense to include here to demonstrate the depth of your team. Make this decision on a case by case basis.

Section E – Resumes. Submit resumes of key personnel by following the instructions in the synopsis. As a rule, resumes are one page each and include no more than five projects. *Tailor the resume to demonstrate the qualifications and experience of each person.* The instructions for this section are found in the Professional Qualifications Selection Criteria. Make sure the role shown on the resume aligns with the roles/disciplines outlined in the RFQ. Also, streamline the format of resumes so that all are consistent with one another.

Section F – Projects. Submit significant projects that align with the requirements in the synopsis and that showcase the team's experience performing work similar to the scope of work and the Specialized Experience and Technical Competence selection criteria.

Section G – Matrix. This matrix crosswalks the personnel submitted in Section E with the projects submitted in Section F. In theory, the reviewer can look at Section G and determine the relationships between the people and projects in the response. As an industry, we often think that Section G should be full of checkmarks for all relevant people and projects; but we know this is not always possible.

Luckily, government reviewers understand the nuances of the form and realize that an essential specialty consultant, such as an archaeologist on a Full-Service A/E indefinite delivery indefinite quantity (IDIQ) response might not have been used on one of the top 10 projects. So, government reviewers acknowledge that a gap in G for that role would be acceptable.

It is a similar situation with a person who only has one year of experience with the firm. They might not have worked on the most-relevant projects.

Section H – Additional Information. This is the section to address the Selection Criteria as outlined in the RFQ. For federal agencies this generally includes: Specialized Experience and Technical Competence; Professional Qualifications; Past Performance; Capacity; Knowledge of Locality; Small Business Participation; Geographic Proximity; and Volume of DoD Awards. It is tempting to start with boilerplate for some of these topics, but with page limits added to the response, boilerplate is not going to make the desired impact.

The Section H is the location in the SF330 where win-themes can be accentuated through highly detailed, precise, and concise content. Use this section to tell the government about your processes, successes, and the reasons why this team is the most highly qualified. Firms often do not have the luxury of presenting a five-page quality control program, nor do the reviewers want to read a five-page plan. Summarize it - What are the most important highlights of your plan? How can you demonstrate that it has worked successfully before? What makes your program stand out from others?

For the technical narratives required in Section H – Past Performance, Management, Quality, Experience, etc. – themes that are woven into each narrative should be developed specifically. What benefit will they get when they work with your firm? Is your management approach strong enough to execute the task orders they require? How have you proven your approach before? Is your specialized experience stronger than your competitors? Do all of your key personnel have advanced degrees? Bring these elements to the top of your narratives to demonstrate your unique expertise at the start of the section.

Section I – Signature block. Do not forget to sign and date the SF330 Part I Section I!

Part II – The part II form is required for each firm and office shown in Section C. It is a snapshot of each firm's personnel and experience. A best practice is to arrange the part IIs in the same order as shown in Section C so it is easy to correlate. Make sure each firm adds the solicitation number to the form and each one is signed and dated.

How are the SF330s Evaluated?

Most agencies follow a similar process for RFQ evaluations. The US Army published the Engineer Pamphlet EP 715-1-7 [18] which details their process for A/E contracting in just over 200 pages.

Generally, the process to select the "most highly qualified firm" starts with the Pre-Selection Board. Consider this the "go / no-go board." This is the agency's first line of reviewers. They are looking for compliance requirements such as, did the firm sign the Part I? do they have the key resumes requested? Did they exceed the maximum of 15 pages in Section H?

Once the packages are reviewed for the baseline criteria, they move to the Selection Board. Selection Boards are most often made up of professional employees with expertise and experience in the type of work being procured, including those who will work with the team after award.

For U.S. Army Corps of Engineers (USACE) review boards, all professional discipline reviewers are registered. These reviewers personally read every SF330 response and evaluate against the selection criteria in the synopsis. Firms with the highest aggregate qualifications are determined to be the most highly qualified. Other firms are ranked according to their aggregate qualifications and may be determined to be highly qualified, qualified or not qualified.

After the Selection Board determines the most highly qualified firms, interviews may be conducted with the top firms. Following interviews, the Board ranks the firms according to selection criteria and makes a recommendation for award.

---

[18] https://www.publications.usace.army.mil/Portals/76/Publications/EngineerPamphlets/EP_715-1-7.pdf

Agency Advice

Follow all instructions. Compliance with instructions is key to making it through the evaluation process. If asked for 10 resumes, give 10 resumes. Do not provide 11 - they will not review that last one. If asked for the date of graduation on resumes, add it even though the form does not require it. If asked for a quality control narrative, make sure to include it. When the synopsis includes a paragraph describing what elements (i.e., cost control, schedule control, subconsultant review process) something for each needs to be written into the narrative, in the order they appear, with subheadings to show the narratives are included.

Tell them your experience. Do not make reviewers assume you have experience with specific codes or processes. Write it out in the resume or project or in Section H. Be precise with your language and clearly demonstrate what your firm did and why it is relevant to the project / contract on which you are submitting.

Make it easy to find information. Put key information in a call out box, highlight keywords; help the reviewers find what they are looking for. Reviewers do not need a dissertation on the subconsultant management plan. They need to know how it works. If a firm has a management plan, it should be easily summarized in a paragraph or two (this is especially important when page count is restricted).

Eliminate fluff. Present what is asked for right up front. Do not hide requested narrative with marketing content. Focus on the selection criteria. This is what is important. Do not focus on what is important to your firm. Tailor resume bios to speak to why the person is the most highly qualified to be the project manager on this contract or the most highly qualified to be the commissioning agent. Tailor firm overviews from boilerplate to say why the firm is on the team. Highlight past working relationships or specialized experience. Remember, space is limited in the SF330 so make each word count.

Provide Proof Points. Develop narratives about how the team executes quality management or project management; knows the geography of the project location; provide examples of success to back up the claim. Where has the team successfully implemented the quality process described? What was the impact on that project?

Top Five Tips for Creating Your SF330 Form

(1) Location. Align subcontractor names and locations in SF330 Section C with the locations shown on the Section E and Section F or not including Part IIs for each of the office locations mentioned in C, E, and F.

#Protip

Crosswalk the firm names and locations in C against the locations for person's resume in E and each project the subcontractor worked on in F, THEN make sure each location that is included has a Part II.

---

(2) Relationships matter. *The SF330 is designed to demonstrate relationships among people and firms.* The Organization Chart in Section D is the first place to show the relationships among the proposed team and how they will work together. The Section G matrix shows past relationships working together. Match employees shown in Section E to the projects they worked on in Section F. At a glance, reviewers can see existing relationships.

#Protip

Arrange your personnel by role, not by firm, so the matrix population is mixed across the board, not by blocks for each firm.

---

(3) Use internal titles *not* roles in the solicitation. Don't use general terms for employee roles on resumes; for example, Project Manager instead of Electrical Engineer. The Role shown in box 13 should match the discipline asked for in the RFQ.

#Protip – use the exact roles from the solicitation for box 13 and repeat that role in the project descriptions on the resume and in Section G.

(4) Not following instructions for Section H. The RFQ is usually direct with the information required in Section H. This is generally found in the selection criteria. Make sure the synopsis doesn't have hidden requirements in other sections (things such as % involvement of each firm, DUNS / SAMMI numbers, points of contact, etc.). Find these items and populate your proposal directive with these details to make sure everything is where they want to find it!

---

(5) Quality Control Check. Build in time to print out the form and do a book check. Make sure the Part IIs are accounted for, make sure the project data is the same from resume to resume and project sheet to project sheet. Have a reviewer run through the document and check keywords to make sure you have included all the criteria.

---

*   *   *

As principal of the award-winning firm Andana Consulting, Carrie Ann Williams, CPSM, works with organizations to guide proposal development and create amazing marketing content.

She has worked with organizations to track, pursue, position, and propose on government solicitations - and private organizations. When not leading proposal strategy, she guides firms to develop lead marketing campaigns with clear goals and implementation plans.

Carrie Ann is known for leading interactive, insightful and actionable training workshops and presentations providing insight into marketing and business strategies for professional services firms. Her sessions have taken her across the country to train companies and organizations including local and national events for SAME, PSMJ, SMPS, AIA, and NVSBE.

A Certified Professional Services Marketer, Carrie Ann has an undergraduate degree in English Literature and a Master of Business Administration degree. Carrie Ann is also "Inbound Certified" and "Content Marketing Certified" from HubSpot. Find her at https://www.linkedin.com/in/carrieannwilliamscpsm/

Episode 24.
Lean Proposal Management

By Michele Atkinson

Principal, Cavalry Consulting

Finding and winning work from the government is not easy. It might feel a bit like learning a new language or learning to ski. The first attempt is awkward and uncomfortable, and it seems as if everyone else gets it, but you are struggling. For companies that are just entering this market, it is important that you open your mind and accept this uncomfortable situation. Everyone starts here.

Even companies with great commercial success start at the bottom in the public sector (unless you are Google, but that is a different topic). Like the star-athlete high school senior who graduates to become an invisible college freshman in a sea of experienced competitors, it can take a few years to find your momentum and shine the light on your special capabilities ... and that's when you will start to win contracts.

As you navigate this unfamiliar terrain, remember that you aren't the first to climb this mountain. The complexity can be so overwhelming at times that you will wonder if it is worth it, but perseverance pays off for those that are willing to stay the course. If you are reading this book, you are already ahead of the curve.

In this episode, you will learn about responding to RFPs and why there is no one-size-fits-all approach to finding success in the federal market.

Traditional Proposal Management

Traditional proposal management is often touted as an approach that requires lengthy and expensive training and ties up a dozen or more people. Significant time and energy is required to identify upcoming opportunities (forecasting). Meeting after meeting is scheduled to identify win themes, evaluate the strengths and weaknesses of your competitors; identify locations for graphics and tables... and all of this before a potential opportunity is even a strong "Go."

As you can imagine, the traditional approach to proposal management is expensive. This type of strategy may make sense for extremely large companies, but it is not efficient or cost-effective for most small firms. Smaller firms have fewer resources and proposal planning and preparation is often delegated to just a handful of people.

The New Alternative

Lean proposal management is not yet an industry-standard, but I guarantee it will be soon. This is a methodology that we use with outstanding results at my firm, Cavalry Consulting. For our team, we implemented Lean Thinking in proposals out of sheer necessity. Our clients are primarily small businesses and they just don't have the luxury of million-dollar business development budgets and 50-person proposal teams like the top 10 defense contractors do. They need winning proposals without all of the hoopla.

As consultants on billable time, we need to deliver the highest quality proposals that bring the most value to our clients and their government customers with the least amount of waste. We were essentially writing the "lean proposals" playbook as we grew the business - which is a large reason for the incredible success seen by our clients over the past four years.

In a world where Lean Processes have revolutionized industries, there is no doubt that eliminating waste in business processes can have a major impact on the bottom line. Consider the competitive nature of government contracts, where multi-million-dollar bids can be won or lost by a margin of only a few thousand dollars. In this scenario, there is no room for waste or error in the proposal.

For this reason, I've always wondered why so many companies are convinced they need the most complex proposal development process. I call this "process for the sake of process," with waste built in at every step of the way. Perhaps it is just an "if it ain't broke don't fix it" methodology that is ripe for disruption.

One thing I am sure about is that lean processes are taking over the way we respond to government RFPs and adding more value with fewer resources. Small businesses have a great advantage here. Small companies have more agility in decision-making and execution. Small companies are able to achieve the full benefits of lean proposals very quickly.

What is Lean?

While there is no single definition of Lean, this one sums it up pretty well in the way that we are using it:

Lean
The core idea is to maximize customer value while minimizing waste. Simply, lean means creating more value for customers with fewer resources." - *lean.org*

When looking at proposal development, it is important to distinguish that "Lean" is not the same as "efficient."

Efficiency means maximum productivity with minimum waste, which appears very similar on the surface. However, *efficiency* only refers to activities and movement, where *lean* digs into desired outcomes (quality and value). This is at the true heart of proposal management.

Lean means eliminating waste from your process to deliver the *highest value to your customer* and the *best quality in your final product*. Instead of simply being faster, it is about using your limited time and resources on the actions that will resonate with evaluators. It means standardizing and automating work that is repeatable to allow more time to hone in on the evaluation criteria and delight your audience.

Fundamental Features of Lean

1. Create Value from the Customer Perspective. This is the most important part of your proposal. To win a proposal, you must show your customer that you understand their needs and their goals. You must show them that you are a company that brings them value. Don't tell them how great you are. Rather, focus on the benefits they get from hiring you.

Hint
Common feedback I hear from contracting officers is that most small businesses get this part wrong (which is a great opportunity to stand above the pack!)

There are Two Types of Value:

- Content (what you say); and
- Process (how you say it)

For **Content**, the words you write in your proposal are just as important as any process that you have in place. You need to create clear communication channels to ensure that the writer has all of the information available without any bottlenecks to slow them down.

Ask yourself - What is valuable to your customer?

- The RFP will tell you what is valuable to them. The evaluation criteria likely tells you what is most valuable to them, and in the order of importance. Use this information to show them you are listening.
- Eliminate extra steps in this process by creating a proposal outline directly from the RFP (example included).

Ask yourself - Who are your customers?

- Who are they as an agency? What is the mission that they wish to accomplish?
- Who are they as individuals? What are their wishes, needs, and desires? Consider the reporting structure in their organization.
- How can you relate to them in a way that shows you are trustworthy, easy to get along with, and low-risk?

For Process, these are the activities that are considered "value" in your process.

- Work that is done correctly the first time
- Work that actually transforms the proposal
- Documents that contain correct information
- Information that meets/exceeds requirements
- Clear and understandable writing

Example of a Lean Proposal Outline

Using the RFP instructions and evaluation criteria below, I created an outline for a proposal that is fully compliant and error-free. It eliminates several extra steps in the process and ensures that every requirement is addressed in the document. To focus on value in your proposal process, consider the following approach.

Solicitation:
Instructions to Offerors (Factor 1 excerpt):

The offeror shall submit a narrative (maximum of three (3) pages) that describes the offeror's technical approach and management plan for the project demonstrating an acceptable understanding of job responsibilities and requirements, and strategy for completing the design and construction within the project limits – in accordance with the scope of work for this project.

Narrative shall include name of design subcontractor, and discuss method for demolition and disposal of existing roof membrane and insulation, recommendation of roofing membrane material, material transport to/from roof level, construction plan, historical building requirements, specialized equipment required, staging of equipment, and proper phasing of the project. Environmental protection due to the close proximity of the Sea Harbor and Cold Creek, must be included.

Narrative must include product information for products that will be used for this project. Manufacturer product information is to be included as attachment to narrative. Narrative is to describe why product(s) being used is the best product(s) for this project's requirements.

Narrative shall describe safety signage and barricades for pedestrian and vehicle traffic and address Federal Building tenant comfort. This narrative must include trades for subcontractors that will be working on this project.

227

Evaluation Criteria (Factor 1 excerpt)

Factor 1 – Proposed plan for replacement of the USA Federal Buildings' Roof(s). This factor considers the offeror's technical approach for completion of the project.

Factor 1 – Proposed Plan [3 pages max]

1.1 Technical Approach and Management Plan

1.1.1 Design Subcontractor: [NAME]

Add text: Introduce company and the value they add.

1.1.2 Method for Demolition and Disposal of Existing Roof Membrane and Insulation

Add text: demonstrate understanding of job responsibilities and requirements.

1.1.3 Recommendation of Roofing Membrane Material

Add text: strategy for completing the design and construction within the project limits in accordance with the SOW.

1.1.4 Material Transport To/From Roof Level

Add text: strategy for completing the design and construction within the project limits in accordance with the SOW, demonstrate understanding of job responsibilities and requirements.

1.1.5 Construction Plan

Add text: strategy for completing the design and construction within the project limits in accordance with the SOW.

1.1.6 Historical Building Requirements

Add text: demonstrate understanding of job responsibilities and requirements.

1.1.7 Specialized Equipment Required

Add text: demonstrate understanding of job responsibilities and requirements.

1.1.8 Staging of Equipment

Add text: demonstrate understanding of job responsibilities and requirements.

1.1.9 Proper Phasing of the Project

Add text: strategy for completing the design and construction within the project limits in accordance with the SOW, demonstrate understanding of job responsibilities and requirements.

1.1.10 Environmental Protection

Add text: Describe environmental protection due to the close proximity of the Sea Harbor and Cold Creek, demonstrate understanding of job responsibilities and requirements.

1.2 Product Information

Include product information for products that will be used for this project.

Describe why product(s) being used is best product(s) for this project's requirements.

[Attach] manufacturer product information.

1.3 Safety Signage and Barricades

Describe safety signage and barricades for pedestrian and vehicle traffic and address Federal Building tenant comfort.

Include trades for subcontractors that will be working on this project.

Reduce Waste

If Lean is known for anything, it is reducing waste. Waste is anything that doesn't add value to your customers or your company. Waste is motion, defects, waiting, extra processing, transferring information from one place to another, double-checking, re-entering data, searching for documents, and under-utilized creativity. Think about it - defects create rework, reinspection, increased cost, and stressed out employees. Efficiency without quality equals defects, rework, and more hassle in the end.

Waste, in a proposal management sense, occurs at every stage during proposal preparation. Every time a writer has to go back and look up a piece of information a second or third time, time is wasted.

It is very likely that half of your current proposal process is dedicated to waste.

If a step in your process isn't creating value (from the customer's perspective), *get rid of it*. As proposal experts, we look at proposals from our customers' perspectives so we don't waste time doing things they don't care about.

How to Reduce Waste

One way to reduce waste is for proposal writers to become Subject Matter Experts (SMEs). For example, if we are writing about heavy civil construction, it is very valuable if we know the difference between cast-in-place and precast concrete. These are not just different words on a page. They have entirely different meanings and require the selection of a different project to show relevance. A detail like this can be the determining factor that wins or loses an award, especially if several companies have submitted proposals that could arguably be considered the best.

To become an SME, proposal writers (whether hired as consultants or in-house) should visit job sites, spend time asking questions of project managers, learn to read specifications, and research the industry.

A final note on reducing waste is to be mindful with assignments. It is often not productive to have two people doing the same thing. For example, proposal review can become a nightmare when multiple reviewers become involved at different times. We have often experienced this situation where a reviewer edits a draft that has become obsolete. This becomes an exercise in mental gymnastics! The way we avoid this is by providing clear instructions to a small, carefully selected group. We make sure these individuals understand the need to respect the assignment and the deadline.

Build Quality into the Process

"We need to be more proactive and less reactive." Have you ever heard someone in your organization say this before?

Working on a proposal right up until the deadline or receiving edits from team member's days past their deadline is the exact opposite. Preparing quality proposals from the start is the proactive way to write and it can literally prevent disaster in the end (we've all been there!). But guess what? Proactive thinking and quality don't happen naturally.

The standard way of thinking is that we build in several rounds of proposal reviews to the schedule. Everyone reads over the drafts and then provides insightful comments during a meeting. Those comments add value to the overall proposal and the effort continues forward on schedule. In reality, many of the team members are busy with billable work or travel and show up to the meeting without having even read the proposal in advance. The meeting goes on, with a few attendees carrying the conversation for the entire group and the review is delayed another day. Slowly, revisions trickle in from team members, and now the proposal manager has to sort through 10 different documents and combine all of the edits.

With built-in quality, each contributor takes ownership of *their part of the proposal*. The process enables them to do the work without errors. This means their templates are good. The software has the right data. They can reach data sources when needed). Inspections (reviews) are not relied on to correct errors. Stop when you find a mistake and fix it right then. Leaders need to provide the equipment, tools, and training so the team can make "defect-free" proposals.

Error Proofing

We use Contract Cloud to detect and prevent errors in our proposal processes with the goal of achieving zero defects. We also use it to search for past projects and know what is relevant, immediately. Contract Cloud eliminates the wasted weeks of preparing a proposal only to find out at the last minute that the company wasn't even qualified.

Automation and Standardized Work

Significant time savings occur by using automation for tasks that are consistently repeated. As an example, a template that includes standard items with built-in macros and styles can reduce document preparation by at least half. And when familiar with the template, all users across the organization will realize similar time savings. We have done this at our own firm and created Standard Operating Procedures that are conducted whenever a proposal is assigned to us. Preparing the compliance matrix,

231

assigning responsibilities and timelines, selecting projects and personnel … all of these tasks fall into place quickly because of our use of such templates.

By documenting our procedures, we are able to consistently apply best practices while remaining agile to the changing nature of each individual proposal. Rather than using a rigid multi-step process, we maintain the flexibility to adapt. For instance, one of the key measurements in Lean is time.

We have mapped out our standard 30-day schedule for a typical government proposal, with each proposal activity that must occur within that timeframe and its correlated place in the workflow. This includes the very first activities (update proposal software with relevant data, prepare compliance matrix, set dates for meetings, etc.) to the very last activities (Ship/hand-deliver proposals, confirm delivery, upload final drafts to proposal software and add final notes).

Using this framework, we can update the proposal schedule with the actual deadline and the number of days that we have to prepare the proposal. The dates automatically populate based on the inputs and we don't have to spend several hours working up a schedule or making decisions before getting started. *This is especially useful in eliminating waste when your team needs to consider the available resources before making a Go/No Go decision.*

If you are interested in viewing our schedule, it is available for download at <u>cavalryconsulting.com/proposalschedule</u>. Our own master schedule is a living document, so it may be revised from time to time. I recommend you consider it a template, then update it to match your own internal processes and best practices.

* * *

Michele Atkinson, CF APMP, is the founder and President of Cavalry Consulting, Inc. She formed the company with her own core values of integrity, quality, and transparency as the foundation of the business. Michele has been perfecting the art of federal proposal writing for over a decade, working closely with executives and subject matter experts to capture their unique advantages in captivating and winning proposals. Since launching Cavalry Consulting in 2016, her expertise in government contracting and proposal development has resulted in over $20 Billion in awards and earned the company dozens of repeat clients. Michele is well versed in the SBA regulations for small business set-aside contracting and is actively involved in the defense acquisition community, where she enthusiastically contributes industry perspective to enhance national security innovation. Find her at https://www.linkedin.com/in/michele-atkinson-45700936/

Episode 25.
Collaboration in the Competitive World of Proposals

By Jay McConville and Cheryl Smith

President, Privia and Head of Marketing, Privia

Crafting a winning proposal is an expensive and time-consuming process. There are experts to wrangle, tasks to assign, and schedules to monitor. There is content to find, write, and tailor to the capture strategy. There are review cycles to referee, version control to worry about, and a relentless commitment to compliance and quality required.

Yet, there is no doubt that the ability to present a cogent, compliant, and motivating proposal is key to every company's success. If you can harness the collaborative energy and enterprise knowledge of your organization, you can win and grow. Thankfully, there are many strategies that can make winning a reality.

What is required is that your process be collaborative - that it maximize the *Intersection* and *Interplay* that occurs among your business development, capture, and proposal teams.

Back in the day, businesses coordinated proposals through the mail or in person. Agencies would snail mail a list of questions to a list of suppliers and weeks later they would receive a box full of binders with answers. In between, there were typists and typewriters, mimeograph machines and printers. There were "war rooms," "wall walks," and team review trips that cost thousands of dollars in airfare, hotels, and meals. All of this was shepherded towards completion with a lot of late nights and last-minute sprints by some pretty darn resilient proposal people.

The internet, personal computer, and email-type applications revolutionized the way we work proposals - making it much faster in putting one together. No longer did everyone have to be in the same office (or "war room") and documents could be shared among the team first by email and shared folders, and later within on-line data repositories.

(Mostly) gone were the days of hardcopy proposals and large "proposal production" operations as more organizations moved toward electronic submission. But with all of this new and revolutionary technology came a new set of unique challenges. These included data overload, lack of team understanding and "mind-share," loss of executive visibility into the process and solution, and task and version control issues.

From its rather humble beginnings to today's crowded arena, what we call the "capture and proposal management process" has certainly come a long way. But like any complex, multi-participant operation, the proposal process must keep pace and evolve as needs, culture, and technology change.

Today's proposal professionals are digital natives - they expect to be able to harness technology to be successful.

- **Digital natives are social, multi-tasking, intuitive learners.** To multitask efficiently they need tools to help them stay organized.
- **Digital natives will not waste time.** Organizations that provide instant access to content will achieve better quality proposals; written faster with more time for reviewers to improve.
- **Digital natives expect to work together anytime, anywhere.** This increased collaboration means experts are in greater lock-step with business development, and reviewers are more in step with expert writers.

Whether your process is home-grown, off-the-shelf, or a combination of the two, one thing is clear: people do not work like they did twenty years ago. The proposal process you choose needs to reflect this new way of working. To win efficiently means giving your teams an easy and secure way to collaborate online and an effective feedback loop so they can focus on the quality work-product craved by today's evaluators.

The Association of Proposal Management Professionals (APMP), the worldwide authority for professionals dedicated to the process of winning business through proposals, echoed this in their recent U.S. Bid & Proposal Industry Benchmark Report[19] - Executive Summary:

"Finding Two: Most organizations have structured and documented fundamental processes in place for business development, including: a dedicated proposal team, established business best practices, and a system of gate reviews for decision-making on proposal bids." - APMP

In other words, your competition is using a "structured and documented" fundamental process to bid new work... and so should you. How you do that in today's environment is what will give you the edge over your competition.

We'll breakdown some of APMP's findings below and explore action items for the next evolution of capture and proposal management.

1. Collaboration and the Gate Review Process

According to APMP, 56% of companies use a gate review process for qualifying bids and executive decision-making.

Qualifying bid opportunities for your team is critical. Putting a proposal together is an investment, so before you go too far down that path, you need to know if the opportunity is the right fit. A gate review process, where key questions are answered in an iterative fashion in order to decide whether to move to the next step in your process, helps you answer those

er is asking for? Is there a relationship known? Is the RFP written and hard-
help your team "face the facts" so

when qualifying a bid and it often t information together. Hence, a

s (APMP), U.S. Bid & Proposal Industry utive   Summary,   (2019) 970763 "collaborative" gate process is best for achieving a more impactful decision and for sharing the results with your proposal team.

We like to think of this step as the *Intersection*: where gate review information is packaged and presented as the capture strategy to the proposal team. Some have called this transition a "hand-off." We disagree with that characterization. Experience shows that if this transition is not collaborative, allowing time for questions and discussions, the resulting work product will be out of alignment with the capture strategy. It will be lacking in information and context which leads to inefficient review meetings. This will then force additional revision cycles.

How do you achieve effective Intersection?

Your on-the-go executives, geographically distributed workforce, and remote working teams may be critical for your expanding business, but they bring some complexity to the collaborative nature of "Intersection." Remote work is rising rapidly, grabbing an ever-increasing share of the workforce.

"Between 2010 and 2017, 16 percent of all white-collar jobs added to the economy were filled by workers working primarily from home."[20] The rising trend in remote workers means organizations are probably relying on email to communicate and come to consensus. As much as an email is considered a "killer app," it is not well suited to this function, causing confusion, frustration, and delays.

There are two simple changes you can make to achieve successful intersection. The key is to begin early in your sales cycle.

Centralize Content

By centralizing gate review documents in an on-line, "virtual" workspace accessed across your secure network, you consolidate all of the resources your executive team requires to make a bid decision quickly. Using a centralized framework means bid documents exist in one "place"

---

[20] The Conference Board; "Teleworking Continues to Expand," https://www.conference-board.org/blog/postdetail.cfm?post=6995; Gad Levanon and Frank Steemers, March 11, 2019

and everyone comes to that place to work on them. Gone are the version control issues.

The benefits of this strategy go far beyond version control. By establishing this framework, you provide 24-hour access to information and team "mind share." You eliminate missed emails, accessing the wrong documents, and losing details. A centralized framework also provides the opportunity for process workflow (see below) for a more controllable and repeatable business rhythm and process.

Centralize Discussion

Years ago, coffee and donuts were enough to entice the team into the big conference room. Today, you're lucky if you can get them all on the same conference call. If you are process savvy, you'll give your decision team the tools they need to collaborate in real-time; i.e. a robust digital environment where they can access materials, review, create discussion threads, comment, come to consensus, and come to the gate review meeting informed and ready to go. You will get to the bid decision faster and you will capture the details you need for the proposal win strategy.

A more seamless intersection of capture and proposal team during the gate review process will deliver a more quality first draft and ease reviewer frustration.

Tip
*Sometimes it's not just where but when your team works.
Centralizing your gate reviews and capture strategy
development with secure 24/7 access will ensure all questions,
and answers, are captured and immediately available to the
rest of the team.*

---

2. There are Lessons to be Learned from the Revision Process

"Access to resources for proposal development is strong, yet many of these tools are not user-ready and require many revisions or are not actively maintained." - APMP

239

We've seen it before. You've identified the challenges and the goals, the win themes and the discriminators, the competition and the experience. You've scoped a winning solution and assembled the right team. From a business development perspective, your capture strategy is a slam-dunk.

The problem is that customers don't read capture strategies. Customers read proposals. Your proposal team may take over, but if you're hoping to "hand off" and walk away and expect a quality proposal, *you're not positioning your organization for the win*. This is because the bid decision and the decision gates leading up to that decision are just steps in a much larger process. You have to keep the information flowing between your capture and proposal team right up until you sign-off on the final document.

We like to think of this step as the *Interplay*. Interplay is where professionals with the deep, long-developed knowledge of the customer and opportunity are working hand-in-hand with those tasked in writing the proposal.

How do you achieve effective interplay?

Writing a proposal from a blank page is daunting. Having easy access to a knowledge base of reusable questions and answers can jump start the process. While this approach is an obvious time-saver, it does come with some risks. For example, establishing the knowledge-base can be time-consuming. Once the knowledge base is live, most organizations realize they must assign a dedicated content administrator to keep the content current. They have to ensure incorrect information doesn't find its way into a submitted proposal. All of this has to be done while continuously back-filling the knowledge-base to address new question gaps.

Too many companies think they can just "push a button" to answer questions automatically from the knowledge-base and that they'll have a winning proposal. As you probably guessed, this is rarely true. The crucial next step in the proposal process picks up where "canned content" falls short; when the knowledge-base is lacking or when more than canned answers are required. When the knowledge-base doesn't deliver, the organization must turn to their team of experts.

Leverage Expertise

So, let's pick up where the knowledge-base left off. You have some of the answers to the questions and now you need to tap into the team to fill the gaps, correct the inaccuracies, meet compliance, tailor, and prepare for review.

In the past - before the age of the internet, teams would meet-up in-house, in a conference room and everything was done on paper. The process was time-consuming and painful.

Today, online proposal management collaboration tools help organizations leverage the team "mind share," avoid miscommunication, and get the writing job done right the first time. By centralizing proposal development, experts discuss details together online and capture the results for reuse. By centralizing their assignments, experts notify other experts for guidance. Communication is more content-centric, more efficient, and targeted. Best of all, by using these collaboration tools, you can reach everyone in your organization exactly when you need them, leveraging their expertise more efficiently for the task at hand.

Expect More from Reviews

Your review team is your gate keeper. They provide feedback on where the team may have blinded themselves to certain compliance issues and solution or strategy weaknesses. Getting them to read takes organization. Engaging them takes quality. Leveraging them takes an effective feedback loop.

Many review teams are merely handed a document. Comments are often hand-written and it is common for critical input to be lost in translation. Things are easier with email and "track changes," but the serial nature of this review process brings significant new challenges, such as miscommunication, disagreement, and serious synchronization and version control issues.

It would kill most executives to know how many review comments are never addressed. In the old days we scribbled them in the margins or on a comment capture sheet. They were mostly useless and many went in the "round file." Today, the proposal team is often overwhelmed by electronically submitted comments. With no way to handle them in a centralized manner, many comments make it to the modern version of the round file, the recycle bin.

A better strategy is to give the team and reviewers an efficient feedback loop; real-time collaboration that builds off differing perspectives and advances proposal quality without messing up your content. Version control is enhanced as the comments live within each document version. There is no serial process pain caused by "sending the documents around" as the documents live in the virtual space, accessible to all.

Furthermore, a collaborative feedback loop can help you better define your review process by guiding participants on their responsibilities. For example, a template should tell reviewers (especially in the early reviews), what is required in each section and what the Win Themes are for that section. They can check to see if themes are coming through, and if they're not…well, you've got yourself a useful comment that won't get lost in the shuffle.

A more seamless interplay of capture and proposal teams will deliver the quality that reviewers expect. You'll avoid endless revision cycles and create greater opportunity for innovation.

Tip

When reviewers review in one centralized place, proposal managers and coordinators skip the "merge" step—buying the writers more time to focus on quality.

---

3. When the Process Works for You (It Works)

"Eight-in-ten say that the process their organization follows for proposal management is working very (23%) or somewhat well (59%)" - APMP

We wrote earlier about receiving RFPs by mail. If you were writing proposals prior to about 20 years ago, you know what we're talking about. RFPs arrived in the mail and there were a lot of typewriters click-clacking. But growing procurement complexity and quantity created a perfect storm of chaos. Enter the standardized proposal management process.

Having a process in place became critical. It got everyone on the same page about the strategy, the tasks, and the deadlines. However, too much process quickly caused a backlash. Teams felt the process was overcomplicated and stifled innovation. Some felt micromanaged and morale suffered.

To fix this many organizations have tried to improve their processes by making them more comprehensive; only to discover the process takes so much nurturing that there is less time for proposal work. Process is key. Without it chaos and poor quality will reign. That said, a process not followed because it is too bureaucratic or onerous is worse than no process at all.

Somewhere along the way, we lost sight of the process goal - a quality, winning proposal. We tried to replace the art of writing a winning proposal with the mechanics of the proposal process. And it just doesn't work.

How do you get the process to work for you?

Implement Workflow

Computers do a lot of things better than humans. They don't, however, do everything better. Smart organizations let humans do what they do best. This strategy applies to the proposal process as well. Let the Proposal Management Software provide the workflow; schedule events, give automatic notifications, enforce deadlines, etc. so that your process moves forward. Let the people create, write, review, and innovate.

Automated proposal workflow doesn't mean the proposal writes itself. It means the computer handles those things best handled by software and humans handle those things best handled by humans.

Automate Communication

Don't let outdated serial communication strategies, like email and voicemail, hijack your proposal schedule. Automate regular communications and keep your team automatically in sync. With fewer communication tasks on your plate, you'll actually have time to get your proposal assignments done. Using workflow notifications, you can alert your team when the proposal is launched, send them their tasks (with instructions), give them access to what they need, and schedule meetings. You can pass tasks among the team after they are reported complete, and so much more.

Get Real-time Status

Is your team working? Have they completed their tasks? The process may help guide your team through milestones, but without a real-time status, you cannot guide them through the bottlenecks that become delays. Use your workflow software to track real-time status and know when your team is working and when they are done.

Tip

Make sure your proposal management process is keeping pace with your needs. Have the ability to analyze process performance, as well as real-time status, and infuse effective improvements into your Lessons-Learned.

Conclusion

Developing a proposal is no easy task. Developing the type of quality proposal that evaluators want to read (not just skim) is downright daunting. It takes a team to define and write *to* strategy and to clearly and concisely demonstrate the benefits of your solution over the competition.

It takes a team to pull it all together, ensure compliance, and present your bid in the best light. It takes a specifically-designed capture and proposal management solution to support the team no matter where or when they work.

Most organizations have defined and documented a fundamental capture and proposal management process. Industry and workforce changes continue to drive the demand for greater efficiency, visibility, and accountability. Organizations that leverage proposal-specific collaboration tools will find it easier to master the intersection, interplay, and evolving standardized process necessary to save time and focus on quality. Organizations who leverage collaboration technology and the benefits of the modern online workforce will win. Those who do not, will not.

Jay and Cheryl are part of the Privia team, "the Proposal Company™," working with clients to provide the best software environment for proposal development possible. Jay is the CEO and Cheryl is the head of Privia Marketing. Each has decades of experience as proposal contributors and managers. Both love to help companies achieve maximum success through the application of tailored technologies to the proposal process.

Jay has twenty-five years of business development, capture management, proposal development, proposal management, and executive experience in the federal government contracting market. Cheryl has twenty years of proposal management, knowledge management, and orals coaching experience in the public sector market. With Privia they are able to increase their output, quality, and efficiency, giving them continued motivation to spread the word about the benefits of content collaboration and proposal management systems.

Find Jay at https://www.linkedin.com/in/jay-mcconville-414b144/

Find Cheryl at https://www.linkedin.com/in/cheryl-smith-1088915/

Episode 26.
Solving the Cyber Security Talent Shortage

By Kathleen Smith

CMO, CyberSecJobs.com and ClearedJobs.net

While cyber security job search and recruitment are challenging undertakings, we often point to the talent shortage in the community as the sole culprit. The state of the industry plays a part in the grand scheme of things, but it's not the only obstacle employers and job seekers face. There are underlying issues hindering the process that merit a deeper conversation, to examine how employers recruit and how candidates search for jobs.

As we begin exploring cyber security job search and recruitment, we can't overlook the current state of the workforce. Through six years of tracking and examination, data shows that "for each cyber security opening, there was a pool of only 2.3 employed cyber security workers for employers to recruit." In comparison, "there are 5.8 employed workers per job opening across the economy in general."[21]

While we have seen an influx of graduates from cyber security higher education programs in recent years, the increases haven't kept up with the growing rate of the market. In fact, cyber job postings have grown 94% since 2013. For reference, cyber security job postings have increased more than three times faster than all IT positions and they typically take longer to fill.

---

[21] "Recruiting Watchers for the Virtual Walls: The State of Cybersecurity Hiring" by Burning Glass Technologies - https://www.burning-glass.com/research-project/cybersecurity/

Many employers find it difficult, time consuming, and costly to hire cyber talent. However, we can't conclude that these hiring struggles are exclusively caused by an imbalanced supply and demand.

The Root of the Problem

CyberSecJobs.com, assisted by The Diana Initiative and Mental Health Hackers, conducted a survey among information security and cyber security professionals and students to better understand the challenges that job seekers face finding a job. When asked if they know how to find a job, 45% responded no.[22]

Though it's easy to assume it's a job seekers' market, numerous professionals in the industry continue to have trouble getting a job because they don't know how to find one. Furthermore, 30% noted they were only passively looking for a job. These findings further amplify the challenges that employers face as they attempt to recruit professionals in our communities.

Talent shortage aside, we have a multilayered problem that affects those on both sides of the process. Ultimately, we need to educate both the people looking for jobs and the recruiters looking to hire them. Through a little strategy and shared understanding, employers and job seekers alike stand to mutually benefit - and successfully hire and get hired.

Navigating Job Search and Career Growth

Career Mapping

So, what can job seekers do to improve their standing in the fight for employment? Most importantly, you must take responsibility for your own career. There isn't a certifications course that teaches you how to plan your career or become an expert job seeker overnight. It's up to you to ensure you take the necessary steps to position yourself for the best outcome. Job search is not a task that can be successfully accomplished haphazardly, as

---

[22] "It's Not as Easy as You Think – Cyber Security Job Search and Recruiting" by CyberSecJob.com - https://www.slideshare.net/CyberSecJobs/cyber-security-job-search-and-recruiting

it's often referred to as a full-time job in itself. It requires self-motivation, introspection, and strategic planning.

The first step of an effective job search is determining what you want to do. This involves planning the next steps of your career and doing some industry research to find out what skills you need to grow and acquire. Getting involved in your professional community is a great way to gain a new perspective, learn new skills, and try things out that you may be interested in. You'll be surprised by how much insight you can walk away with after attending or helping out with a professional event in the cyber security community. As you acquire more industry knowledge and experiences, this will help you map your career path and determine your long-term goals.

Networking

Once you've planned what you want to do, the 'search' in job search really comes into play. CyberSecJobs.com's job search survey found that the most common ways that job seekers search for jobs include networking, social media, referrals, and job boards. You can always check for listed positions on social media, job boards, and company websites on your own. However, your network will greatly expand your prospects; revealing the hidden job market and increasing your chances for those sought after referrals.

Volunteering in your professional community offers vast opportunities for building an expanded industry network. Consider volunteering, presenting, and competing at local or regional cyber security conferences and events to meet face-to-face with other security professionals and employers. This is vital to continuous job search success. 79% of survey respondents reported the most common way they find jobs is by asking their network of friends.

In another survey, CyberSecJobs.com, assisted by a network of security conferences including Security BSides (a global network of hacker cons), HackInParis and HackWestCon, examined industry professionals who spend time volunteering at cyber security conferences and other activities in the cyber security community. This survey found that 95% of respondents believe volunteering improves networking and social skills - both invaluable assets to an effective job search.

While we all call upon our network of contacts for recommendations on restaurants and vacation destinations, why not also benefit from having a network of recruiters to help recommend jobs? As you progress through your career, be sure to develop a list of recruiters to keep in touch with. They might not have the right fit for you now, but if you build the relationship, they may have another recommendation, or reach back out in the future with the perfect position.

Professional Development

There's truth to the saying 'it's all about who you know,' as an expanded industry network will improve your odds of gainful employment. But we can't rely solely on our network to bring all of our goals to fruition. Though career progression is typically seen as education, certification, and job moves, we need to build both technical and non-technical skills in different environments to continually advance. This is increasingly important as LinkedIn's 2019 Global Talent Trends Report found that 92% of talent professionals agree that soft skills matter as much as hard skills, if not more.[23]

Without specific tasks, it's difficult to build the soft skills employers seek and we don't always have opportunities to build these effectively in our day jobs. New challenges give us opportunities to learn and volunteering in your professional community offers a leading venue to build these vital skills. The most reported skills that respondents say they take away from volunteering include teamwork, organizing, planning, and communication.

Participating in Capture the Flag (CTF) competitions is another resource you can use to build skills. This is especially valuable if you are new to your field and lacking formal work experience to list on your resume. They provide an opportunity to practice technical skills, to network, and to obtain work experience.

After each competition or volunteer experience, take time to reflect and jot down the challenges you faced, what you might have failed at and also where you were successful. Be sure to outline your competition or volunteer work and responsibilities on your resume and social media profiles. In your

---

[23] 2019 Global Talent Trends Report by LinkedIn Talent Solutions - https://business.linkedin.com/talent-solutions/blog/trends-and-research/2019/global-recruiting-trends-2019

interviews, include key opportunities where you learned a new valuable skill that makes you perfect for the job.

As you can see, being active in your professional community has become a must have benefit for cyber security job seekers. When leveraged through a career development lens, professionals stand to reap numerous benefits through volunteering. Spending just a few hours a month volunteering provides personal fulfillment and opportunity; e.g. learning new skills, building an industry network, and even finding a new job.

As you navigate your job search remember to continually build your network and actively pursue multiple avenues to find the best opportunities. Contribute to projects that fuel your career trajectory and make you a more desirable candidate. Develop qualities such as leadership, time management, delegation, and problem solving. Continue learning and developing both hard and soft skills and keep abreast of developments in your profession. If your search doesn't pan out immediately, stay diligent and don't be discouraged. You want to evaluate, refine, and improve your technique until you reach success.

Recruiting and Retaining Top Talent

Finding Prospects

On the other side of the equation, we have employers and recruiters racing to hire top talent. Understandably, recruiting in the cyber security community (and most other industries) comes with its fair share of challenges. At the end of the day, people hire people. They must be able to find one another to take the first steps, whether that be through a job board, job fair, referral, or some other means. Knowing where tech talent searches for jobs and where they network will allow your organization to be present in the right place at the right time.

Being active in the community is a great way to reach those coveted prospects. Local and regional events attract the talent you're searching for and brings them all together in one easily accessible place.

Being active in the community does not require sponsoring large commercial conferences. Instead, tap into the large network of volunteer conferences and meet-ups. Most conferences and programs in the cyber security community are completely volunteer run. As we discussed, volunteers form an attractive talent pool of top tier candidates with valuable skillsets. Furthermore, many job seekers look into companies they already know about to find jobs. Thus, being present at industry events and conferences will help you find the talent you seek and also boost your visibility among potential candidates.

Leveraging Support

If you are looking for an effective way to retain your employees and recruit great talent, re-examine your support of volunteer activities and volunteer organizations. Savvy employers understand their employees can build valuable skills through volunteer work and skilled employees are vital to the continued success of any company. Having your employees volunteer in the community reflects well on your organization and builds your employer brand.

CyberSecJobs.com's volunteer survey found that nearly 60% of respondents stay with their current employer because they support their volunteerism in the community. Employer support is vital to these individuals and it can be the determining factor when considering possible career moves… as over 97% stated they would move to a company that supported their volunteer efforts.[24]

So how can you lend support to encourage retention? The most prevalent employer support, at 62.3%, is in the form of paid time off. Employers that offer this kind of support become immediately more attractive to active community volunteers, as many typically use their allotted personal PTO days for volunteer purposes instead of rest and relaxation. With busy work and family schedules, volunteering can bring added stress to participants, but they do so nonetheless because the benefits and the added sense of fulfillment make it worth it.

Add a dash of employer support to the mix and you have volunteers operating in the community *who serve as your brand ambassadors*. Thus, offering your support for volunteer pursuits can affect the outcome of recruiting your top candidate and keeping them on board.

---

[24] "Volunteering Impacts Your Cyber Security Career" by CyberSecJobs.com - https://www.slideshare.net/CyberSecJobs/cyber-security-community-volunteering-survey-results-2018

In addition to providing paid time off for volunteering, find out more about your existing employees' volunteer activities. Which activities and events do they attend or support? You might consider sponsoring these events. You can also provide support to employees who want to submit proposals to speak at conferences by assisting with the Call for Proposals process or helping to create a slide deck for their talk. You do not have to break the bank with exorbitant costs in order to support community involvement. Existing budgets for recruiting, training, marketing and bonuses can all be leveraged to more effectively retain and recruit talent.

These additional efforts will help you better understand and connect with your current workforce and attract prospective candidates that operate in the community. So, give your candidates an opportunity to share their community activities on their resume or application. This will help you identify top talent while also conveying your support and making a great impression on your candidate.

Recruiting Veterans

In addition to tapping into the volunteer talent pool, employers have another source of talent that is highly underutilized. If you're looking for skilled and hard-working candidates, military veterans are a great fit. They have some of the best technical training and hands-on experience that can't be readily learned in an academic setting. Consider expanding your recruitment strategy if you haven't already, to recruit veterans that bring leadership, teamwork, and the technical skills that are important to cyber security.

Tapping into Leading Motivators

Now that we've found talent to recruit, what actually motivates a job seeker to move to a new company? CyberSecJobs.com's job search survey identified the top reported motivators that draw job seekers to one company or another. With the high cost of living in most tech centers, the top response was salary (84%), as you might expect. A close second was a good working environment (80%), followed by company support of work/life balance (76%). Considering the sheer number of hours that professionals devote to work, it's understandable why they urgently seek a good working environment and work/life balance. Sharing a little about your company culture can go a long way in helping a prospect imagine how they might fit in.

CyberSecJobs.com's job search survey also asked how employers can make it easier to recruit professionals. The top two survey responses included providing remote work and making the recruiting process more transparent. While remote work may not always be possible with high security work, it is a fairly common request in the community and it can make the difference between hiring your first or second choice candidate. So, consider adding remote work when possible to promote optimal recruitment and retention.

Also, review your hiring and recruitment process to ensure it's transparent. Your candidates won't know what your hiring process looks like unless you clearly communicate the steps. This kind of proactive transparency will benefit your candidate experience and your overall recruitment process.

Setting Career Paths

Another key piece of information from the survey is to promote retention. When asked about career plans for the next year, only 29% of survey respondents communicated they plan to stay with the same employer, in the same role. This is because job seekers desire career paths and professional growth rather than a mere job. Nearly half of the respondents said they want to change their current role, whether that be at their current company or somewhere new.

Career mapping is not something that managers are taught. However, it is a valuable activity that supports your company's continued retention efforts. It's a shared responsibility between the employer and employee to determine goals, strategies, and how to accomplish them.

For example, an attendee on a cyber-security career panel explained how they had worked for a large financial institution for 17 years. Their growth had topped-out in their area of expertise and for many, this would prompt a job search for new opportunities. Being a financial institution, the professional had worked extensively with regulation compliance. Their employer presented them a career path in security and offered to pay for their certifications so they could guide them through regulation compliance. The individual was thrilled to have a new career at a place they really enjoyed working. Because the employer worked with their employee to help map the next steps of their career, they were able to retain a valuable asset.

Considering the rate of turnover in the industry and how long security positions can take to fill, it is vital to prioritize retention. By offering support, you help employees continuously grow and lessen the risk of losing talent to opportunities outside of your organization.

Supporting the Growth of the Industry

While all of these strategies provide job seekers and employers with tools to better reach their immediate goals, the security industry will benefit in the long term by unclogging the talent pipeline that has aggravated the talent shortage we face today. Until companies can acquire the talent they need, they will find themselves exposed to the risk of cyber-attacks, a detriment to us all.

How might we all work to increase the existing talent pool and strengthen the cyber security industry? First and foremost, we must demystify the stereotype of a man wearing a hoodie working on nefarious tasks in a basement. In reality, security is a space for innovation that welcomes and requires a diverse workforce. We have a great need for more women and people with diverse backgrounds for the sake of successful security. Diversity facilitates a more productive, engaged, and innovative workforce.

As we make the cyber security realm more accessible and work together to support our workforce, we'll begin to see a more prosperous industry unburdened by talent shortage. If job seekers take responsibility for their own careers and employers help build talent rather than simply buying it, together, we stand ready to shape the next generation of cyber security professionals.

* * *

Kathleen Smith is the CMO for ClearedJobs.net and CyberSecJobs.com. Founded in 2001, ClearedJobs.net is a veteran-owned career site and job fair company for professionals seeking careers in the defense, intelligence and cyber security communities. Find her at https://www.linkedin.com/in/kathleenesmith/

Episode 27.
Society of American Military Engineers

By Mario Burgos

President and CEO, Burgos Group

Burgos Group was founded in January 2006 as a marketing and management consulting firm. It quickly gained traction by taking an equity position in lieu of fees in a couple of companies. Unfortunately, the recession hit just as the firm was achieving momentum. By June of 2008, I found myself in a very unique position. For the first time, I did not see a clear market opportunity. It was as if someone had pressed pause on the U.S. economy. Companies were closing their doors from Main Street to Wall Street. The vast majority of those that remained open were taking a wait and see attitude. This equated to inaction - particularly as it related to retaining marketing or management consulting services.

Around this time, the Government had launched the American Recovery and Reinvestment Act of 2009 (ARRA) as a catalyst to jump start the economy. Having always been a market entrepreneur, I decided to pivot and chase this promise of "shovel-ready" opportunities in the business to government (B2G) sector. My brother, David Burgos, joined me in January of 2009 as a co-owner of the company, and by December of that year, we were certified as a Small Business Administration (SBA) 8(a) and Small Disadvantaged Business (SDB). Our primary reason for seeking the certification was that we had been advised by numerous sources that set-asides were an easy way to win federal contracts. In hindsight, I can tell you without any doubt the words "easy" and federal contracts" should never be used in the same sentence.

The SBA 8(a) program is a nine-year business development program, and there are consultants galore that will tell you the secret to winning government contracts and growing your federal government business is to get your company 8(a) certified. What they rarely tell you are the cold hard facts about the 8(a) program.

Anecdotally I have learned over the years that approximately 50% of the companies that get 8(a) certified will go through the entire nine-year program without ever landing an 8(a) contract. Of the 50% of those companies that do land a contract, it will take about half of those companies four years before they land their first contract. So, if you're following the math, that means only 25% of the universe of 8(a) companies land a contract in the first four years of certification.

Think about that for a minute.

How many small businesses do you know that can wait four years to land their first contract? Consider the time and opportunity investment required for a business development cycle of that length. These anecdotal statistics are supported by the data that is available online. For example, the SBA's, *FY2020 Congressional Budget Justification and FY2018 Annual Performance Report* notes that in FY2018 there were 6,789 firms participating in the 8(a) program and 3,590 of those 8(a) firms were awarded federal contracts – 52.87% of participants received a contract.[25]

Now as luck would have it, I was not aware of these statistics at the time. Sure, I had attended the requisite "Doing Business with the Government" type training sessions. The same type of sessions where the seasoned speaker inevitably advises the audience that you are likely facing an uphill battle if you choose to pursue government contracts as a prime contractor without any past performance working on a government contract. This advice is often coupled with the counsel that the attendees would be wise to get started by seeking subcontracting opportunities with an established prime contractor.

---

[25] U.S. Small Business Administration, "FY2020 Congressional Budget Justification and FY2018 Annual Performance Report," pp. 74, 75, at https://www.sba.gov/document/report--congressional-budget-justification-annual-performance-report

But I was convinced that if I just applied sound, consistent, and targeted marketing efforts, our company could break into the federal market. So, we bid, failed, requested a debrief, refined our proposals and bid again. This cycle was repeated over and over and over again. In fact, by the end of our first 12 months in the 8(a) program we had responded to over three dozen opportunities and submitted dozens more responses to sources sought notices. Oh, and it is probably worth mentioning that it took us fourteen months to receive our 8(a) certification. So, we had not only burned through our limited savings, but we were piling up credit card debt at an unfathomable rate just to keep the lights on – the lights in our respective home-based offices.

Then, in April of 2010, we landed our first federal contract. It was a $650,000 roadwork project for the Bureau of Land Management (BLM). It was an 8(a) set-aside competitive contract. While it was small enough to have been direct awarded through the 8(a) program, it was a project funded by ARRA dollars and that came with a mandate for BLM to compete the contract. *Even though we won, we requested a debrief – something I highly recommend whether you win or lose.*

Through that debrief we learned two very important lessons that would play a huge role in our strategy and ultimate success in the 8(a) program. First, we learned that there had been a total of nine bidders on that opportunity, but seven of those bidders had been eliminated for non-compliance with the Request for Proposal (RFP) instructions. There is a lesson there for everyone. While you may be the best at the product or service you provide, if you cannot submit a proposal exactly as the government requests it, you will never get a chance to prove just how great your company can perform.

The second lesson came from a simple question asked during our debrief, "Would you please tell us about any weaknesses identified in our proposal?" The answer from the contracting officer was both simple and painful, "Burgos Group."

That's right, the only weakness in our proposal was our company. She went on to add that we had absolutely no past performance, and she was right. But we had put together a great team and that team's technical response, past performance, and competitive price was sufficient to meet the evaluation criteria and be awarded the contract.

This is a key consideration every time we pursue a federal contract. We start with Section L (Instruction to Offerors) and Section M (Evaluation Criteria). In the latter, we are looking for any reason that would exclude us from being eligible for contract award. If we find one, we make a "no go" decision on the opportunity. But, if we can check all of the boxes, either on our own or with teaming partners, then we move forward with deciding to pursue the contract.

If you are going to pursue federal contracts, I cannot emphasize enough how important it is to build a large network of potential teaming partners and suppliers. Once a solicitation is posted on SAM.gov you will rarely have more than 30 days to respond, and that is barely enough time to put together the bid and definitely too late in the game to start identifying teaming partners.

When money was tight, we started building those networks in our respective backyards. Dave was going to every outreach event he could find in New Jersey and the surrounding states and I was utilizing the same approach in the Southwest. We would even go to site visits for opportunities we had no intention or capability of bidding because we could exchange business cards with business development people from other companies. This was an inexpensive way to network with people in the sector - something I am always surprised more people don't do.

By the end of FY2010, our efforts and strategy had paid off. We were an exception to the 8(a) statistics. We had won our first 8(a) set-aside contract five months after entering the program, and we went on to be awarded a total of eight prime contracts valued at $2.3M dollars. The contracts were for doing everything from landscaping and construction to property management.

An interesting side note is that of those eight contracts, five were small business contract awards. In other words, we did not need any special certification to compete for those contracts other than to qualify as a small business in the NAICS code under which it was solicited. Of the three 8(a) contracts we were awarded, only one of them was direct awarded (i.e. without other competition), and the value of that contract was only $12,000. The takeaway is that you can win contracts without special set-aside designations, and you will be hard-pressed to find an agency that is going to direct award large contracts to any company without past performance.

I would like to say that winning those contracts was the turning point which alleviated the pressure on our company, but nothing could be further from the truth. We were personally leveraged to the hilt. We had employees coming onto our payroll and realized that the government is billed 30 days in arrears and has 30 days to pay. That meant we were faced with cash flowing 60 days of contract value and that was if our invoice was submitted correctly into the Wide Area Workflow (WAWF) system the first time. If not, cash flow needs would be much higher.

But I was not really worried. After all, I was confident that when I took our $2.3M in newly signed contracts into a bank, it would be easy to have our existing $25,000 credit line doubled or more to provide the necessary cash flow.

I was 100% confident, *and 100% wrong*.

Bank after bank turned us down. This was the height of the economic recession and neither our business nor personal financials supported the underwriting needed for a bank loan. When it comes to small business banking, banks make loans based on past performance, credit worthiness, and assets. They do not make loans based on future projections alone. The only reason we even had a $25,000 line of credit was because it was an SBA Guaranteed loan. But from a bank perspective, nothing warranted increasing that. We could not even qualify for the various microlending programs that existed in our communities.

So, we turned to family and friends. We presented our success to date - namely our ability to land $2.3M in contracts. We relied on the fact that they knew our work ethic to make them comfortable that we could service those contracts and that we would pay them back before paying ourselves. We took advantage of the fact that their money in a bank account was returning 1% if they were lucky and we were offering a 10% return on their investment. This strategy worked and we raised sufficient capital to cash flow our contracts.

When we won another eight contracts valued this time at $3.3M by the end of FY2011, I thought for sure the banks would get on board and realize we were not one-shot wonders. Again, I was wrong. One bank president actually told me, "I can lend you money when you stop growing." So, we found ourselves back to raising subordinate debt from friends and family for another two years.

It was not until mid-2014 that circumstances really changed for us. We continued to win more contracts at higher dollar values, and our profit, which we were reinvesting in the company, had generated enough money to meet most of our cash flow needs. We had retired the subordinates raised in the early years and were finally eligible for adequate conventional financing from a local bank.

The Society of American Military Engineers (SAME)

Luck happens when you are at the right place at the right time, but you have to show up in the first place for that to happen. One of the places I showed up was at the Society of American Military Engineers (SAME) Albuquerque Post monthly luncheon. At that lunch, the speaker was talking about upcoming contracting opportunities with his agency and several of his colleagues were in attendance. Other attendees included a mix of potential small and large business partners. It was this first lunch where I recognized there was an opportunity to take an active role in a national security dialogue between industry and government which has been taking place since 1920.

It was a no-brainer to pay the $100 Individual Membership (we are now a Sustaining Member) and keep going to those monthly luncheons. When the Post President solicited members to get involved with the local Post Board, I raised my hand. I kept raising my hand and in a couple of years, I went on to become the Albuquerque Post President.

In 2011, when we had a little bit more money available in the budget for marketing our capabilities, we chose to invest it and attend the national SAME Small Business Conference (SBC), which that year was held in Kansas City.

At this one event, there were military leaders, important agency points of contact, and some of the most successful prime contractors in the business. We also gained a ton of knowledge from the education sessions and from visiting with key service providers (such as surety agents, attorneys, and capital sources). As I delivered my elevator pitch while walking up and down the exhibitor aisles and during the networking events, I was wondering if this was truly a good investment of our company's very limited resources.

In hindsight, I can tell you unequivocally that it is the relationships that I developed by attending SAME local, regional and national conferences, year after year, that has been the key to our company's continued exponential growth. What we learned and who we met at these conferences was invaluable as we continued to pursue federal opportunities.

At that first conference, we met the bonding agent that finally said "yes" when EVERYONE else was telling us "no." We began the dialogue with many of the teaming partners with whom we have since successfully pursued dozens of federal prime contracts. During this time, no one on our senior management team had served in the military or worked in the government sector. So we learned "the language" and expectations of our customers at this event and future SAME SBCs. Most importantly, we have found (and continue to find) many informal mentors and champions among the friends we have made at SAME.

SBC has become a *MUST* attend event for our company. As we have had more money to invest, we chose to add attendance to SAME's other national events (the Joint Engineer Training Conference, the DOD & Federal Agency Program Briefings, and the Facilities Management Workshop). And now that our company has a national presence, we also attend as many regional industry day events as our schedule allows. My own personal volunteer commitment to SAME has also grown. I am currently serving on the SAME National Board as the Chair of the Small Business Community of Interest.

I have found that whatever we have invested into SAME pays back exponentially. When we enter a new market, I find I always have someone local whom I trust that I can call for subcontractor referrals. When we are considering a new partner, my friends from SAME are invaluable in helping me do my due diligence. Then, there have been those times when I've found myself facing a unique contracting challenge and I've called a contracting officer or small business representative I've met though SAME to get a government perspective on finding a win-win to a "hypothetical" situation.

Today, Burgos Group has over 125 employees from coast-to-coast and we're growing. We continue to focus on meeting the general & electrical construction needs of various federal agencies and commercial clients throughout the country. Our customer-centric focus and results driven performance has been widely recognized over the last few years:

- Inc. 5000 list (2014-2019) – only 3% of companies have made the list six times
- Albuquerque Business First's Fastest Growing Companies (2014-2019)

- 2017 Society of American Military Engineers Industry Small Business Award
- 2017 SBA Small Business Persons of the Year for New Mexico
- 2015 SBA Prime Contractor of the Year for Region VI (Texas and surrounding states)
- New Mexico Flying 40 (2014-2018)

Within the federal sector we have been awarded more than 80 prime contracts and executed on over 225 task orders. In December 2018, we graduated the SBA 8(a) program, and since doing so, **we have been awarded $10.2B in Indefinite Delivery Indefinite Quantity (IDIQ) multiple award task order contracts (yes, that's a "B")**.

If you're in the architecture, engineering, or construction fields, joining the Society of American Military Engineers (SAME) should be one of your first steps.

* * *

Mario Burgos is the President and CEO of Burgos Group. Headquartered in Albuquerque, New Mexico, with operations in seven states, Burgos Group is a Small Disadvantaged Business. They offer general and electrical construction, facilities operations, logistics and professional technical services to federal, state, and municipal agencies as well as many private industry clients.

Since the inception of Burgos Group, they have experienced significant growth through a commitment to delivering excellent performance. Thirteen different federal agencies have awarded Burgos Group more than 80 prime contracts with the largest single award to date being a $160M IDIQ construction contract for the Defense Threat Reduction Agency. Find him at https://www.linkedin.com/in/marioburgos/

Episode 28.
Contract Novation

By Steve Meredith

Government Contract Procurement Program Manager, Southwestern Pennsylvania Commission

In the business world, mergers and acquisitions occur on a daily basis. Some small business owners may be looking to move on from the labor of love that they've helped build over their career. Other small business owners may want to expand their current offerings. Either way, sometimes a merger or acquisition is the best way to bring about a smooth transition for all involved. While the merger and acquisition processes are complex in their own right, if the party selling their assets has a federal government contract, it is important to know that the contract in question will need to be novated.

Novation, as defined by Cornell Law School's Legal Information Institute, is "an agreement made between two contracting parties to allow for the substitution of a new party for an existing one." In the context of government contracting, novation is the process by which the government formally recognizes a new party as the company under contract with the government.

While that definition is succinct, it does not address why contract novation is necessary in the first place. When a company wins a government contract, the government is essentially stating that the winning contractor represents the best value to the government for that particular good or service. What is inherently the best value to the government should in theory also be the best value to the American taxpayer. From a common sense perspective, novation is necessary because the government needs to do its due diligence and ensure that it is still getting the best value for the taxpayers if and when the new contractor is recognized.

The novation process can be time-consuming, but it can be broken down into five basic parts:

1. The company selling its assets informs the federal government contracting officer associated with their contract that they wish to have that contract novated. This must be done in writing.

2. The government requests documentation from both the company selling assets, as well as the company receiving assets, in order to evaluate the proposed agreement.

3. The government contracting officer notifies each contracting office within that specific agency that will be affected by the merger, and requests the submission of comments and/or objections within 30 days of that notification

4. The government makes a determination as to whether or not it is in their best interest to recognize the successor.

5. If the recognition of a successor is approved, the government then forwards a signed copy of the executed novation agreement, as well as a Standard Form 30 (Amendment of Solicitation/Modification of Contract) to all necessary parties.

While the steps outlined above are relatively simple to understand, step three requires some clarification. When a government contracting officer notifies each contracting office affected by a potential merger or acquisition, they only notify contracting offices within that officer's particular agency. In other words, a Department of Veterans Affairs (VA) contracting officer is only going to go around to other VA contracting offices affected by a potential novation to ask for any comments or objections to the proposed merger.

It is important to recognize that if a business has multiple contracts with different government agencies, the company selling the assets will have to approach a contracting officer for one of the contracts with each separate agency and request novation in writing. For instance, if a business has contracts with the VA, the Department of Energy, and the U.S. Department of Agriculture, that business owner is responsible for contacting three separate contracting officers (one at each agency) to request novation of those respective contracts.

As a business owner, adding the responsibility of the novation of your business's government contracts can be daunting. With that said, there are a few essential considerations that all business owners need to take into account when considering the novation process in the context of selling their business's assets.

1. Contract novation should be a part of your overall exit strategy. If you know that you will be considering retirement five years from now, you need to take a look at where your current government contracts will be at that time, as well as which ones will need to be novated. If a business owner knows they are going to retire in five years, you may want to focus on winding down your government work until the transition is complete. That way, you will have fewer contracts to novate, which means less paperwork to turn over to the government, and a smoother transition for all involved.

2. Allow at least a year for the entire process to take place. The government will ask both parties for an extensive list of documents ranging from sales agreements, all affected contracts, evidence of transferee's capability to perform, articles of incorporation, balance sheets, etc. It will likely take time for both the seller and the buyer to find these documents and once everything is submitted, there will be at least a month waiting period while the government receives feedback from the contracting offices affected by the proposed merger.

3. Know where your documentation is located. Once you receive the list of documents requested from the contracting officer(s) for the contract(s) in question, you can shorten the novation timetable by locating the requested documents quickly and submitting them to the contracting officer in a timely manner.

4. The seller needs to ensure that the company to whom they are selling assets can perform on the government contracts being novated. While this seems self-explanatory, any government contractor selling their assets to a successor needs to realize that the decision as to whether or not the successor is recognized ultimately rests with the government. One thing that the seller can do to

ensure a smooth transition is to make sure that the buyer has the manpower, know-how, and stamina to comply with the government's requirements.

5. Companies acquiring assets should ensure that they update their System for Award Management (SAM) profile once the novation is complete. If your company is acquiring assets, you may also want to talk to Dun and Bradstreet, and later, the SAM.gov team, and discuss how best to preserve the DUNS number / SAM Managed Identifier (SAMMI) tied to the novated contract. If your company acquired another company's assets and your company is also a government contractor with your own DUNS number or unique identifier, ask Dun and Bradstreet or the SAM.gov team how you can associate your company's identifier with that of the identifier listed on the novated contract.

In addition to the five tips listed above, one tip that may or may not go without mentioning is to stay in contact with the contracting officer assisting with the novation process. As I mentioned at the beginning of the episode, mergers and acquisitions happen on a daily basis, which means the novation process happens on a daily basis as well.

Learning about the novation process is crucial to contractors who have already won government work. If you're new to the world of government contracting, the process of registering as a government vendor can be an overwhelming task, let alone marketing yourself to government buyers and pursuing government contracts.

Luckily, the U.S. Government recognized this, and in 1985, Congress authorized the Procurement Technical Assistance Program (PTAP) which facilitated the establishment of Procurement Technical Assistance Centers (PTAC) across the United States. Today, there are over 300 local PTAC offices and each PTAC is responsible for assisting business as they pursue government contracts. Furthermore, because PTACs are funded through a cooperative agreement with the Defense Logistics Agency as well as with a match from their host state governments, PTACs offer their services free of charge to their clients.

In FY2019, the PTAP received $42.3 million dollars from the U.S. Government along with roughly $27 million dollars from their host state governments. For that investment, the PTAP helped clients win over $26 billion dollars in federal, state, and local government contracts. This represents a Return on Investment of over 600%.

While the PTAP's assistance is wide-ranging in nature, it can be condensed into five basic areas. On a daily basis, PTAC staff across the nation assist businesses to:

1. Register as government vendors. This includes registering as a vendor in the Federal System for Award Management (SAM), as well as state and local government vendor registration processes.

2. Market themselves to the government agencies that buy what the company provides.

3. Provide bid-match services that result in a daily email that matches a company's capabilities with federal, state, and local government solicitations.

4. Provide solicitation read-through services so that our clients understand government requirements and regulations.

5. Provide bid proof-reading services so that clients can be sure that they've answered all of the government's questions prior to submitting their bid for consideration.

When I counsel my PTAC clients, I often tell them that there are two things that a PTAC counselor cannot do. First, we cannot tell you how to price your product or service. As mentioned previously, PTACs can certainly help you proofread your bid to ensure that you've answered all of the government's questions in any given solicitation. However, we are not allowed to tell clients how to price their product as the client has to determine that on their own.

Second, we are not allowed to tell a government agency to give you a contract. The contractor has to win the work on their own merits.

With those two restrictions out of the way, there are some general tips that I often give my clients whenever they express a desire to pursue government contracts:

Make sure that you have the time to devote to government contracting. While this tip seems self-explanatory, just because you register as a vendor in SAM, or with your respective state and local governing bodies, it does not mean that you will be handed a giant bag of money. There is a fair amount of time and effort that goes into pursuing government work and you may find that your efforts are not immediately rewarded. On average, it can take 12-18 months for you to win your first government contract. Have patience and be persistent.

Government contracting is an 80/20 split. This means that 80% of the time, new government contractors should be reaching out to government agency small business representatives and 20% checking government bid-boards like SAM.gov (beta.sam.gov). Much like selling commercially, government contracting has more to do with the relationships you build than bidding on opportunities you see online. Furthermore, one of the most effective ways to be successful in the government marketplace is to engage government agencies *prior* to solicitations hitting the aforementioned bid-boards. If you know about a government requirement before its open to the public, you'll be in a better position to respond to the solicitation and hopefully win the work.

Don't be afraid to start small. There is an entire slice of the government contracting pie that is automatically set-aside for small businesses every year. Procurements valued at $10,000 to $250,000 fall under what is known as the Simplified Acquisition Threshold (SAT). As the name suggests, the procedure for bidding and winning these opportunities are meant to be as simple as possible.

I often tell my clients that pursuing simplified acquisitions is a great way to start for a couple of reasons. First, every government opportunity is going to have what's known as a "Statement of Work (SOW)" included in the solicitation. Generally speaking, the lower the dollar amount on the SOW, the easier it will be for a sole-proprietor or a small firm to manage. The easier the work is to manage, the greater the chance a new contractor has at performing well and eventually winning more contracts.

The second reason that I tell my clients to pursue simplified acquisitions is because of the selection process for these acquisitions. If you are a small business and you submit a bid on a Request for Proposal valued *above* the SAT, most (not all) of the time your bid will be reviewed by a source selection team. The source selection team is made up of multiple individuals with different goals for the acquisition. The bottom line is that your bid may impress multiple people on the source selection team but if you fail to impress the decision maker, you stand a high chance at losing out on that opportunity.

With simplified acquisitions, *there is one person*, the contracting officer, who has the authority to select the winning bidder. That alone gives a small business a greater chance at potentially winning a government contract.

As I mentioned earlier in this episode, PTAP assistance is wide-ranging in nature. Fortunately for small business owners, your local PTAC is closer than you think. You can find your local PTAC by visiting www.aptac-us.org, and searching for your local PTAC by state. Once again, PTACs *never* charge for their services so it is really in a small business's best interest to take advantage of the PTAP program.

*   *   *

Steve Meredith serves as the Program Manager for Government Contract Procurement at the Southwestern Pennsylvania Commission (SPC) Procurement Technical Assistance Center (PTAC), located in Pittsburgh, PA. In his role, Steve has helped SPC's Government Procurement clients register to do business with federal, state, and local government bodies. He provides clients with daily bid-match emails, helps interpret government solicitations, and provides other technical assistance.

This free assistance has helped Steve's clients win million's of dollars in government contracts. Steve holds a Verification Assistance Counselor certificate from the U.S. Department of Veterans Affairs; a Bachelor's Degree in Music, and a Pennsylvania Education Certificate from Seton Hill University. He lives in Monroeville, PA with his wife Kelly and his son Preston. Find him at https://www.linkedin.com/in/stevenemeredith/

Episode 29.
Compensation for Unanticipated Costs and Delays

By Maria L. Panichelli, Esq.

Partner and Chair of the Government Contracting Practice Group at
Obermayer Rebmann Maxwell & Hippel

Disclaimer: Nothing in this article should be construed as legal advice, or as establishing an attorney/client relationship between Ms. Panichelli and the reader.

After you've won a federal government contract award, what comes next? As any contractor will tell you, the contract award is only the beginning - performance presents a whole new series of challenges. There may be changes to the contract, defective specifications, delays and disruptions, differing site conditions, or any number of other problems that arise. Each of these issues may cause a contractor to experience delays, or incur additional costs, that it had not anticipated when it responded to the solicitation.

Dealing with these challenges - and recovering the unanticipated costs incurred - requires contractors to understand a complex web of statutes and regulations, including the Federal Acquisition Regulation (FAR) and individual agencies' supplemental acquisition regulations. These acquisition regulations provide a legal framework that governs every aspect of doing business with the federal government.

The regulations control how a contractor must compete for and perform a contract, as well as how a contractor must handle issues that arise during performance. The regulations also limit the manner in which a contractor can seek compensation, resolve a dispute, or litigate against the government. Understanding this body of regulations and other relevant laws is critical to success in the government sector. A contractor who truly understands the FAR, the obligations it imposes, and the approved methods of resolution and recovery can often avoid conflict with the agency.

Below, I discuss two interrelated tools contractors can use to seek compensation for unanticipated costs incurred on Federal government projects: namely, Requests for Equitable Adjustment (REAs) and Claims under the Contract Disputes Act (CDA). I also discuss the most common defenses raised by the government when refusing contractor REAs and Claims, the contractor mistakes these defenses are based on, and how to avoid these mistakes to maximize your chances of recovery.

Requests for Equitable Adjustment and CDA Claims

The FAR provides that a contractor who, during contract performance, incurs unanticipated costs, or suffers schedule changes, for which it was not responsible, can seek relief. Specifically, that contractor can request an "equitable adjustment" to the contract to make up for the problems it encountered.

However, unlike in the private contracting context, a federal government contractor cannot just file a lawsuit against the government in the state or the local US District Court when an issue arises. Suits against federal agencies, which arise out of performance of federal contracts, are heard before either a Board of Contract Appeal (like the Armed Services Board of Contract Appeals, or the Civilian Board of Contract Appeals, depending on the agency from which a contractor is seeking compensation) or the United States Court of Federal Claims. Moreover, before a contractor can file suit before these bodies, the contractor must exhaust certain administrative remedies. That is where REAs and Claims come in.

Both REAs and claims involve a contractor's demand – submitted to the agency itself – for an equitable adjustment to account for issues that arose during performance. The relief sought can take a variety of forms. A contractor may seek relief in the form of an equitable adjustment of the contract time - i.e. extension of the contract's period of performance. A contractor could also request an equitable adjustment of the contract price - i.e. an increase in contract price.[26] The legal authority for these equitable adjustments exists in different issue-specific sections of the FAR itself. For example, the Changes clause at FAR § 52.243-4 provides that a contracting officer may make any number of changes to a contract; however, if any such change "causes an increase in the Contractor's cost of, or the time required for, the performance of any part of the work . . . the Contracting Officer shall make an equitable adjustment and modify the contract in writing."

Similarly, under the Differing Site Conditions Clause, FAR § 52.236-2, if a contractor encounters, during performance, conditions that are materially different than those expected, which "cause an increase or decrease in the Contractor's cost of, or the time required for, performing any part of the work. . . an equitable adjustment shall be made . . ."

In short, through these types of clauses, contractors are entitled to seek relief for costs and delays arising out of issues that occur during performance. The question then becomes whether it makes more sense to submit a REA or file a claim.

There are several important differences between REAs and Claims. As a general matter, REAs are less formal. They do not normally require contractor certification (except REAs submitted to DoD agencies that are over the Simplified Acquisition threshold). REAs are often used as an opening salvo - a preamble to negotiations between a contractor and the government. As such, REAs are generally thought of as a normal part of performance – they are considered a creature of contract administration.

In contrast, claims are a bit more formal. They require certification if over $100,000. They are not a creature of contract administration; rather, they represent the first step in the dispute resolution process. Unlike REAs, which do not trigger any obligations on behalf of the government, agencies must respond to a claim within a certain timeframe, or face consequences. So, how do you decide which to submit?

The key thing to remember is that a contractor must file a *claim* before it may initiate a lawsuit before the Court of Federal Claims or the Boards of Contract Appeal. A REA is not sufficient. Now, that does not

---

[26] Less often, the relief sought will take other forms, such as a declaration that the government has breached the contract, and/or permission to cease work on the project without giving rise to a termination for default.

mean that a claim has to be the contractor's first step. Many contractors actually *start* by submitting a REA first, hoping to invite negotiation and resolve the situation without getting too adversarial. If that REA receives no response, or if the government denies the REA, then the REA can be converted to a claim.

Of course, in the alternative, if a contractor believes that the government is unlikely to negotiate, it may consider a REA a waste of time. In those types of circumstances, a contractor may skip the REA all together, and start by submitting a claim. There is no requirement to begin with a REA. Other situations in which a contractor may choose to skip a REA and proceed directly to a claim are if the contractor wants to put pressure on the government to respond, or if the contractor is about to run up against the 6-

REAs	Claims
Less Formal	More Formal
No Certification (Unless DoD/Over Simplified Acquisition Threshold)	Certification over $100,000
Creature of "Contract Administration" – Considered Part and Parcel of Contract Performance	The First Step in Litigation
Opening Negotiations	The First Step in Litigation
Does Not Trigger Governmental Obligation to Respond	Does Trigger Governmental Obligation to Respond

REAs v. Claims: A Summary Comparison

year statute of limitations.

Both REAs and claims usually take the form of a letter to the contracting officer responsible for the project from which the REA or claim arises. The letter should lay out the factual circumstances or issue(s) that gave rise to the claim, provide an explanation of why the contractor is entitled to relief, describe the damages and/or delays incurred, and include a request for relief that outlines the specific number of additional days, dollars, or other relief requested. Ideally, claims should also include detailed legal analysis, highlighting the applicable FAR sections and explaining how and why the contractor is entitled to relief pursuant to those regulatory provisions.

Claims are more likely to be successful if they include an analysis of relevant case law demonstrating that contractors in similar situations have received compensation from the government in the past. This is one of the reasons why, although many contractors feel comfortable preparing their own REAs, the vast majority engage legal counsel when submitting a claim.

When submitting a claim, the contractor should always make sure any required certification is completed. The claim should include a clear and unequivocal written statement that puts the contracting officer on notice of the basis and amount of the claim. It should also explicitly request a contracting officer's final decision (aka a "COFD").

After a contractor submits its claim, the agency will consider it and issue a COFD. That COFD may: accept the contractors position and agree to provide the compensation or relief sought; partially accept the contractors position and agree to provide partial compensation/relief; or deny the claim, refusing to provide compensation/relief.

If the contractor is not satisfied with the outcome, it can appeal the determination by initiating suit before a Board of Contract Appeal or the Court of Federal Claims. Many clients ask what happens if the government simply fails to provide a COFD, or takes an unreasonably long time to issue it. In that case, the contractor can take what is called a "deemed denial" appeal, which allows it to initiate a lawsuit the same way it could have done had the agency affirmatively denied the claim.

In either case, it is absolutely vital that the contractor submit its claim prior to initiating litigation before the Boards or Courts, as any litigation based on a claim that was not submitted to the contracting officer will be immediately dismissed. After initiation of the appeal, claims litigation proceeds before a Board of Contract Appeal or the Court of Federal Claims and afterwards, if either party is unhappy, they have the option to appeal to the United States Court of Appeals for the Federal Circuit.

Common Government Defenses Precluding or Reducing Contractor Recovery on REAs and Claims

As previously explained, after a contractor submits its claim, the agency will consider and analyze the claim before issuing a COFD. During that period, the government will analyze, among other things, whether it has any defense – i.e. a basis to deny (in whole or in part) the contractor's claim. Three of the most common defenses raised are based on Lack of Notice,

Lack of Authority, and Waiver/Release. Therefore, it is critically important for contractors to understand what these defenses are as well as how to avoid making the very common mistakes that enable the government to raise these defenses.

Notice

Notice - or, more precisely the lack thereof - is an extremely common government defense to contractor claims. Many of the FAR clauses that permit a contractor to seek an equitable adjustment also require the contractor to provide some sort of notice. Failure to provide that notice can bar recovery.

For example, previously, we examined the Changes Clause (FAR § 52.243-4) and the Differing Site Conditions Clause (FAR § 52.243-4), and saw that both provisions included language allowing a contractor to seek an equitable adjustment of the contract if circumstances "cause[d] an increase in the Contractor's cost of, or the time required for, the performance of any part of the work." The Changes Clause goes on to state, however: ". . . no adjustment for any change under paragraph (b) of this clause shall be made for any costs incurred more than 20 days before the Contractor gives written notice as required."

Similarly, the differing site conditions clause provides, in relevant part, that: "No request by the Contractor for an equitable adjustment to the contract under this clause shall be allowed, unless the Contractor has given the written notice required." Accordingly, if a contactor fails to provide the requisite notice, they have significantly reduced their odds of receiving an equitable adjustment.

Now, there are certain arguments that can be made to try and rebut a (lack of) notice defense, but their success is far from certain. Contractors are far better off taking care to provide appropriate notice at the applicable times. The most successful contractors are diligent and consistent in sending notice letters any time an issue arises. If you have questions about what type of notice is required, and when, it is best practice to consult a legal professional familiar with government contracting and the FAR.

Authority

Dealing with a federal agency always involves a varied cast of characters. There is, of course, the Contracting Officer ("CO"). In addition, during day-to-day performance, a contractor may be dealing with a Contracting Officer's Representative ("COR") or a Contracting Officer's Technical Representative ("COTR"). Contractors must keep in mind the different levels and types of authority each of these individuals possess. Most critically, only contracting officers have the authority to change a contract. They can bind the government only to the extent of authority granted to them and only up to the amount of their warrant.

This difference in authority can become important in a variety of circumstances. For example, let's take a situation in which a contractor is dealing with a very hands-off CO. He or she rarely gets involved in project performance and allows the COR to handle much of the day-to-day interaction with the contractor.

Now, remember from above that a contracting officer may make changes to a contract, but if such change "causes an increase in the Contractor's cost of, or the time required for, the performance of any part of the work . . . the Contracting Officer shall make an equitable adjustment and modify the contract in writing." As explained previously, this allows a contractor, through a REA or claim, to seek compensation for damages or delays incurred as a result of the changes made by the CO.

However, in our example, the CO is rarely around; it's not the CO but *the COR* who instructed the contractor to perform out of scope work or deviate from the contract provisions in some way. If the contractor incurred additional costs, or schedule delays as a result, and tried to seek an equitable adjustment from the government, the government would likely use the authority defense to bar recovery. That is, the government would likely take the position that the COR did not have the ability (authority) to change the contract and the contractor should not have followed instruction to deviate from the contract. Therefore the contractor is not entitled to an equitable adjustment in connection with that change.

For this reason, contractors must be wary about going forward with any work that constitutes a change to the contract without explicit instruction *from the contracting officer*. Otherwise, the contractor might be impeding its ability to recover additional costs, or time, associated with performing the changed work. Sometimes a contractor finds itself in a situation where it cannot proceed without instruction, but instruction is coming from someone without the requisite authority. If you find yourself in this tricky spot, a legal professional can assist you.

Waiver/Release

Finally, we come to the waiver/release (sometimes called the accord and satisfaction) defense. This is when the government argues that a contractor has "waived" or "released" its claims by agreeing that no further compensation or relief was due. This defense is very common and usually arises because of language included in a contract modification signed by the contractor; most often in the "closing statement" section of the modification.

Often, when the government issues a modification, the closing statement will include language along the lines of:

> "It is understood and agreed that...the contract time is extended the number of calendar days stated, and the contract price is increased as indicated above, which reflects all credits due the government and all debits due the contractor. It is further understood and agreed that this adjustment constitutes compensation in full on behalf of the contractor and its subcontractors and suppliers for all costs and markups directly or indirectly attributable for the change ordered, for all delays related thereto, for all extended overhead costs, and for performance of the change within the time frame stated."

If a contractor signs a modification with that language, it likely just gave up any right to claim additional time or money relating to the change ordered in the modification. Sometimes, the waiver language will be even broader. It will waive not only claims for money or time relating to the change described in the modification, but *all* existing claims on the project. Therefore, the key is not to sign a modification that contains waiver language unless you are, in fact, receiving complete compensation and consent to waive further claims. If you have questions about how to preserve your claim rights, consult a legal professional.

In summary, REAs and Claims are two tools that contractors can use to seek additional time, additional money, or other relief relating to issues that arise during contract performance. If contractors familiarize themselves with the REA and claim processes, and take care to avoid the common mistakes outlined above, they likely will be successful in getting relief for the damages or delays incurred.

If you have questions about REAs or claims, how to avoid common pitfalls relating to authority, notice, waiver, or any other issue effecting performance and dispute resolution on a federal government job, reach out to a government contracting attorney.

*   *   *

Maria Panichelli is a partner and Chair of the Government Contracting department at the law firm of Obermayer Rebmann Maxwell & Hippel. She focuses her practice exclusively on federal government contracting, guiding her clients through every stage of the procurement process. Maria's practice includes pre- and post-award bid protests, contract interpretation and performance counseling, preparation of Requests for Equitable Adjustment and Claims, Contract Disputes Act (CDA) claim litigation, statutory and regulatory compliance counseling, resolution of subcontractor disputes (including the use of pass-through claims, and Miller Act claims), contract terminations, and all aspects of small business procurement.

She provides comprehensive legal counseling that allows her clients to successfully navigate complicated legal requirements while still fulfilling their business goals. Maria is active in a number of federal contracting associations, and is a frequent lecturer at agency, government contracting, and small business conferences. She blogs about government contracting topics weekly at govconexaminer.com. Find her at https://www.linkedin.com/in/mariapanichelli/

Episode 30.
Bouncing Back from a Losing Streak

By Courtney Spaeth

CEO, growth[period]

Too many times it is easy to blame your staff or, for that matter, anyone else but yourself, when you lose a proposal. Winning new work as a government contractor is hard because the process is lengthy and complicated and riddled with delays, protests, politics, and inevitable blunders. Even harder is achieving success in lateral growth markets - government departments and agencies where you have never been an incumbent and where your relationships with the customer are just beginning to form.

As we will discuss in this episode, blame is the last place to start when you are working to regain your winning streak. A strong and refined sense of self-awareness is usually where the road to bouncing back needs to begin.

Growth is a strategic mindset that requires a high degree of discipline, investment, patience, and the ability to take calculated risks. There is no shortcut to growth. Companies with leadership teams that understand and foster growth have more vibrant cultures and tend to be more successful on their journey to grow to $350M+.

Many "C" suite executives in the government contracting space are more comfortable with familiar tasks such as program management or engineering than the adoption of a long-term mentality that combines the art and science required for successful growth. As such, leadership tends to make poor hiring decisions, is quick to blame others, and does not invest in the proper areas. In some cases, leadership may not invest in growth at all and instead completely relies on luck or good fortune to win new and significant work. This is a dangerous hole to fall into. Luck is not repeatable. Your mindset and culture are notoriously difficult to change once these characteristics become ingrained in the leadership's long and short-term growth strategies.

Growth is a science. It requires repeatable processes, metrics, formulas, research, and the successful application of all these factors to achieve the desired result. If your company has been losing for quite some time, the first place to look is the underlying science of your approach. Do you have processes in place? Are they the correct ones?

One of the important fundamentals of being successful in government contracting is your ability to use process to drive your bid decisions and resource investment including the timely performance of gate reviews.

Confirm that your staff is providing all the correct information necessary at the various stages for you to have multiple data points from which to evaluate the opportunity. Make sure that you have performed an honest assessment of the incumbent's performance (if there is one), and of equal if not greater importance - an assessment of your competition.

Too many times the staff will tell the CEO whatever they think the CEO wants to hear instead of providing the full picture. Ensure that you are engaged and asking the right questions. If you are not sure if your process is as sound as it needs to be, then hire an expert to perform a third-party assessment.

The next place to look is your organization's structure and staffing. Business development is not the same as sales. Business development is the strategic execution of a strategy to drive revenue over time in a repeatable fashion. Sales are the tactical implementation of a short cycle revenue plan. Did you hire a business developer to head your company's efforts to go to market? Or did you "cheap-out" on how/who you hired for that role?

A lot of times CEOs in government contracting will invest more money in the hiring of program executives than they will in their business development staff. However, if you do not grow you decline or die, underlining the fact that the right level of investment in the correct talent is essential for success.

Sometimes a losing streak reflects the fact that the right people are not in the correct roles. A talented business developer is not an inexpensive resource and is always employed. They are in high demand so it is useful to procure the services of a recruiting firm with expertise in GovCon to help lure them to your organization.

In order to make the correct hire, it is also essential that the leadership team recognize that placing unrealistic expectations on this individual and his/her team will only lead to failure and disappointment. There is no such thing in government contracting as "low hanging fruit" so if your recent losing streak reflects the fact that you have pressured your BD staff to bid a volume of opportunities to "prove their worth" or to demonstrate that they have "value," then your expectations and approach need a major course correction.

Even having the most talented BD leadership and team in place does not guarantee that you will win right away. However, it is a necessary step in the right direction. Talent needs to be enabled in order to succeed and right-sizing your views on what constitutes "value add" is essential for your whole company to get back on the path to winning.

Losing streaks can also be indicative of too much organizational self-confidence and not enough reality about the importance of fostering personal and strong relationships, especially with new customers. Too many times we have heard a CEO state that because his/her organization was performing so well with one agency that the sheer competency of their company in completing the work would be enough to get them over the finish line with another customer.

Past performance matters tremendously, especially as it relates to execution and effectiveness and highlights how much your government customer values you. While past performance is necessary to be successful at winning additional work, it is not sufficient to ensure winning similar work with new customers. If no one in an authoritative position with the target customer has ever heard of you or does not really know what you do, who you are, or why they should trust you with their work - you are guaranteed to have a much harder battle ahead of you to win.

Customer intimacy is extremely important in achieving repeatable and measurable success and without it, government contractors tend to fail more often than succeed. This is just as applicable to the big systems integrators with great past performance at other agencies.

If you have been losing because you are bidding work where your firm or your key leadership have no name recognition, no past performance, and no critical insights into that customer's culture, challenges, and needs, then you should consider pausing for a moment and figuring out why you truly believe you will win, *not why you should win*.

Just because you can bid something does not mean that you should and saying no is often just as important as saying yes. Be honest with yourself about how effective your brand has been in establishing a leveraged position for key leadership with lateral growth customers. Take a step back and see if you have been drinking your own marketing Kool-Aid, which while potentially effective with future customers and teaming partners, has provided you with a false sense of security about your position with current targets.

We recently had a company come and see us who had lost their last 16 bids in a row! We were astounded. At what point do you stop the madness? Well for them it was at their not-so-sweet sixteenth loss. They were a $35M government contracting firm still run by its founder who had been historically very successful winning work with one agency in the U.S. intelligence community. They talked themselves into the idea that the word "community" follows intelligence for a plausible reason. But as any seasoned government contracting business development leader will tell you, there is literally nothing communal about the intelligence community. Despite this, they chose to simultaneously bid two different major programs at two separate intelligence agencies.

The company had no prior existing relationships with either agency and no customer intimacy. They simply assumed that their past performance at their longstanding customer would be sufficient for them to leapfrog into a prime position with the other two agencies. As a critical aside, both programs had incumbents who were well-liked by the customer and consistently scored high marks on their CPARs. One of the incumbents had been the incumbent for 15 years in a row and had recently won a Contractor of the Year award for outstanding service! Despite this, the company truly believed that on the merit of their performance at the lateral agency, they could unseat the incumbent and sachet in the door.

Unsurprisingly they lost both bids and at the same time managed to be outbid by one of the Big 5 on their incumbent prime work! They had been so busy running around in circles they forgot that customer intimacy also matters when you are also the incumbent! All of this underscores the point that performance is not always everything. The art of creating and maintaining relationships is an important part for reversing losing streaks as it is for preventing them in the first place.

Relationships matter and the best and most productive ones are anchored in mutual trust and respect. Losing streaks sometimes reflect a company's leadership that has been stretched too thin or has lost focus on what matters most - their people and their relationships with their customers and teaming partners.

The adage "Do unto others as they do unto you" is just as applicable to relationship management in government contracting. Too often we see executives at large systems integrators patronize or blow off their peers at small businesses. They are simply too important (in their own minds) and too busy to treat them with respect.

The government contracting space is a small world. Individuals tend to stay in the field for a long time and gather expertise and advanced schooling that enables them to advance their titles while staying in the industry. There is not as much job-hopping as there is in the tech industry, for example, and people in government contracting value loyalty and longevity more than almost any other industry in world today.

We have been around long enough to see so much industry consolidation that yesterday's small business Vice President of Business Development is tomorrow's new Chief Growth Officer. Where the companies in government contracting used to be staid and were characterized by enormous market longevity, e.g. Lockheed Martin, Boeing, Northrop Grumman, etc., they are now a confusing mix of entities that were the results of spin-offs, platform company roll-ups, and private equity machinations.

An enormous number of government customers, as well as their industry peers, do not have a clear understanding of what exactly Peraton or DXC does, or what the difference is (still after all these years) between SAIC and Leidos. Customer confusion leads to opportunities for smaller and more agile government contractors to swoop in and unseat incumbents who now have confusing brands and high attrition rates among their key program staff. This has led to a very fluid talent market in government contracting and has allowed former small business executives to transition more seamlessly into large company roles. These individuals, like Santa, remember who was naughty and who was nice to them when they worked for a smaller company.

In such a "small" world industry pettiness can often lead to poor teaming decisions and make for bitterness, animosity, and unsuccessful partnerships. Applying a strong sense of self-awareness of how you, your staff, and your company are viewed by your peers and past, current, and future customers can help you avoid losses based on poor market positioning.

In the end, stopping a losing streak often comes down to the actions of the CEO. It is his or her responsibility to stabilize the bid and capture process, include BD and marketing, and calm everyone down. Parsing out blame just leads to accelerated attrition. It does not help you win.

If you are losing consistently, something in your approach is flawed and needs to have a course correction. It may not necessarily be your people. It may be that the expectations you have set are ill-advised or inappropriate. Attempt to do a review without assigning blame. Identify the issues. Work to correct them and then forge ahead without ruining morale. You very well may need the people who are already there and putting them will fail to create a culture that encourages growth.

* * *

Courtney Spaeth is the founder and CEO of growth[period], a business development and transaction advisory services firm with expertise across a range of industries including Aerospace and Defense, Sports, Entertainment, Hospitality, Tech, Cyber, Telecom, Cloud, Global Health and Wellness, Construction, Architecture, and Engineering.

Founded in 2007 and headquartered in Washington DC, the firm's clients include General Dynamics, Verizon, Nemacolin Woodlands Resorts, the Stagwell Group, Sokolin Wine, Stanley Black and Decker, and more.

Prior to founding growth[period], Courtney served as Corporate Vice President of Homeland Security for Raytheon Company. While at Raytheon she was responsible for developing the company's homeland security business in North America, the Middle East, Eastern and Western Europe, and Asia, and in less than two years her efforts resulted in new revenue of over $1 billion USD. Before Raytheon, Mrs. Spaeth served as Director of Homeland Systems Solutions for Lockheed Martin, where she won over $3 billion USD in new business. Find her at https://www.linkedin.com/in/courtneybspaeth/

Episode 31.
How to Accelerate in the Government Marketplace

By Carroll Bernard

Co-Founder, Govology

I am sure many people would agree that doing business with the government is *no picnic*. It's complicated, confusing, and expensive. Several studies have shown that it takes an average contractor 18 to 24 months and approximately $80k to $130k to land their first contract. No wonder many small businesses get frustrated and quit before they see any return on their invested time and money.

"What a nightmare!"

"Why would any small business owner in their right mind pursue government contracts?"

"It seems like such a waste of time, money, and energy."

If someone expressed these sentiments a couple of decades ago, I might have agreed with them. But not today! Not after seeing what government market opportunities can do for small businesses that know how to play this game.

I can tell you from experience that winning government contracts does not have to take 18 to 24 months and cost $80k to $130k. If you follow a simple set of principles that I'm about to share with you, you'll be able to achieve the same results in half the time and at a fraction of the cost.

These fundamental truths, which I call "acceleration principles," are simple but very powerful. They have no magical powers to bring you overnight success. They are not "feel good" advice or secret hacks to riches. They are enduring truths that, when applied diligently and consistently, will transform your business into a strong, steady, and growing enterprise that can win and sustain business in the government marketplace.

But before I delve into the acceleration principles, I want to share a personal story so you can understand why I am a passionate believer in their transformative power.

My journey in federal acquisition began a couple of decades ago when I joined the U.S. Navy as a Supply Officer. It was a stressful but rewarding role, and as long as I kept my ship stocked up with parts, food, fuel, and anything else we needed to carry out our mission, everyone was happy with their "Support" (i.e., me) - from the sailors to the captain.

After I left active duty, I relocated to the state of Washington with my family. First, I took a job as a buyer at the City of Vancouver, Washington, and then, a couple of years later, I joined the Department of Veterans Affairs as a Contracting Officer. In both roles, my main job was to acquire construction services, although I also procured other items as needed.

During my time as a Contracting Officer, I watched many businesses struggle to understand the ins and outs of federal contracting. As a lifelong entrepreneur at heart, I felt a calling to help them, but, unfortunately, there wasn't much I could do in my capacity as a Contracting Officer. So, I took a new position in the federal government as a Business Development Specialist (now called a Business Opportunity Specialist) with the U.S. Small Business Administration. I was very excited about landing that job and dreamed of all the ways I would be able to support entrepreneurs pursuing government market opportunities.

I wore many hats at the SBA, which included managing a portfolio of forty 8(a) firms. I also maintained collateral duties as the primary HUBZone liaison and a Veterans Business Development Officer. In addition, I held a government purchase card and took care of my local office's needs for small buys below the micro-purchase threshold.

When I was at the SBA, I made a few curious observations. First, we were right at the end of the last great recession, and business owners were flocking to the government marketplace just as B2B opportunities dried up. On the flip side, the Federal government was spending more money than ever in an attempt to stimulate the economy through the American Recovery and Investment Act of 2009.

I also observed that companies with an already established presence in the government marketplace not only survived the recession, but had their best years ever. In contrast, those with no presence were desperate. Many went out of business and declared bankruptcy after draining their life savings to save their business.

I often recall one particular contractor who pleaded for help to get government contracts to save his business. Once he blew through all of his savings, unfortunately, he drained his mother's entire retirement account as well. It was heartbreaking to watch some of these events unfold before my eyes. Despite our best efforts to help these businesses, there was only so much we could do.

Selling to the Federal government can be a great way to grow your business and diversify so that you can survive and potentially flourish during a recession (which is as inevitable as death and taxes). However, if you choose to ignore the government marketplace during the good times, it will not be there to save your business in bad times. Why? Because the Federal government procures goods and services at multiple levels, some of which take years to get a company positioned in. During a recession, much of the big-spending happens through higher-level contract vehicles that newcomers can't access - they are just too late to the party!

Another thing that blew my mind was the transformative power of a well-matched and executed team, especially when it involved a small business and a larger company forming a joint venture under the auspices of the SBA's Mentor-Protégé Program. At that time, the benefits of this program were available only to minority firms that participated in the 8(a) program. But now, any small business can benefit from this program, as long as they have the right mentor and they know how to use the program to their advantage.

You may be asking, "What's so special about the SBA's Mentor-Protégé Program?" Let me explain.

The SBA's Mentor-Protégé Program is the only program where the government allows small firms to form joint ventures with large firms, which then become eligible for small business set-aside contracts. Do you understand what that means? It means that when you're bidding on a small business set-aside contract, you are not competing against other small businesses that have comparable resources and capabilities. No! You are competing with small businesses "on steroids" that can draw on the support of their larger mentors to crush their competition.

In 2011, my local PTAC was looking for a part-time counselor in my area and I jumped on the opportunity. Though I lost half my pay and excellent benefits as a federal employee, this move allowed me to pursue my true passion for helping small businesses. To supplement my loss of income resulting from the job change, I established a consulting firm where I worked with companies outside of my PTAC service area who sought my unique experience. Through the consulting side of my business, I worked as a contractor supporting the City of Vancouver's acquisition team, and in 2012 provided training and consulting support to the SBA grant-funded program called the Small Business Teaming Pilot Program.

I thoroughly enjoyed serving as a PTAC counselor and working as a coach and consultant, but there was still something bugging me. I noticed that contractors struggled to get the training they needed. So, in 2015, I made another shift and went full time in my business. Together with my awesome wife Elena, we launched an online training platform (Govology), where companies can find some of the best government market education (it's true, our customers told us that) online, on-demand, 24/7. At the time of this writing, we have produced over 85 webinars and on-demand training sessions that have benefited over 6000 business professionals.

My professional life has taken many twists and turns, but it has also presented many valuable lessons that I apply in my own business and share with others. The acceleration principles I'll discuss next are rooted in these lessons and reflect years of observing, implementing, and learning what works and does not work.

How to Accelerate Your Small Business Success in the Federal Marketplace

Before I lay out my acceleration principles, I want to address one critical assumption they are built on - your small business has the basic structure needed at the foundational level to be successful as a business in general.

I've seen more small businesses fail in the government marketplace, not because it was too much for them to handle, but because they failed in business. Plain and simple.

Government market superstars tend to share certain characteristics - they have a great leader at the helm; a solid business foundation with an established (proven) product or service, sales outside of the government marketplace, and good people who consistently do the hard and sometimes uncomfortable work required of them.

With a strong leader, a dedicated team, and a solid foundation in place, you'll be ready to take on the government marketplace. But that's not enough. If you want to break into the government market faster and without spending a fortune, you need to focus on the following acceleration principles:

1. Build knowledge
2. Get clarity
3. Build and leverage strategic relationships
4. Take action daily

Your success will largely hinge on the people you meet, the things you know, and how consistently you put those to work in your business. So, let's take each of these principles and break them down.

Knowledge

You've likely heard the old saying "knowledge is power" and when it comes to the government marketplace - if you don't get educated, you'll be at a considerable disadvantage. For starters, there are a myriad of rules you must know to make sure your business processes, as well as your products and services, are compliant with government requirements and regulations.

It's not enough to understand the language of procurement - and successful businesses know this. They use their knowledge and the rules to gain a competitive advantage. They understand how to get compliant, stay compliant, and challenge their competitors who are not...in many cases, getting them kicked out of competitions through protest.

You don't have to earn a Ph.D. in government contracting. A little time and effort applied consistently to learning about compliance requirements related to your product or service will do the trick. Remember, learning is a journey - not a destination. You'll need to keep up with the regulatory changes each year as they may pose either a threat or an opportunity for your business.

Compliance aside, there are also many competitive advantages built into the regulations governing the world of small business set-asides. The SBA's Mentor-Protégé Program, that allows a small business to form a joint venture with a large firm to compete for small business set-asides, is just one such example. Many firms will never see these opportunities because they are unwilling to dedicate the time required to learn this market.

Clarity

The next acceleration principle is gaining clarity on several fronts.

First, you should get clear on where you want your business to be in the future. I start with a ten-year vision; dial it back from there to three-year goals; then a one-year plan with quarterly goals, weekly targets, and daily activities focused on moving me to where I want to go.

Then comes the WHY question. Why do you want to pursue and capture government market opportunities. Specifically, how will this help you get to where you want to go? Your "WHY" will sustain your efforts when you feel down and frustrated. Start asking yourself questions like "Is this the best use of my time," or "Is this worth the time and financial investments I'm making?"

Next, you should gain clarity on the environment in which you are operating. Part of this is general knowledge about the government market, but another big piece is knowing the facts that pertain to your specific sales and marketing efforts to government agencies.

Ultimately, you want to develop a proven process that is repeatable and profitable. It is hard to establish a proven process for your sales and marketing team if you don't understand how your buyers acquire the type of products and services you sell.

You should know who buys what you sell, what contract vehicles they buy through, how much they buy, who they buy from, and what price they've paid in the past. You also need to understand what subjective factors outside of price they consider when selecting a vendor or a group of vendors to be "the chosen one(s)."

Getting these answers will require that you perform some market research. The good news is that the federal government provides access to free historical spend and contract data. It is not that hard to find and analyze the data if you know where to look or who to ask for help. Check out www.usaspending.gov and get some training on how to analyze historical spend data.

Relationships

One of the big reasons why many small businesses fail is that they don't establish and leverage the right relationships. Just like in B2B markets, relationships in the government marketplace are also a critical factor for acceleration.

You can spend hours tweaking your website, polishing your capability statement, and sifting through bid leads. Still, at the end of the day, if you are not getting out there and connecting with people and building relationships, you will not be fully empowered.

We have a course on Govology called Marketing to Government Agencies and Prime Contractors that goes into more detail about specific relationships you need to develop and how to leverage them. If you want to take this training, visit www.govology.com/marketing. If you don't already have a free access code, email us at support@govology.com, and we'll be happy to provide free access to this training as a bonus for purchasing this book.

In addition to developing relationships with key stakeholders at government agencies, you need to form a government market mastermind and consult them as often as possible. Some of the folks in your government market mastermind will be free. Some may be fee-based. Here is a list of potential candidates:

1. Your local PTAC counselor
2. Specialized subject matter experts (depending on targets)
3. A legal expert versed in federal contracting
4. An expert in federal accounting matters (if required)
5. An expert in cybersecurity (if required)
6. Teaming partners

If you need help finding members for your mastermind, check out our directory of the people we know, like, and trust (directory.govology.com).

Many of these people are also Govology faculty members. If you have trouble finding an expert in a specific area of need, feel free to reach out to me at support@govology.com.

Action

The final element of Acceleration is "ACTION."

If knowledge is your launchpad, clarity is your mission, and relationships are the vehicle to help you get where you want to go; action is the spark that ignites the fuse and launches you from the land of problems into the realm of possibilities.

Developing the knowledge, clarity, and relationships you need to be successful requires dedication and consistency. By the same token, even if you already have the requisite knowledge, clarity of direction and purpose, and strategic relationships, you won't get anywhere if you don't take action every month, every week, every *day*.

At Govology, we have a program called *Govology Accelerator* where we help our members through the process of planning, prioritizing, and taking consistent action on the most critical activities. We also keep them accountable to make sure they stay focused on their priorities and don't get sidetracked by every-day minutiae.

Thank you for reading this episode and allowing me to share my principles for business acceleration. I've used these principles in my own business for years and found them very helpful in keeping me grounded and focused on my goals. There have been times when I'd get distracted by fleeting opportunities, but these principles are like an old friend you can always count on. They've never failed to bring me back on course.

* * *

Carroll started his acquisition career in the U.S. Navy Supply Corps providing logistic support and acquisition management while serving as a supply officer. After leaving active duty, he continued his acquisition career as a Procurement / Contract Specialist with the City of Vancouver, Washington and the U.S. Department of Veterans Affairs. He also worked for the U.S. Small Business Administration where he served as a Business

Development Specialist for 8(a) companies in the Business Development Program.

Through his duties in contracting and at the SBA, Carroll became a subject matter expert in Small Business Programs, Federal Certifications, Mentor Protégé Programs, Teaming, and Small Business Contracting with Federal Agencies.

Carroll and his team at Govology built and continue to expand their world-class training platform to help business professionals get the know-how they need to be successful in the government marketplace. Carroll also provides support as a national GovCon Guide, Coach, Consultant, and Trainer. Find him at https://www.linkedin.com/in/carrollbernard/

Episode 32.
Preparing for an Exit

By Erin Andrew

Managing Director of Government Contract Lending, Live Oak Bank

The number one issue business owners face, from small mom and pop shops to fast-growing government contracting businesses, is planning for an exit. Unlike the world of high-tech startups where you launch a business with an exit (an investor and an IPO in mind), many small businesses, especially those in the government contracting space are left on their own to figure it out. This often happens at a point in time when it is too late to have control over the graceful and profitable exit they desire.

That is why planning for an exit early and often is critical. You want to think through these steps, as well as the timing and strategy, before you have to go through them. The five Ps of an exit are important steps to think through if you are: just starting your business; you are in the thick of organic growth and don't anticipate an exit for a decade or two into the future; or you are nearing retirement age and starting to think about what is next.

Planning

Start planning earlier rather than later. This is tough because most business owners are so immersed in the day-to-day activities of running the business that it can be challenging to take time to think about the future. You should know where you want to be in the next one, five years, ten years, etc. Even for folks who love what they do and say they will never retire or leave the business; you should remember that sometimes an exit isn't by choice as a health or personal challenge may arise.

When is the best time to sell your company?

In the government contracting world there are several events or circumstances where it is advantageous to sell your business. Understanding and identifying these potential circumstances allows you to maximize the profitability of your exit. Missing these opportunities can be costly if they coincide at the same time that you desire to exit. These include:

1) When you have won many new contracts and your backlog is more robust than typical.

2) When your potential pool of buyers increases because of the type of work or set asides or lack of set asides.

3) When you still have room to grow in your size standard that corresponds to the North American Industry Classification System (NAICS) codes applicable to your business.

Let's briefly look at each of these scenarios.

a) Large and New Contract Backlog

The more work you have in your backlog the more money you will get for your company. It is quite the conundrum for most potential sellers because the moment you win new work is usually followed with the desire to keep building on the new wins. It is a hard decision to make, but it is important to review the options on your contracts and look for the next best window to potentially sell. If you decide to continue working, you might end up waiting five years for a recompete to experience the same robust backlog. Some folks might want to sell in two years instead of waiting another five years, so they decide to sell right after the first win rather than waiting for the recompete. It is a very personal decision requiring that you weigh financial and retirement perspectives.

b) Large Number of Buyers

The larger the pool of potential buyers, the higher the price. The market will often determine the price while taking into account factors such as the ability for buyers to leverage debt. For example, if you are a small business with full and open contracts, both small and large prime contractors will buy you. These types of businesses usually see larger multiples because larger entities with deep pockets can pay a higher premium for the company. A small business with primarily set asides will experience a buying market that most likely consists of other small businesses who can continue to perform the set-aside work on the contracts.

Timing your exit to maximize the sales price gets a little messier when products or intellectual property (IP) are a part of a company. Sometimes, a large prime contractor might pay a premium price for that product due to the value of the IP or product. They may even buy that small business even if they can't perform on the set-aside contracts.

Sometimes, businesses contemplate splitting off their product from their service to avoid realizing a lower multiple on their product piece. I will talk more about this in the *Pricing* section. Another example - if you are a service-disabled veteran-owned small business (SDVOSB) with the majority of your contracts being SDVOSB set asides, you will most likely be selling to another SDVOSB who can perform the work on the contracts and be able to bid on the recompete. The same goes for 8(a) companies, women-owned small businesses (WOSBs), etc. If you are an SDVOSB, 8(a), woman-owned, or HUBZone company with all full and open work, the market is much more open because anyone could buy you.

c) Room to Grow in NAICS

The combined revenues of a transaction determine if a company remains small after a transaction. Consequently, if you're a small business, it is better to sell when you have some room left in your NAICS size standard codes. If a company has small business set asides, those with high-size standard NAICS codes, whether dollar or employee based, usually have a larger pool of buyers who can buy them and remain small.

For example, if you are a company with small business set aside contracts in the 541611 NAICS (which has a $16.5M size standard with five-year average revenues at $16M), there really aren't many people who can buy your company and maintain those contracts. You might be better off planning to go after work in some of the higher NAICS like the 541 series with a $30M size standard so someone could buy your firm that currently has $15M in revenues on a five-year average and can maintain the contracts after the transaction. You may also decide to try to win full and open work in the 541611 NAICS in order to be an attractive target for a larger prime or mid-size company that could do the work on those contracts without the restriction of a small contractor.

It is important to think of these scenarios well before you are a year out from exiting as a shift in strategy can take years to accomplish. You want to maximize your options and potential pool of buyers.

How Often Should I Plan?

Often. I recommend that companies build a valuation exercise into their annual strategic planning process. This provides you with the discipline to check the pulse of your exit plan every year as markets, size standards, and clients change. This process shouldn't take a lot of time but will allow you to assess if you are on the path you set out for a few years earlier or if you might anticipate some challenges based on rule changes or contract losses.

For example, the change from the three-year to the five-year revenue average forced some small businesses to change strategies because of the impact on their size status. This completely changed their timing and strategy for an exit and forced them to reevaluate how to change their timeline to sell. Sometimes it makes sense to revisit this valuation exercise on more than an annual basis if changes in government policy or regulation occur throughout the year. At the very least, you should review your valuation on an annual basis.

Professionals

If you are having heart surgery, you wouldn't go to your primary care physician to do it, would you? The point of having specialists is that they provide very specific expert advice at pivotal times in your life based on their unique experience with a certain situation or problem.

In the government contracting merger and acquisition (M&A) space, professionals who specialize in government contracting M&A can help save you time and money on a transaction if they are engaged at the right time. This doesn't mean you have to kick your day-to-day attorney or accountant to the curb. Rather, it means that you are about to embark on a very important and specialized task that requires a professional who has done this type of transaction many, many times. This means you need to find an attorney who understands the challenges in the small business government contracting M&A space with proven past performance. Also look for an accountant who specializes in understanding the tax implications of a GovCon small business M&A transaction or an M&A advisor who understands the size implications of your transaction. Find an accountant that knows how to find buyers in the government contracting space who can actually buy your company and capitalize on its assets.

It is also important to ask how these professionals are compensated. Is it by the hour, by month, or is there a flat fee? Negotiating a flat fee or asking for a rough estimate of the cost based on the parameters of the transaction, up-front, will allow you to budget for the transaction. Your agreements should always be memorialized in a contract.

If you don't already have a financial advisor, it is imperative that you find one. Your first conversation should be with your financial advisor to determine how much you need to net out of any sale transaction based on your personal financial situation and expectations. This number can then be cross walked with your internal valuation process. This will help you understand and plan for the timing of your sale and any strategy shifts you should employ to add value and increase your net gain at time of sale.

Pricing

This is the most sensitive and most important topic for many interested in eventually exiting - *how much will I get for my company?* This is an important topic for sellers to study and understand because coming into a transaction without the knowledge of what the market will support will cost you time and money. This cost is usually in the form of drawn-out retainers because the price the seller wants isn't in line with what the market will support. To better understand this, let me present how you usually value a small business government contracting firm.

Unlike high-growth tech startups, valuation is typically measured by bottom line vs topline revenues. In the government contracting space, a price is determined by a multiple of earnings before interest, tax, depreciation, and amortization (EBITDA) - plus addbacks. It is an indicator commonly used by prospective buyers or investors to measure a company's financial performance. In its simplest form, EBITDA is calculated by adding the non-cash expenses of depreciation and amortization back to a company's operating income. Below is the basic formula:

EBITDA =
Operating Profit (EBIT) + Depreciation (D) + Amortization (A)

To arrive at the true value of the company for a prospective buyer, potential addbacks are identified. These are expenses that will either go away once the company is in the hands of a new owner or won't be incurred again. These types of expenses include things such as:

- Owner's salary
- Taxes and benefits, and
- Personal expenses an owner passes through the company as well as other non-recurring expenses.

It is important to make sure you support the potential addbacks; it should be logical and verifiable that the addbacks are reasonable and provide valuable data to help prepare a valuation of your company.

Addbacks are added to the EBITDA number and that number is then multiplied by "the multiple." The "multiple" for GovCon small businesses is usually between 2-6x EBITDA, plus addbacks, depending on factors such as number of small business vs full and open contracts, applicable size standards, type of set aside work, length of contracts, etc.

Sometimes folks ask why the multiple can't be higher. The main reason is if a small business is going to buy another small business, they generally need to leverage debt from a banking institution. If they are leveraging debt, the debt service ratio needs to be within a realistic range for a credit department to approve. The debt service coverage ratio (DSCR) is a measurement of the cash flow available to pay current debt obligations. For example, if the debt service coverage ratio (DSCR) is 1.15, which is the minimum requirement for SBA loans, then a borrower must have $1.15 of free and open cash to cover every $1 of debt.

If a small business has all full and open contracts and a large prime is going to buy them, the debt service coverage ratio will most likely not matter as much, especially if the prime is self-funding the purchase. This allows for the multiple to increase depending on the demand of the product or service the small business is selling. All the above factors contribute to the actual multiple for your business. If debt is not leveraged and / or the buyer cannot self-fund, the other option is significant seller financing or an earn-out structure, which often leaves the seller with little to no cash at close.

People

"It's not the tools you have faith in - tools are just tools - they work or they don't work. It's the people you have faith in, or not." ~Steve Jobs, Apple

Businesses in the government contracting space succeed or fail based on their ability to hire and retain good people. In the services space, your business is your people. Every owner is defined by the strength and depth of their team, which can also impact the price of your business. As you move closer to an exit, you need to determine who, if anyone, on your team you want to bring into the initial conversations.

If you have team members who have some equity in the business, they are typically included in the early conversations. As you prepare your team for your eventual exit, whether it is one year or four years in advance, it is important for you to start finding ways to automate your role.

Identify key players on your team who can start to take over some of the day-to-day activities you have been covering. The goal is to ensure the business is running on its own without you needing to be in the day-to-day by the time of sale. You want to identify key employees, something any buyer will want to know about. These key employees are individuals who are critical to the operation of the business whether it is your CFO, your business development representative or others. Many times, the buyer wants to ensure that some or all the key employees will stay around after the sale to ensure that business operations continue to run smoothly. Some buyers will provide equity deals to these key employees to encourage them to stay on as well.

The process of selling your business is a very personal and confidential process. You don't want to notify employees of the transaction until you understand what the transition might look like and you have a confirmed buyer. Buyers can pull the offer during due diligence. As a result, determining the appropriate time to discuss a potential sale and / or which employees should be included is unique to your situation and your relationship with your employees. You must maintain their trust and manage their expectations. Only you, as a business owner, can know what is best for your business, who to bring into the conversation, and when to notify your team. You need to understand and anticipate their reactions; be prepared to address their insecurities and be proactive in talking about the deal once at the right time.

Preparing for a Marathon

M&A is not for the weak of heart. It is a long and arduous process and roughly fifty percent of deals fall through before they make it to closing. Understanding how to plan, hire the right professionals, price your company ahead of time, and prepare your people for a transition can help increase your chances of success. You must be prepared for the marathon and set aside time to get your books and documents in order to ensure a smooth and timely transaction.

Business owners often share that they want to do a transaction in a few months and it is important to understand that it may take several months for due diligence alone, let alone finding the right target and making sure they have financing in place to go through closing.

Since you are following the first 'P' and planning on an annual basis by performing a valuation exercise, you should be in a good position to start planning one year out from your actual sale. It is at this point that you should prepare to hire an M&A advisor, attorney, and an accountant, in addition to a financial advisor. These professionals will help you properly plan to go to market.

Once you are on the market, it can take anywhere from a month to 12 months to find a good target buyer. When you've identified the target buyer, you still need to receive and execute a Letter of Intent (LOI) that is agreed upon by all parties, which can take some time. The bottom line is be prepared for many ups and downs throughout the process.

Some Final Thoughts

If you are contemplating an exit in the near future, below are several recommendations for questions that will be important for you to answer to better determine how close you are to making this leap:

1. Have I talked to my financial advisor and do I have an idea of a rough price range of where I would want to exit?

2. Am I more interested in the purchase price or the cash up front? Sometimes, people have a price in mind and are willing to take a very aggressive earn out structure while others care more about the cash they can put in their pocket at the time of sale.

3. Do I care more about price or a cultural fit? Most people will say both, but some people are really committed to finding someone who can help continue their legacy with their employees and their company and will sacrifice a little on price to find that right person. Others will simply go with the highest bidder.

4. Am I realistic about the price that I want and have I talked to multiple folks to ensure I have a realistic assessment of this price? If you go into the selling process with too high a price, like pricing a house too high, it will sit for a long time and could cost you quite a bit in attorney and other fees. Make sure to educate yourself on market multiples and other factors that may be included in the price.

Selling your government contracting firm can be a taxing event both emotionally and financially. It is important to understand the steps you need to perform to position yourself for the best possible exit. If you have any questions or want to discuss your approach, please email me at erin.andrew@liveoak.bank or reach out on LinkedIn at https://www.linkedin.com/in/erinandrew/.

* * *

Erin Andrew is a Managing Director with Live Oak Bank's Government Contracting Division where she manages M&A advisory activity. She represents buyers and sellers who are looking to acquire or sell and helps them with due diligence, financing, and negotiations. Erin joined Live Oak Bank with over 6 years at the U.S. Small Business Administration (SBA). Most recently she was Associate Administrator for Capital Access, where she oversaw the Agency's lending efforts that included $100 billion of government loan programs for small businesses. She also held positions at the SBA as Assistant Administrator for the SBA's Office of Women's Business Ownership where she oversaw the agency's efforts to promote the growth of women-owned businesses; Acting Executive Director of the National Women's Business Council; and Director of the Innovation Clusters and Skills Initiatives in the SBA's office of Entrepreneurial Development. She was also a part of Booz Allen Hamilton's federal government IT practice and held other positions at the state and local levels of government. She is a Project Management Professional (PMP) and a Kauffman Fellow (Class 20).

Episode 33.
10 Reasons You Need a Government Coach

By Michael LeJeune

Partner at RSM Federal, Federal Access PM, and Podcast Host
for Game Changers for Government Contractors

When companies reach out to us, they often have one question: "How do I make more money?" The question can come in many forms, but the fundamental desire to make more money, become more successful, and GROW is the same.

My answer to this question is always the same. Hire a coach. Why a coach? Because a coach is going to help you with every area and every challenge you have in your business. It's what we do. Our purpose is to help you achieve the results you want.

How is it possible for a coach to touch every area of your business? It's possible because we are *experts in business*. In the case of RSM Federal, we are not only experts in business, we are also subject matter experts in government contracting.

It's hard to place a dollar value on working with a coach. Each client is different and the potential for growth varies based on business model, stage of the business, and other factors. But you should expect to see at least a 10x return on any coaching investment. What you won't see on a profit and loss (P&L) or balance sheet are the intangible benefits of working with coach. This episode will cover the top 10 benefits you will receive from working with a quality coach.

#1 – They Will Reduce the Learning Curve

The average business takes 3 to 5 years to simply learn the ins and outs of government. That doesn't even include how to be a good business owner. You may be good at your trade/craft; but you need to be good at business.

My goal as a coach is to reduce that 3 to 5-year number to about 6 months or less. You will always need to learn more, but after 6 months, you will be grounded in the fundamentals and off to the races.

#2 - Access to Resources

Great coaches create what we refer to as *artifacts*. These are documents, templates, videos, libraries, and other resources that you can use to accelerate your knowledge and revenue. These items are key because companies spend years creating these type of resources from scratch. You should not have to waste a lot of time building a capability statement or figuring out what goes on your government landing page. You should be able to follow a template or guide and quickly knock it out.

For clients and members, our Federal Access Knowledge-Base has more than 300 documents and templates, over 100 training videos and webinars, and a very robust search engine to quickly locate the tactics, strategies, or tools you need. The resources are based on years of government contracting best practices – all designed to save time and accelerate your revenue. There are many resources on the market. Whether you use Federal Access or other resources, having access to these tools is critical. If you want a free account on Federal Access and poke around, visit https://federal-access.com/join/

#3 – They Will Show You Your Blind Spots

You don't know what you don't know. Our job is to be masters in both business and the market. We combine our knowledge with your skills to grow an amazing business. Along the way, we help you avoid costly mistakes by showing you what you don't know.

#4 – Accountability

Most business owners got into business for themselves so that they didn't have to report to anyone anymore. It's dangerous when you don't have anyone to push you. We will hold you accountable. Often just having someone to meet with is enough. This will push you down the track faster. Accountability brings you results. It's a key growth strategy. It forces you to perform the right activities that facilitates progress.

#5 – A Sounding Board

How many things are rolling around in your head? It feels like you can't share your thoughts with most people. It's outside their box. Spouses don't usually make good sounding boards. Their focus is on family, security, etc. You need someone you can talk to about depression, frustration, your hopes, dreams, etc. *without judgement.*

You can't share this kind of stuff with your business team.

Your coach will help you put things in perspective and help you create an action plan to address your concerns. A coach may need to point out if you're being crazy or need to slow down and focus. Great ideas can be great, but you have to be cautious. You don't want to derail the company just because you had a great idea in the shower.

#6 – Perspective

Your coach has an outside perspective where they can view the entire field. On the field, you are nose to nose with your team and the opponent. We can see the forest through the trees. We can see what's a big deal and what's a blip on your radar. We can see when you are close to a touchdown. As we become more assimilated with your team, the team will share more and more with us. We will have a 360-degree view of your team. No-one is going to share things with you like a quality business coach.

#7 – Answers

What's not working? What's wrong with your service? Why can't you find good people? Perpetual questions. What, why, how.... sometimes you just need direct answers that are tailored specifically to your situation. Generic advice will only get you so far...

You need someone who can explain HOW to do something. What should your bid-matching settings be set to look for? What should be in your SAM profile? What goes on your capability statement? These are the basic answers.

You're scheduled to meet with a program manager at the Department of Homeland Security (DHS). What is your focus? How will you map the value of your products and services to the requirements you've identified in pre-acquisition? How do you prepare to collect information and intelligence before, during, and after the meeting? These are the more advanced pieces that a quality coach will help you identify and execute.

A great coach wants you to learn along the way.

#8 – Your Mindset

A huge part of getting you to be successful is getting you to think differently. People often think you need the best product, quality, service, etc. But what matters most is attitude and beliefs. Evolving your thinking is critical to this because if you think you can do it, you will.

As you achieve more, your mindset will start to shift. Have you ever heard the story of the 4-minute mile? The short version is that up until Roger Bannister broke the 4-minute mile in 1954, it was thought to be an impossible feat. Then in 1954, Bannister did it. Since then, the 4-minute mark has been broken countless times. The current world record is 3:43.

The difference between today and before Bannister did it is the mindset. People are not necessarily faster. They just know what's possible. A coach will help you see what's possible in your business and more importantly, what YOU are really capable of.

A business coach should change your perceptions.

#9 – Personal Development

If people understood that they have to work harder on themselves than they do on their business, they probably wouldn't be in business. The better you get, the better your business will get.

Your coach will help you develop as a business owner and a person; your character, traits, the things you hold important. Someday, you will move on to other challenges. Whatever you are doing now is either preparing you to take on the next challenge or it will serve as a funding mechanism.

#10 – Financial growth

Your business should grow leaps and bounds. My expectations are for clients to double their business in 12 to 18 months. It's not always possible, but that's my goal.

You don't want a business that's really *just a job*. You want to make an impact in your life that is going to last generations. That won't happen if you aren't seeing significant financial growth in your business.

A quality business coach is how many small businesses become large companies.

* * *

Michael LeJeune is a Partner with RSM Federal and Program Manager for the Federal Access Knowledge-Base and Training Platform. He is an award-winning business coach, author, and host of the podcast Game Changers for Government Contractors. He has been consulting and mentoring companies in the government market for twenty years. Michael is also an Army Veteran. Find him at www.linkedin.com/in/michaeljlejeune/

Final Thoughts

This book covered a lot of information! It's very easy to feel overwhelmed by the number of items on your action / to do list, but don't worry. You don't have to implement everything in the next 24 hours or even this month.

I would suggest that before you dive into your action list, that you go back and reread the episodes that resonated with you the most. Then sit down and *prioritize your list.*

The most important thing right now is not to fall into the trap of putting this book back on your shelf with a plan to "come back to it later." In fact, I recommend that you leave this book on your desk for the next three months - even if it sits in the back corner. Keep it handy. Let it be a reminder that you have twenty-nine industry experts at your fingertips.

If you have questions about these episodes, reach out directly to any of our authors. We are all here to help you. If you have questions and don't know who to approach, reach out to me directly (Michael LeJeune). My *direct business email* is mlejeune@rsmfederal.com and my office number is (636) 577-5005. If I don't know the answer to your question, I guarantee I'll point you in the right direction.

Next Steps

Get some coaching - whether it's RSM Federal or someone else – strengthen your business maturity and request help! If you don't know where to start, you can sign up for a *free Business Breakthrough session* on our website. Just visit: https://rsmfederal.com/breakthroughcoaching

As soon as you close this book, please go subscribe to the podcast Game Changers for Government Contractors. If you even remotely enjoyed this book, you will *love* the podcast. Subscribers and downloads help us continue this free resource.

Finally, thank you for picking up this book. We really appreciate it! I cannot thank you enough for helping get our message out to the masses. In that spirit, if you enjoyed this book and know someone who could benefit from it, please make them aware of it or just buy them a copy.

Thank you again! Don't hesitate to contact us if you have questions.

Other Resources

An Insider's Guide To Winning Government Contracts

#1 Amazon Bestseller
Visit https://www.amazon.com/dp/1733600922

Federal Access (FA)
Knowledge-Base and Training Platform

The flagship solution of RSM Federal. Federal Access (FA) is an award winning and nationally-recognized training platform that helps companies win government contracts.

FA has more than 300 essential documents, 100+ training videos and webinars, and the best Subject Matter Expert (SME) support for government contractors. You can start your journey with us today for FREE by visiting https://federal-access.com

Podcast
Game Changers for Government Contractors

Available on any podcasting app. Just search for Game Changers for Government Contractors. This podcast is #1 podcast in the Nation for small business government contractors.

Every month, industry subject matter experts provide game-changing strategies for winning government contracts. Game Changers was designed BY government contractors FOR government contractors.

Connect with us on LinkedIn

If you gained value from the content and concepts in this book, I highly suggest that you connect to EVERY author on LinkedIn. We all provide similar value via articles and posts on a regular basis. Be sure and mention that you heard about us via this book!

One Last Thing... or Two?

There are 29 of us that spent a year writing this book! We want to thank you for trusting us with your time.

If you enjoyed and gained value from this book, we would be *very grateful* if you help us in return.

1. **Post a review on Amazon.** Even if you did not buy this book on Amazon, you can still leave a review! This is the most important.

2. **Take a picture of yourself holding this book and post the picture to LinkedIn** *and* say why you enjoyed the book. Publishing and marketing a book is difficult. Our ability to share your picture with our network is 100 times more powerful than our own marketing. (Just make sure to tag us - Michael LeJeune and Joshua Frank.

Your support really does make a difference. We read and respond to all LinkedIn posts personally.

Thanks again for your support!

About RSM Federal

The Art and Science of Government Sales™

RSM Federal is an award-winning coaching and consulting firm that works with small, mid-tier, and large companies to accelerate their understanding of the government market and learn how to position for and successfully win government contracts - with exceptional results. Our clients have won over $2.6 Billion in government contracts since 2008.

Providing the **Art and Science of Government Sales**™, RSM Federal has quickly become a nationally trusted educator, trainer, coach, and consultant to other companies, associations, and coalitions.

We emphasize basic and advanced strategies tailored specifically for your company to accelerate success and revenue. We leverage a proven combination of industry expertise and measurable strategies to deliver cost-effective and high-value results for our clients.

With nationally recognized and award-winning expertise and hundreds of resources, tactics, templates, and step-by-step strategies, your company can immediately accelerate your marketing, prospecting, sales, teaming, and proposal activities - literally overnight.

About Michael LeJeune
Editor-in-Chief

MICHAEL LEJEUNE is a Partner with RSM Federal and the Program Manager for the Federal Access Knowledge-Base. He is an award-winning business coach and author. He has been consulting and mentoring companies in the government market for nearly twenty years.

Michael specializes in breakthrough-coaching. He works primarily with companies that are either new to the market or have plateaued and don't know what to do next.

You have likely heard Michael on the nation's leading government contractor podcast - Game Changers for Government Contractors. Michael started this podcast with co-host Joshua Frank in 2016. Thousands of contractors listen to Game Changers every month. Game Changers is available on every podcasting app.

Michael served four years in the Army at Ft. Hood. First in the 2nd Armor Division and then with the 4th Infantry division from 1995 to 1999. Michael received numerous awards while working on the FORCE XXI project for the Army testing new equipment and technologies. This is how Michael was introduced to government contracting.

Michael started his corporate career in 1999 with GTE/General Dynamics in the highly competitive collaboration space. His primary clients were the Department of Defense, Intelligence Agencies, and the Joint Forces Commands.

Michael currently resides in the small town (5,500 people) of Monticello, IL with his wife, two daughters, and two puppies. He hates the cold and looks forward to moving to someplace warm after his daughter finishes high school.

About Joshua Frank
Executive Editor

JOSHUA FRANK is managing partner for RSM Federal. Bestselling author, trainer, and management consultant with 30 years in the government market, Josh is a recognized authority on government sales and speaks nationally on business strategy and business acceleration. He lives in St. Louis, Missouri with his wife, son, and daughter. Josh loves educating business owners on how to accelerate their government sales.

Josh specializes in the development and implementation of tactics and strategies required to differentiate, position for, and win government contracts. His passionate keynote presentations are consistently rated as one of the strongest sessions at national conferences and events. His training, with hundreds of testimonials, is consistently rated as being real-world, highly educational, and thought provoking.

Due to the number of contracts won by Josh's clients, he was awarded the Veteran Business Owner of the Year by the Small Business Administration (*a first for a business coach*); the National Industry Small Business Advocate of the Year by the Society of American Military Engineers; and Josh's company was awarded "The 50 Most Trustworthy Companies of the Year" by Silicon Review.

Other books authored by Josh:

An Insider's Guide To Winning Government Contracts
#1 Amazon Bestseller
https://www.amazon.com/dp/1733600922

The Government Sales Manual
Available on Amazon
https://www.amazon.com/gp/product/061541348X

Author Websites

michaellejeune.com and authorjoshfrank.com

Learn more about RSM Federal

rsmfederal.com

Learn more about Federal Access

federal-access.com

FREE podcasts for government contractors at

https://soundcloud.com/gamechangersforgovernmentcontractors

Made in the USA
Columbia, SC
29 May 2020